EXODUS RETOLD

Ancient Exegesis of the Departure from Egypt in Wis 10:15–21 and 19:1–9

HARVARD SEMITIC MUSEUM PUBLICATIONS

Lawrence E. Stager, General Editor

HARVARD SEMITIC MONOGRAPHS

edited by
Peter Machinist

Number 57
EXODUS RETOLD
Ancient Exegesis of the Departure from Egypt
in Wis 10:15–21 and 19:1–9

by
Peter Enns

Peter Enns

EXODUS RETOLD

Ancient Exegesis of the Departure from Egypt in Wis 15–21 and 19:1–9

Scholars Press
Atlanta, Georgia

EXODUS RETOLD

Ancient Exegesis of the Departure from Egypt in Wis 10:15–21 and 19:1–9

by
Peter Enns

© 1997
The President and Fellows of Harvard College

Library of Congress Cataloging in Publication Data
Enns, Peter, 1961–
    Exodus retold : ancient exegesis of the departure from Egypt in
Wis 15–21 and 19: 1–9 / Peter Enns.
        p.   cm. — (Harvard Semitic monographs ; no. 57)
    Includes bibliographical references and index.
    ISBN 0-7885-0403-7 (cloth : alk. paper)
    1. Bible. O.T. Apocrypha. Wisdom of Solomon X, 15–21—
Commentaries. 2. Bible. O.T. Apocrypha. Wisdom of Solomon XIX,
1–9—Commentaries. 3. Exodus, The. I. Title. II. Series.
BS1755.3.E56   1997
229'.307—dc21   97-35988
                                       CIP

Printed in the United States of America
on acid-free paper

To My Family,
Past, Present, and Future

TABLE OF CONTENTS

Preface

This monograph is a revision of my doctoral dissertation completed in May, 1994, under the direction of Prof. James L. Kugel in the department Near Eastern Languages and Civilizations at Harvard University.

There are many people whom I would like to acknowledge. Although to mention some would risk offending many others, I am nevertheless eager to give due recognition to those who made my graduate work both possible and enjoyable, and to those who aided in bringing this monograph to completion.

I owe a deep debt of gratitude to the faculty of the department of Near Eastern Languages and Civilizations at Harvard University. Their teaching has had a tremendous impact on me. To a large extent, this work represents the faculty's influence in shaping the fundamental questions I ask when I approach the interpretation of ancient texts. I would like to mention in particular James L. Kugel, whose teaching and interests are reflected throughout this study, and my careful and conscientious readers, Jon D. Levenson and Paul D. Hanson. These three have had more than an academic influence on me and I am grateful for the chance to offer my thanks to them. I am also indebted to Peter Machinist whose thorough and incisive comments have no doubt greatly increased whatever value this study might have. I would also like to acknowledge *Biblica* for their permission to include in this study a slightly revised version of my treatment of Wis 10:20-21 ("A Retelling of the Song at the Sea in Wis 10,20-21," *Bib* 76 [1995] 1-24).

My colleagues at Westminster Theological Seminary have been most supportive over the past several months as I have worked to bring this project to completion. The faculty, both presently and during my years there as a student, is a continual reminder to me of the high standards and holy calling of Christian scholarship. In addition, I would like to thank my research assistant, John Makujina, for proofreading the manuscript and compiling the index of ancient works.

A passing sentence or two in a book's preface can hardly express my thoughts and feelings about the people closest to me, who have had a significant hand in everything I have accomplished. For the nine years I spent in seminary and graduate school, my parents were kind enough never once to mention (at least in my presence) that other sons had by now begun generating a steady income. My wife, Susan, has had sagely patience that

1

defies reason with a husband who never seemed to get enough of school. My children, Erich, Elizabeth, and Sophia, have been a constant reminder that there is a higher calling than writing books—raising children to follow the path of wisdom.

A word about references and the use of translations is in order here. For commentaries on the Wisdom of Solomon, I have chosen to cite in the footnotes only the author and page number, or, if the author is already mentioned in the text, typically only the page number. This is to avoid the tedious repetition of *Wisdom*, *Sagesse*, or *Weisheit* with each mention of a commentary, of which there are many. I have also abbreviated some of the standard reference works throughout (see list of abbreviations). N. Turner's volume on syntax, vol. 3 in J. H. Moulton's *A Grammar of New Testament Greek*, will simply be cited as "Moulton, 3." followed by the appropriate page number in that volume. Full references are given in the bibliography. All other works comply with accepted standards.

All translations of biblical, apocryphal, targumic, and rabbinic material are my own, although I have consulted regularly standard scholarly translations of these materials. I should make special mention of two rabbinic works. All citations of the *Mekilta de-Rabbi Ishmael* are according to J. Z. Lauterbach's bilingual edition. I have, however, supplemented Lauterbach's text where necessary with the text from the edition by H. S. Horovitz and I. A. Rabin. Likewise, my citations of the *Memar Marqah* are from J. MacDonald's two-volume bilingual edition, where I have included the page number both to his translation and his Aramaic text. I have also included the corresponding page number of Z. Ben-Ḥayyim's newer critical edition (*Tibat Marqe*). Also, any Aramaic will be reproduced from Ben-Ḥayyim's edition. The pseudepigraphal material is taken from Charlesworth's two volume *The Old Testament Pseudepigrapha* with ancient language supplied where appropriate. Citations from Philo's *De Vita Mosis* and Josephus' *Jewish Antiquities* are from Colson's and Thackeray's translations in the Loeb Classical Library Series (*Philo VI* and *Josephus IV* respectively). For the sake of brevity, references to ancient texts will normally include simply the appropriate sections, paragraphs, and tractates, etc., without supplying any further bibliographical information.

July, 1997
Westminster Theological Seminary
Philadelphia, Pennsylvania

Abbreviations

1 Clem	1 Clement
AB	Anchor Bible
ABD	*Anchor Bible Dictionary*
'Abot R. Nat.	*'Abot de Rabbi Nathan*
AGJU	Arbeiten zur Geschichte des Antiken Judentums und des Urchristentums
AJSR	*Association for Jewish Studies Review*
AnBib	Analecta biblica
ANRW	*Aufsteig und Niedergang der römischen Welt*
Apoc. Ab.	*Apocalypse of Abraham*
Aq	Aquila
'Arak.	*'Arakin*
Aram.	Aramaic
ATANT	Abhandlung zur Theologie des Alten und Neuen Testaments
b.	Babylonian Talmud (followed by tractate)
BAGD	W. Bauer, W. F. Arndt, F. W. Gingrich, and F. W. Danker, *A Greek English Lexicon of the New Testament*
BASOR	*Bulletin of the American Schools of Oriental Research*
BDF	F. Blass, A. Debrunner, and A. Funk, *A Greek Grammar of the New Testament and other Early Christian Literature*
Besh.	*Beshallaḥ*
BETL	Bibliotecha ephemeridum theologicarum lovaniensium
Bib	*Biblica*
Bib. Ant.	Ps-Philo, *Book of Biblical Antiquities*
BJS	Brown Judaic Studies
BKAT	Biblischer Kommentar: Altes Testament
BTB	*Biblical Theology Bulletin*
BZ	*Biblische Zeitschrift*
BZAW	Beihefte zur Zeitschrift für die alttestamentliche Wissenschaft
Cant. Rab.	*Canticles Rabbah*
CaSi	*Cahiers Sioniens*
CBC	Cambridge Bible Commentary

CBQ	*Catholic Biblical Quarterly*
CBQMS	Catholic Biblical Quarterly Monograph Series
CRINT	Compendia rerum iudaicarum ad novum testamentum
DBSup	*Dictionnaire de la Bible, Supplément*
Deut. Rab.	*Deuteronomy Rabbah*
EHAT	Exegetisches Handbuck zum Alten Testament
ErIsr	Eretz Israel
ETL	*Ephemerides theologicae lovanienses*
ETS	Erfurter theologische Studien
Exod. Rab.	*Exodus Rabbah*
Frg. Tg.	*Fragmentary Targum*
FRLANT	Forschungen zur Religion und Literatur des Alten Testament
GKC	W. Gesenius, E. Kautzsch, and A. E. Cowley, *Gesenius' Hebrew Grammar*
Gen. Rab.	*Genesis Rabbah*
HAT	Handbuch zum Alten Testament
HR	*History of Religions*
HSS	Harvard Semitic Studies
HTR	*Harvard Theological Review*
HTS	Harvard Theological Studies
HUCA	*Hebrew Union College Review*
ICC	International Critical Commentary
IDBSup	Supplementary volume to *Interpreter's Dictionary of the Bible*
IRT	Issues in Religion and Theology
ITQ	*Irish Theological Quarterly*
JBL	*Journal of Biblical Literature*
JBLMS	Journal of Biblical Literature Monograph Series
JJS	*Journal of Jewish Studies*
JNES	*Journal of Near Eastern Studies*
Jos., *Ant.*	Josephus, *Jewish Antiquities*
Jos. *J. W.*	Josephus, *The Jewish War*
JPS	Jewish Publication Society
JQR	*Jewish Quarterly Review*
JRAS	*Journal of the Royal Asiatic Society*
JSHRZ	Jüdische Schriften aus hellentisch-römisher Zeit
JSJ	*Journal for the Study of Judaism in the Persian, Hellenistic and Roman Period*

JSOT	*Journal for the Study of the Old Testament*
JSOTSup	Journal for the Study of the Old Testament— Supplement Series
JSP	*Journal for the Study of the Pseudepigrapha*
JSPSup	Journal for the Study of the Pseudepigrapha— Supplement Series
JTS	*Journal of Theological Studies*
Jub	*Jubilees*
LCL	Loeb Classical Library
Lev. Rab.	*Leviticus Rabbah*
LS	H. G. Liddell and R. Scott, *Greek-English Lexicon*
LXX	Septuagint
m.	Mishnah (followed by tractate)
Mek.	*Mekilta de Rabbi Ishmael* (followed by tractate)
MGWJ	*Monatsschrift für Geschichte und Wissenschaft des Judentums*
Midr. Teh.	*Midrash Tehillim*
n. (nn.)	footnote(s)
NCB	New Century Bible
NCE	*New Catholic Encyclopedia*
NRT	*La nouvella revue théologique*
NTS	*New Testament Studies*
Num. Rab.	*Numbers Rabbah*
OTL	Old Testament Library
OTM	Old Testament Message
OTS	*Oudtestamentische Studiën*
Pesaḥ.	*Pesaḥim*
Pesiq. R.	*Pesiqta Rabbati*
Pesiq. Rab. Kah.	*Pesiqta de Rab Kahana*
Pirqe R. El.	*Pirqe Rabbi Eliezer*
Pr. Ev.	Eusebius, *Praeparatio evangelica*
PTMS	Pittsburgh Theological Monograph Series
Qoh. Rab.	*Qoheleth Rabbah*
RB	*Revue biblique*
RevistB	*Revista biblica*
RevQ	*Revue de Qumran*
RSPT	*Revue des sciences philosphiques et théologiques*
RSR	*Recherches de science religieuse*
Sanh.	*Sanhedrin*

SBLDS	Society of Biblical Literature Dissertation Series
SBLSCS	Society of Biblical Literature Septuagint and Cognate Studies
SBLSP	Society of Biblical Literature Seminar Papers
SBS	Stuttgarter Bibelstudien
ScrHier	Scripta hierosolymitana
Shab.	*Shabbat*
Shir.	*Shirata*
SJ	Studia judaica
SJLA	Studies in Judaism in Late Antiquity
SPB	Studia postbiblica
SSEJC	Studies in Scripture in Early Judaism and Christianity
Sym	Symmachus
t.	Tosephta (followed by tractate)
T. Benj.	*Testament of Benjamin*
T. Levi	*Testament of Levi*
T. Reub.	*Testament of Reuben*
TextsS	Texts and Studies
Tg. Neof.	*Targum Neofiti I*
Tg. Onq.	*Targum Onqelos*
Tg. Ps.-J.	*Targum Ps-Jonathan*
TGl	*Theologie und Glaube*
TLZ	*Theologische Literaturzeitung*
Tg. Ezek.	*Targum Ezekiel*
TTZ	*Trier theologische Zeitschrift*
TU	Texte und Untersuchung
TZ	*Theologische Zeitschrift*
USQR	*Union Seminary Quarterly Review*
V. Mos.	Philo, *De Vita Mosis*
VTSup	Vetus Testamentum, Supplements
WBC	Word Biblical Commentary
WTJ	*Westminster Theological Journal*
WUNT	Wissenschaftliche Untersuchungen zum Neuen Testament
ZAW	*Zeitschrift für die alttestamentliche Wissenschaft*
ZKT	*Zeitschrift für katholische Theologie*
ZNW	*Zeitschrift für die neutestamentliche Wissenschaft*
ZTK	*Zeitschrift für Theologie und Kirche*
ZWT	*Zeitschrift für wissenschaftliche Theologie*

Part I

Ps-Solomon and His Exegetical Traditions

Introduction

Purpose of the Present Study

As with most any book of antiquity, the Wisdom of Solomon (Book of Wisdom) has enjoyed a long history of expert commentary and analysis. In this century alone, nearly forty commentaries on this biblical apocryphon[1] have appeared along with the expected countless articles and monographs. Is there any justification in adding another pebble to this mountain of scholarship?

The focus of this study is specifically biblical interpretation in the Wisdom of Solomon. The questions addressed are: how does the author of this work (conventionally referred to as "Pseudo-Solomon," hereafter Ps-Solomon) understand the biblical texts he discusses or alludes to, and where do his ideas come from? To put it another way: why does Ps-Solomon say what he does about Scripture? To be sure, these questions have not been entirely neglected in previous scholarship, and, hence, no pretense is made that they are unique to the present study. Nevertheless, a perusal of the secondary literature demonstrates that most commentators have, at best, assigned a secondary role to answering these questions. More significantly, many of those who have dealt in substantive fashion with these exegetical questions have, in my estimation, neglected factors essential to the investigation; they have tended to view the author of the Wisdom of Solomon as an interpreter working in isolation, implying that what he says

---

[1] My assumptions regarding the extent of the biblical canon are those traditionally shared by Judaism and Protestantism. The pleasant irony, that so much of my own understanding of the Wisdom of Solomon depends on the thoughtful and penetrating work of Roman Catholic scholars, has not escaped my notice.

about the Bible is, for better or for worse, largely his own imaginative exposition of Scripture—or sheer fantasy. The central aim of the present study, however, is to investigate Ps-Solomon's comments on Scripture in the context of the interpretive milieu which certainly shaped his understanding of Scripture. This study seeks to demonstrate the extent to which Ps-Solomon's comments on Scripture reflect Second Temple traditions and exegetical techniques.

Overview of Previous Scholarship
Among the more prominent older commentaries on the Wisdom of Solomon, four works stand out in their detailed and substantive handling of the book: C. L. W. Grimm (1860), W. J. Deane (1881), P. Heinisch (1912), and A. T. S. Goodrick (1913).   These works continue to be valuable sources of information, particularly concerning issues of translation, textual criticism, and interaction with the history of scholarship at the time. Only occasionally, however, do they make reference to other sources of antiquity whose comments on Scripture parallel those of Ps-Solomon at a given point.   Nevertheless, despite some idiosyncrasies (e.g., Goodrick's all-too-frequent cavalier dismissals of Ps-Solomon's comments), these works still represent among the best of the scholarship on the Wisdom of Solomon.   Two more recent commentaries include those of D. Georgi (1980) and A. Schmitt (1986), which are essentially brief, scholarly annotations to their own translations.   Georgi's commentary is especially helpful in providing biblical references to Ps-Solomon's comments as well as cross-references within the Book of Wisdom, but neither Georgi nor Schmitt focuses on the questions that concern this study.

The commentaries by J. A. F. Gregg (1909) and J. Reider (1957) are similar in presentation to those of Georgi and Schmitt, but have a bit more to say concerning biblical interpretation in the Wisdom of Solomon. Gregg, for example, mentions "Palestinian *Midrashim*, or Commentaries" as sources for some of Ps-Solomon's comments (pp. xiii; 95).   He does not, however, specify which midrashim nor does he develop his thoughts here to any significant degree.   Reider occasionally makes a point to mention parallels to rabbinic exegetical traditions, but his commentary offers nothing approaching a systematic handling of this phenomenon.   In fact, at times he even seems to disparage any value these traditions might have for understanding the Wisdom of Solomon.[2]   Three relatively recent

---

[2]For example, see pp. 40-43 in Reider's introduction ("Rabbinic Sources"), where one gets the impression that he will deal with this issue much more substantively than he does.

commentaries are the popular expositions by J. Geyer (1963), E. G. Clarke (1973) and J. M. Reese (1983). The nature of these commentaries precludes detailed scholarly interaction with the text, but they are nonetheless thoughtful presentations. To these may be added G. Ziener's very readable 1970 commentary, which complements his earlier, more detailed treatment of the book.[3] These works—many others could be mentioned as well—are representative of the rich and variegated reflection on the Wisdom of Solomon over the years and are foundational to any further contribution, including the present one. Nevertheless, the broader issues of Ps-Solomon's interpretation of Scripture, and, more specifically, the interpretive traditions to which he certainly had access, are routinely either lacking in these commentaries or treated all too briefly.[4]

There are two commentaries, however, that stand out against this background: C. Larcher's 1983, three-volume *Le Livre de la Sagesse* (1983), and D. Winston's *The Wisdom of Solomon* (1979). Both of these works are important for this study, since, in addition to dealing thoroughly with the issues that have occupied previous commentaries, they also draw attention throughout to early Jewish interpretive traditions that parallel the Wisdom of Solomon. Winston's work is especially valuable in that he seeks out parallels not only with early Jewish sources, but with Hellenistic philosophy as well, both of which are immediately relevant for understanding the Wisdom of Solomon.[5] Winston draws upon his breadth of learning, and successfully and admirably locates the Wisdom of Solomon in its literary and cultural milieu. Yet even these two commentaries, it seems to me, have not gone far enough in discussing Ps-Solomon's interpretation of the Bible. This is no doubt due, at least in part, to the limited space that can be allotted to any one verse in a commentary on the whole of the Wisdom of Solomon. Hence, one goal of this study will be to

---

Compare this, however, to his apparent disparagement of these traditions cited below (p. 37 and n. 62).

[3] *Die theologische Begriffssprache im Buche der Weisheit* (Bonn: Peter Hanstein, 1956).

[4] Other commentaries are listed in the bibliography. C. Larcher's commentary provides an exhaustive bibliography of commentaries and other secondary literature up to 1982 (*Le Livre de la* Sagesse, 11-48). J. A. Emerton provides a brief assessment of commentaries up to 1965 ("Commentaries on the Wisdom of Solomon," *Theology* 68 [1965] 376-80).

[5] Perhaps the most comprehensive treatment of the Hellenistic setting of the Wisdom of Solomon is J. M. Reese, *Hellenistic Influence on the Book of Wisdom and its Consequences* (AnBib 41; Rome: Biblical Institute Press, 1970). Other important studies on the influence of Hellenism on Judaism in general and on the Wisdom of Solomon in particular are included in the bibliography.

bring into sharper focus what Larcher and Winston have drawn attention to in only a cursory manner.

Apart from commentaries, several works have appeared in recent years that do treat more fully, albeit in varying degrees, the issue of biblical interpretation in the Wisdom of Solomon. For example, along with Larcher's commentary is his excellent introduction to the Book of Wisdom, where he draws many fine parallels between the Book of Wisdom and the Old Testament, *Enoch*, Qumran, selected Hellenistic texts, and Philo.[6] It is, however, outside of Larcher's purpose either to treat extensively Ps-Solomon's comments on the departure from Egypt or to engage the rabbinic sources.[7] Several articles have been written that touch somewhat on the topic, but these otherwise valuable contributions offer little in the way of uncovering the nature of the biblical interpretation that we see in the Wisdom of Solomon, especially Ps-Solomon's use of Exodus traditions in chaps. 10-19 and the exegetical process that underlies these traditions.[8]

Although several excellent monographs have appeared in recent years on a variety of topics related to the Book of Wisdom,[9] there is to my knowledge only the monograph by Udo Schwenk-Bressler devoted, at least in part, to Ps-Solomon's treatment of the Exodus.[10] Despite what the title

---

[6] *Études sur le Livre de la Sagesse* (Paris: Librairie LeCoffre, 1969) 86-178.

[7] See also E. Des Places's review of Larcher's monograph ("Le Livre de la Sagesse et les influences grecques," *Bib* 50 [1969] 536-42).

[8] E. Burrows, "Wisdom X 10," *Bib* 20 (1939) 405-7; F. Feldmann, "Die literarische Art von Weisheit Kap. 10-19," *TGl* 1 (1909) 178-84; P. Grelot, "Sagesse 10,21 et le Targum de l'Exode," *Bib* 42 (1961) 49-60; J. Schaberg, "Major Midrashic Traditions in Wisdom 1,1-6,25," *JSJ* 13 (1982) 75-101; A. Schmitt, "Struktur, Herkunft und Bedeutung der Beispielreihe in Weish 10," *BZ* 21 (1977) 1-22; R. T. Siebeneck, "The Midrash of Wisdom 10-19," *CBQ* 22 (1960) 176-82; E. Stein, "Ein jüdisch-hellenistischer Midrash über den Auszug aus Ägypten," *MGWJ* 78 (1934) 558-75. See also the monograph of H. Maneschg, *Die Erzählung von der ehernen Schlange (Num 21, 4-9) in der Auslegung der frühen jüdischen Literatur: eine traditions-geschichtliche Studie* (Frankfurt am Main: Peter Lang, 1981).

[9] J. M. Reese, *Hellenistic Influence*; M. Kolarcik, *The Ambiguity of Death in the Book of Wisdom 1-6: A Study of Literary Structure and Interpretation* (AnBib 127; Rome: Biblical Institute, 1991); M. Gilbert, *La critique des dieux dans le Livre de la Sagesse (13-15)* (AnBib 53; Rome: Biblical Institute, 1973); G. Ziener, *Die theologische Begriffssprache*; U. Offerhaus, *Komposition und Intention der Sapientia Salomonis* (Rheinischen Friedrich-Wilhelms-Universität Bonn, 1981).

[10] *Sapientia Salomonis als ein Beispiel frühjüdischer Textauslegung: die Auslegung des Buches Genesis, Exodus 1-15 und Teilen der Wüstentradition in Sap 10-19* (Beiträge zur

of this work might suggest, however, there is little to no substantive overlap with my study. Schwenk-Bressler's monograph (a reworking of his 1991 University of Munich dissertation) is an admirably comprehensive treatment of biblical passages either commented on or alluded to in the Wisdom of Solomon, but there is essentially no interaction with intertestamental and rabbinic evidence, both of which are central to the present study.   For Schwenk-Bressler, Ps-Solomon's comments on Scripture reflect *his* interpretation of the *biblical* texts in question, i.e., his conscious, isolated, and direct adaptation (*Rückgriff*) of *biblical* themes and passages.   Exegetical traditions current in Ps-Solomon's day that might have influenced his comments are, somewhat remarkably, left out of the discussion entirely.   Apparently, one is left to conclude that what Ps-Solomon says about Scripture is to be understood in terms of his own, individual, creative interaction with the biblical texts.

Thesis and Methodology

It is the thesis of this study, however, that the content of what Ps-Solomon says about the Exodus cannot be understood in isolation.   Many of his comments on Scripture demonstrate that at the time that the Wisdom of Solomon was written,[11] there already existed an extensive and well-

---

Erforschung des Alten Testaments und des antiken Judentums 32; Frankfurt am Main: Peter Lang, 1993).

[11]There is a broad unanimity among scholars to date the Wisdom of Solomon between 100 BC and AD 50. Of all the arguments that attempt to date the book more specifically, D. Winston's is the most convincing to me (20-25; see also Goodrick, 5-17, and H. van Broekhoven, "Wisdom and World: The Functions of Wisdom Imagery in Sirach, Pseudo-Solomon and Colossians" [Ph.D. diss.; Boston University, 1988] 84, n. 93). Winston dates the book to the reign of Gaius 'Caligula' (AD 37-41), on the basis of (1) Ps-Solomon's extensive use of certain words that do not appear in secular Greek literature before the first century, and (2) the "desperate historical situation" that must have prompted Ps-Solomon's call to faith and his condemnation of the wicked (20-25). Winston's second point is quite valuable for our understanding of the nature of biblical interpretation in the Wisdom of Solomon, and this issue is discussed in more detail in Part III. The date of *composition* of the book, however, tells us very little concerning the antiquity of the exegetical traditions contained therein. Therefore, since the focus of this study is the interpretive traditions found in the Wisdom of Solomon, deciding on an absolute date is not a major concern. A summary of the arguments on the date of composition may be found in B. J. Lillie, "A History of the Scholarship on the Wisdom of Solomon from the Nineteenth Century to Our Time" (Ph.D. diss.; Hebrew Union College, 1982) 149-79. For a brief discussion on the date of the Wisdom of Solomon, see W. H. Horbury, "The Christian Use and the Jewish Origins of the Wisdom of Solomon," *Wisdom in Ancient Israel: Essays in Honor of J. A. Emerton* (eds. J. Day, R. P. Gordon, and H. G. M.

developed set of exegetical traditions concerning the Pentateuch in particular. Fragments and reflections of such exegetical activity can be seen in other Second Temple works (some earlier than the Book of Wisdom), particularly "retellings" or "expansions" of biblical narratives found in such books as Judith, Ben Sira, *Jubilees*, *Biblical Antiquities* and others. I hope to show, by way of his treatment of the Exodus, that Ps-Solomon, although he was most probably a resident of the Greek city of Alexandria in Egypt,[12] was thoroughly versed in these ancient exegetical traditions (even to a greater extent than his apparent contemporary and neighbor, Philo).[13] There was, in a manner of speaking, a stock of existing interpretive traditions to which Ps-Solomon had access and which guided[14] his exposition of Scripture in the second part of his book, chaps. 10-19.[15]

Williamson; Cambridge: Cambridge University Press, 1996) 183-85.

[12]Ps-Solomon's home is routinely considered to be Alexandria, since his writing is "steeped" in Middle Platonism, which was "influential at that time in Alexandria" (Winston, 3; see also pp. 25-63).

[13]See also Vermes's view that "the literature of Hellenistic Judaism was built upon Palestinian foundations" (*Scripture and Tradition in Judaism* [SBP 4; 2nd ed.; Leiden: E. J. Brill, 1973] 124 and n. 1). See also below pp. 35-37, esp. n. 60.

[14]As Vermes puts it, these exegetical traditions "*governed*" biblical reading and understanding" in the centuries that followed their inception (ibid., 176; my emphasis). Ps-Solomon's retelling of Israelite history, in particular the Exodus, certainly bears this out, as will be shown below.

[15]Although these issues will not prove central to my study, I am making two assumptions here concerning the nature and origin of the Wisdom of Solomon: that the book was authored by one person and that the book can best be understood to consist basically of two parts. Concerning the first issue, the unity of authorship has been the dominant view of most 20th century scholars. The arguments have been conveniently summarized in several works including B. J. Lillie, "A History of Scholarship," 53-81, and the commentaries by Reider (15-22) and Winston (12-14). Perhaps the most convincing attempt to establish the unity of authorship is that of J. M. Reese (*Hellenistic Influence*, 122-52). Reese argues for the book's unity on the basis of words and phrases that appear in both chaps. 10-19 and chaps. 1-9, what he calls "flashbacks." Reese's work is a far fuller version of a similar view put forth by earlier by G. Ziener (*Begriffssprache*, 95-96). Concerning the division of the book into parts, there is much less agreement. The discussion essentially centers around whether the book should be considered a two- or three-part work. Advocates of the latter approach include Heinisch, who divides the book: 1:1-5:23, 6:1-9:18, and 10:1-19:22 (XIV; see also van Broekhoven, "Wisdom and World," 87), and Winston (1:1-6:21, 6:22-10:21, 11-19 [9-12]). B. M. Metzger is one of many who have argued for a two-part division, 1:1-9:18 and 10:1-19:22 (*An Introduction to the Apocrypha* [New York: Oxford University Press, 1957] 68-73). A. G. Wright likewise has a two-part division but makes the division at 11:2 rather than 10:1 ("The Structure of the Book of Wisdom," *Bib* 48 [1967] 165-84). Regardless of how one divides the first nine chapters of the Book of Wisdom, it seems that a clear break should come at 10:1, since it is here that Ps-Solomon

Moreover, just as important to this study is the evidence from rabbinic literature. It will be shown that some of Ps-Solomon's comments are in fact early witnesses to interpretive traditions that only surface fully in later rabbinic works. The relevance that midrashic compilations might have for understanding Second Temple texts should not be ignored simply because the dates of these compilations are later than the 1st century AD. [16] This, however, is not to suggest that there is any direct dependence of one upon the other. Rather, where we find later rabbinic texts to offer interpretations similar to those offered by Ps-Solomon, the conclusion to be drawn is that both texts are independent witnesses to interpretive traditions that originated with neither. Rabbinic evidence, then, will be brought into the discussion at various points throughout this study (albeit judiciously), not only to highlight particular interpretive traditions in the Wisdom of Solomon, but the interpretive techniques that lie behind these traditions.

Biblical Motives behind the Traditions
In addition to investigating the identity of the exegetical traditions in the Book of Wisdom, considerable attention is also paid in this study—as will be illustrated below—to the biblical motives that gave rise to these traditions. From an exegetical point of view, the Wisdom of Solomon exhibits characteristics of other Second Temple texts: much (but by no means all) of what Ps-Solomon says about Scripture is ultimately motivated by words and phrases in the biblical narratives themselves, particularly by what would have been considered irregularities or problems in the texts. Early interpreters offered "explanations" for these problems, which eventually became associated with the biblical story itself, so that the

---

begins his "retelling" of Israel's history, first generally (10:1-14) and then the Exodus/Wilderness specifically (10:15-19:22). Although every scheme has its own inherent logic, Metzger's division seems the most straightforward. This two-part division at 10:1 is even more convincing when we see chaps. 1-9 as Ps-Solomon's attempt to recontextualize the Exodus, something Reese alludes to in his discussion of flashbacks but does not develop fully. The appendix to this study is a preliminary attempt to support Reese's tantalizing thesis. The issue will also be touched upon somewhat in Part III of this study.

[16]As Vermes puts it: "The present enquiry clearly shows how unwise and unscholarly it is to neglect, in the study of early Jewish exegesis, the testimony of a midrashic collection merely on the grounds of its late appearance." Vermes refers specifically to *Sefer ha-Yashar* (which Vermes dates to the 11th century) and its comments on the life of Abraham, which "preserves a valuable amount of pre-Tannaitic exegetical traditions" (*Scripture and Tradition*, 95). Although the strength of Vermes's assertion would need to be evaluated on a case-by-case basis, the general thrust of his argument is completely sound.

explanation was included as part of the retelling. Many of Ps-Solomon's
comments on Scripture are evidence of his affiliation with pre-existing
exegetical traditions that grappled with the data of the Bible. For early
interpreters, sacred Scripture was to be read closely. It was such close
readings that brought to the surface problems in the sacred texts that
needed to be solved. It is within this larger hermeneutical framework
that Ps-Solomon's comments ought to be understood: they are witnesses to
ancient exegetical traditions whose hermeneutic called for a closer reading
of the biblical text than is sometimes appreciated by modern interpreters.[17]
As J. L. Kugel puts it:

> [T]here is a tendency in readers—perhaps encouraged by the very form of
> these narrative expansions—to regard them as mere "poetic flights," or as
> expressions of some political/theological program that came to be
> associated, more or less at random, with one part or another of the biblical
> text, or again, as leftover bits of popular folklore that eventually became
> fused with this or that biblical figure or incident....so it seems worthwhile
> here to assert once again, without seeking to denigrate any of these interests
> and fields, that the *exegetical* side of these texts deserves our primary
> attention: anyone seeking to come to grips with such texts must first reckon
> with the exegetical motives of their audiences before turning to these
> other concerns.[18]

---

[17]Perhaps an extreme example is L. Hammill, "Biblical Interpretation in the Apocrypha
and Pseudepigrapha" (Ph.D. diss.; University of Chicago, 1950). Hammill seems to treat
biblical interpretation in the intertestamental period as largely an unwelcome deviation from
an earlier, more straightforward, literalistic approach. His bias becomes clear in his
introduction by means of a series of questions: "To what extent is early exegesis
acceptable? How soon did *misuse* of the Scriptures or *aberrations* in method of
exegesis begin? What was the nature of these *departures from the natural sense*, and what
gave rise to them?" (1; my emphasis). The title to his second chapter, which forms the
lion's share of his dissertation, is also telling: "Unacceptable Haggadic Interpretation" (iii).
In this chapter he treats such topics as "The Application of Scripture Passages to Persons or
Subjects Entirely Different from That for which They Are Used in the Bible," "Deliberate
Misconstruction or Mistranslation of Biblical Passages," "Attempts to Explain
Contradictions and Difficult Passages," "Midrashic Elaboration of Scriptural Passages,"
and others. It is the view expressed in the present study, however, that any judgments
concerning the "appropriateness" of the methods employed by early biblical interpreters are
entirely beside the point. Moreover, it is certain that these early interpreters did not
"deviate" from an earlier "natural sense," as Hammill argues. Evidence from within the
Hebrew Bible itself demonstrates that the foundations for their midrashic approach has
roots extending into the biblical period itself. It is a far more interesting question to ask
why these early interpreters handled Scripture the way they did rather than asking whether
they ought to have handled it so.
[18]*In Potiphar's House: The Interpretive Life of Biblical Texts* (San Francisco:

I wish to emphasize Kugel's qualification in his assertion, namely, that comments made by early interpreters in general (and Ps-Solomon in particular) cannot be fully understood simply as exegesis (there were also other forces at work, and occasional examples will be mentioned in Part II), nor can every comment be convincingly attributed to a "problem" in the biblical text. Nevertheless, fully in keeping with Kugel's observation, my investigation into the Wisdom of Solomon has brought me to the conclusion that seeking such triggers in the biblical text is the most profitable place to start if one hopes to understand why and how these traditions arose. Suggesting possible biblical motives for the exegetical traditions found in the Wisdom of Solomon receives considerable attention throughout this study.

The Midrashic Character of the Wisdom of Solomon
The extent to which Ps-Solomon's retelling of the Exodus interacts with the history of interpretation up to his time touches upon questions that have been discussed in recent years, both in general and as they relate specifically to the Wisdom of Solomon: what is midrash and what is the midrashic character of the Book of Wisdom, particularly chaps. 10-19? A proper treatment of these important questions is far beyond the scope of this monograph, yet a comment or two will put into sharper focus the approach taken in this study to the issue of biblical interpretation in the Wisdom of Solomon.[19] Concerning the question of what is midrash, there is a basic disagreement on a continuum between two poles. On the one hand, midrash is thought to be a rabbinic genre, and therefore a phenomenon that comes into existence no earlier than the 1st or 2nd centuries AD. This narrow definition may be contrasted to a broader definition: some have argued at length for the presence of midrash going back several centuries BC and into the biblical period itself.[20] One's

---

HarperCollins, 1990), 247-48. See also Vermes, *Scripture and Tradition*, 83: "Before any other consideration, homiletical or doctrinal, the task of the [ancient] interpreter was to solve problems raised by the Bible itself."

[19]For the following discussion, see also F. Murphy's concise reflections on the genre of Ps-Philo's *Book of Biblical Antiquities* (*Pseudo-Philo: Rewriting the Bible* [New York/Oxford: Oxford University Press, 1993] 4-5). His approach dovetails well with that taken here.

[20]The broad definition is ably defended in by R. Bloch ("Midrash" [*DBSup* 5; Paris: Letouzey & Ané, 1950] and "Note méthodologique pour l'étude de la littérature rabbinique" *RSR* 43 [1955] 194-227) and R. Le Déaut ("A propos d'une definition du midrash," *Bib* 50 [1969] 395-413) (see bibliography for references to English translations).

approach to this question will then certainly influence how one answers the second question, namely, the midrashic character of the Wisdom of Solomon.[21] Since the Book of Wisdom, however one chooses to date it, is certainly no later than the first half of the 1st century AD (perhaps barely qualifying under the narrow definition), those who understand midrash as a rabbinic phenomenon, particularly as a literary phenomenon that interacts overtly with a biblical text, are correct in rejecting any identification of midrash and the Wisdom of Solomon. Those who allow for the presence of midrash in the centuries before the destruction of the Second Temple, however, are also correct in claiming the Book of Wisdom as a midrashic text, provided it meets other criteria judged to be characteristic of midrash in general.

At the risk of entering the fray, I should state plainly that I align myself with those who allow for an understanding of "midrash" as an *interpretive* phenomenon present in texts of great antiquity, even extending to the Hebrew biblical literature itself, rather than as a specifically *literary* phenomenon. To be sure, the term "midrash" has come to enjoy such broad application that it has come to mean very little, and recent attempts at clarifying the terminology (such as Porten's) are needed. To make the distinction between midrash as a *genre*, which certainly flourished after the destruction of the Second Temple, and midrash as an *interpretive approach*, which is certainly much older, seems to me to be a basic first-

---

M. Fishbane's landmark study, *Biblical Interpretation in Ancient* Israel (Oxford: Oxford University Press, 1988) is a strong defense of the pervasive presence of midrashic exegetical activity within the biblical period itself (what he calls "Inner Biblical Exegesis"). The narrow definition is espoused, for example, by A. G. Wright on the basis of genre ("The Literary Genre Midrash," *CBQ* 28 [1966] 105-38; 417-57. Reprinted, New York: Society of St. Paul, 1967). G. Porton argues that midrash proper should pertain only to literature that interacts overtly with a biblical text ("Defining Midrash," *The Study of Ancient Judaism I: Mishnah, Midrash, Siddur* [ed. J. Neusner; New York: Ktav, 1981] 55-92; "Midrash: Palestinian Jews and the Hebrew Bible in the Greco-Roman Period," *ANRW* II.19.2 [1979] 103-38; "Midrash," *ABD* 4.818-22.) Porton's definition of Midrash serves to bring some order to the debate, but also restricts the discussion by excluding from his definition allusions to Scripture that might themselves be evidence of earlier interpretive, i.e., midrashic, activity, such as we see in the "retelling" genre. Van Broekhoven discusses the midrashic flavor of 11:1-19:22 ("Wisdom and World," 93-100, esp. nn. 109 and 110). The bibliography to the present study contains a number of other articles and monographs that touch upon this issue in varying degrees.

[21]For example, R. Bloch includes the Wisdom of Solomon as an example of midrash ("Midrash.," Eng. trans. p. 42). G. Porton, on the other hand, finds little evidence for entrenched midrashic activity before the 1st century AD ("Midrash," esp. pp. 112-18). In saying so, Porton is certainly consistent with his definition of midrash.

step in addressing the issue. This comment notwithstanding, the point I wish to make here is more subtle, and perhaps less controversial. Whether or not the Wisdom of Solomon can be called "midrash" ("yes" under the broad definition, "no" under the narrow), it certainly contains in its comments on Scripture interpretive traditions that were developed independent of, and therefore earlier than, the writing of the book. These traditions represent interpretive activity that we may freely refer to as "midrashic," thereby perhaps avoiding the label "midrash," which, for some, should be reserved for a particular genre of literature. Evidence of such midrashic activity, of course, is not unique to the Book of Wisdom but is characteristic of the "retelling" genre as a whole, which does not simply repeat or reproduce the biblical text but retells it in an augmented manner; it is not merely Scripture, but "Scripture plus." This interpretive phenomenon is the focus of this study, and any preoccupation with labeling the genre of the book at the expense of examining the midrashic comments contained therein overlooks a valuable mine of information concerning the nature of biblical interpretation represented in the Wisdom of Solomon and the state of biblical interpretation at the time of its composition.

Exegetical Traditions in Wis 10:1-14

What I propose to do in this study, therefore, is to examine a particular theme in Wisdom 10-19, the departure from Egypt in 10:15-21 and 19:1-9, in an attempt to document parallels to the Wisdom of Solomon in other sources, earlier and later, as well as to unfold the exegetical thinking that underlies what Ps-Solomon has to say. By focusing on the Exodus, I hope not only to be able to devote more attention to the passages in question than can a commentator treating the entire book, but to shift the discussion somewhat from Ps-Solomon's own interaction with the biblical text to the interpretive traditions that form the backdrop to this interaction and to the exegetical processes that these traditions represent.

Toward that end, I would like to begin by giving just a few examples of early Jewish exegetical traditions apart from the Exodus that have found their way into Wis 10:1-14 (Ps-Solomon's retelling of Israelite history from Adam to Joseph), in order to show the extensive role that these traditions play in his exposition of Scripture. An exhaustive discussion of these verses would take us far beyond the scope of this study. We will focus, rather, on the verses that present Abraham, Lot, Jacob, Joseph, and the Flood. Even a brief investigation will make manifest the importance of early Jewish traditions for understanding Ps-Solomon's comments about the Patriarchs and the Flood, and will establish the proper perspective from which, then, to view his comments on the Exodus.

Abraham

Wis 10:5a-b reads as follows:

> And she [=wisdom[22]], *when the nations in wicked agreement had been confounded* (ἐν ὁμονοίᾳ πονηρίας ἐθνῶν συγχυθέντων), recognized the righteous man [=Abraham] and kept him blameless before God.

The "confounding" (συγχέω) of the nations of which Ps-Solomon speaks certainly refers to the Tower of Babel story. In Gen 11:7 and 9, as given in the LXX,[23] God is said to confound (συγχέω) the language of the people building the Tower, who then scatters the "nations" over the face of the earth.[24] The question, however, is why Ps-Solomon would connect this incident to Abraham.[25] Abraham is not at all mentioned in the Tower narrative; in fact, his name does not appear in the Bible until Gen 11:26, well after the Tower story is over.

Ps-Solomon's apparent displacement of Abraham is not unique. In fact, to ask why *Ps-Solomon* would put Abraham in the tower narrative deflects the discussion from its proper focus, since a similar tradition is found in a number of other ancient texts, most prominently perhaps in Ps-Philo's *Biblical Antiquities* 6-7. This text, likely stemming from the 1st

---

[22]Throughout this study, "Wisdom" will be capitalized when the word refers to the Wisdom of Solomon (i.e., Book of Wisdom) or when designating the genre Wisdom literature. Hence, to avoid confusion, the lower case "wisdom" will have to be used when referring to either the concept of wisdom or the personification of wisdom (i.e., "Dame Wisdom"). Some confusion may arise, however, when quoting the works of others, since most scholars that treat the topic of Wisdom literature tend to capitalize "Wisdom" (since they are not working on a book by that name) when referring to the concept or to its personification. This cannot be avoided, but the context in which the term is used will leave no doubt in the reader's mind as to its referent.

[23]The critical edition of the LXX consulted throughout this study is the multi-volume *Septuaginta: Vetus Testametum Graecum* (Göttingen: Vandenhoeck & Ruprecht).

[24]See, too, F. W. Farrar, *The Wisdom of Solomon* (Apocrypha; ed. H. Wace; London: J. Murray, 1888) 480.

[25]That this "righteous man" is to be identified as Abraham is obvious not only from the context (v. 5c clearly refers to the "Binding of Isaac" episode), but from the term "blameless" (ἄμεμπτος), which alludes to Gen 17:1 ("Walk before me and be blameless," LXX ἄμεμπτος). See Schwenk-Bressler, *Sapientia Salomonis*, 71; Winston, 214.

century AD,[26] also makes Abraham a contemporary of the Tower of Babel incident. In his expansive retelling of the Genesis narrative, Ps-Philo has Abraham and eleven others actively resist the effort to build the tower; as a result, they are threatened with death by fire if they do not recant (6:1-5). The group is given a seven-day respite to decide, and during this time they have an opportunity to escape (6:6-10). Abraham alone refuses to flee, trusting rather in God's justice (6:11-12). God delivers him from a fiery fate by causing a great earthquake (6:15-18). This, however, does not deter the builders from trying once again to construct a tower to reach up to heaven. This time God punishes them by confusing their language (7:1-5). Whether or not Ps-Solomon knew this exegetical tradition in precisely the same form we find in *Biblical Antiquities* is beside the point. Nor is it important to argue for any direct dependence of Ps-Solomon on Ps-Philo. What is important to note, and what Wis 10:5 makes quite clear, is that Ps-Solomon was at least familiar with that part of the tradition that placed the patriarch in Babel at the time of the building of the Tower. Apparently, Abraham's resistance to idolatry, guided by wisdom, is what "kept him blameless before God" (ἐτήρησεν αὐτὸν ἄμεμπτον θεῷ) in Wis 10:5b.

The question is why such a tradition would have arisen in the first place.[27] Of course, ancient interpreters only gave to posterity the results of their interpretive activity, not the exegetical logic behind those traditions. Still, is there a place in our discussions of these fascinating interpretive phenomena for reasoned attempts to discern this exegetical logic? Can anything be said concerning "what went on in the minds" of early interpreters that might have justified such an understanding of Abraham? It seems that this connection between Abraham and the Tower narrative serves a particular purpose by explaining a difficulty introduced in another portion of Scripture. Although the precise biblical source for this

---

[26]Ps-Philo's work is typically dated to the 1st century AD. D. J. Harrington argues for the likelihood of a date before AD 70 (*Old Testament Pseudepigrapha*, 2.299). See also F. Murphy, *Pseudo-Philo*, 6, and C. Perrot and P. M. Bogaert, *Pseudo-Philon: Les Antiquités Bibliques* (vol. 2; Paris: Éditions du Cerf, 1976) 66-74. H. Jacobson, however, rehearses the arguments for a pre-AD 70 date and finds them wanting. He prefers a date somewhere between AD 70 and the middle of the second century (*A Commentary on Pseudo-Philo's* Liber Antiquitatum Biblicarum, *With Latin Text and English Translation* [AGJU 31; Leiden: E. J. Brill, 1996] 1.199-210). Deciding on a firm date is of no real importance here.

[27]J. L. Kugel also discusses this tradition (at greater length), although he does not mention Wis 10:5 (J. L. Kugel and R. A. Greer, *Early Biblical Interpretation* [Philadelphia: Westminster, 1986] 85-90).

exegetical tradition may be difficult to determine, there can be little question that Josh 24:2 plays a central role.   This verse abruptly, and somewhat matter-of-factly, mentions that Abraham and his ancestors worshipped other gods before they left for Haran.[28]   What makes such a statement problematic, of course, is that, although Abraham's *Vaterland* is mentioned in Gen 11:27-32, there is no direct indication there, or anywhere else in Genesis, that Abraham's family partook of any idolatrous activity.   One can see how this fact would have impelled ancient interpreters to develop an explanation designed to fill in this gap in Genesis, thereby reconciling it to Josh 24:2.   Moreover, the precise form that this explanation took arose from exegetical activity surrounding certain particulars within the Abraham narrative itself.   In other words, seeing the need for a story of idolatry on the part of Abraham's ancestors before their westward journey across the Euphrates (i.e., to "explain" Josh 24:2), early interpreters set about the task of constructing such a story, and to do so, they seized upon a number of elements in Genesis that seemed ready and waiting for such an interpretation.   The result was an interpretation that made Abraham not merely a resident among idolatrous peoples in general, but, more specifically, an actual contemporary of the Tower of Babel episode.

Still, how could ancient interpreters justify placing Abraham in the context of the Tower of Babel? At least two passages in Genesis, working in tandem, were available to yield the desired result. The first is Gen 15:7: "I am YHWH who brought you out of Ur of the Chaldeans." What does God mean by telling Abraham that he has taken him "out of Ur of the Chaldeans?" Why should God mention this apparently irrelevant fact in the context of Gen 15:7?   "Surely," an early interpreter might have thought, "Abraham knows the name of his own birthplace!   Would he really need to be reminded?"   Such a superfluous remark might have encouraged early interpreters to seek another meaning. The name "Ur" is a homonym for one Hebrew word for fire, אוּר (see Isa 31:9; 50:11). Hence, Gen 15:7 can be read as if God were saying that he took Abraham out of the "fire" of the Chaldeans. God is not reminding Abraham of his birthplace, but saying that, in removing him from that place, he also saved Abraham from some sort of fire.

---

[28]They were, according to Josh 24:2, בעבר הנהר. This is no doubt a reference to the land of Abraham's ancestry, which, according to Gen 11:31, is the region of Ur. The river referred to in Josh 24:2-3, therefore, is the Euphrates (see J. A. Soggin, *Joshua: A Commentary* [OTL; Philadelphia: Westminster, 1972] 220, 223).

The association of Abraham and fire is a widespread exegetical tradition that actually takes two forms. In some texts, the fire is one of Abraham's making for the purpose of destroying the idols, which is not in view in Wis 10:5b.[29] Elsewhere, the fire is that into which Abraham was cast by the tower builders, and from which he was delivered by God.[30] This second version is certainly the story Ps-Philo has transmitted, and likely Ps-Solomon as well, particularly in light of the fact that Wis 10:1-21 as a whole is concerned to show how wisdom delivers from hardship those who serve her (cf. 9:18 and 10:9).

If, then, the latter tradition is represented in Wis 10:5, what more can be said about the fire itself into which Abraham was cast? The answer is found in a second passage, Gen 11:3. The identity of the fire from which Abraham was delivered is the very same fire used to burn the bricks for building the tower. The verse reads: "Come, let us make bricks and *let us burn* [*them*] *thoroughly*" (ונשרפה לשרפה). Since Gen 11:3 takes place in *Babylon*, and since it is the only mention of *fire* before Gen 15:7, this episode would seem to provide the logical identity of the "*fire* of the *Chaldeans*" from which Abraham was delivered. The close juxtaposition of the two narratives plus the "fire" connection between them apparently led ancient interpreters to see in this phrase a convenient (if also discreet) allusion to the "fire of the Chaldeans" in Gen 15:7 from which Abraham was delivered. This view may be contrasted, for example, to that of J. Reider:

---

[29]This tradition may be found in *Jub* 12:12-14, where Abraham, at the age of sixteen, is said to have "burned the house of idols" (v. 12; Charlesworth, *Pseudepigrapha*, 2.80). The presence of this tradition in *Jubilees* attests to the antiquity of a tradition that links Abraham with some fiery activity in Babylon. In *Apoc. Ab.* 1-8, the inhabitants of Chaldea also meet a fiery doom, but there it is a fire from heaven rather than one that Abraham set. Abraham's resistance to the idolatry of the Chaldeans is also recorded in Jdt 5:6-9, albeit without the mention of fire. In any event, this form of the tradition is not alluded to in Wis 10:5b.

[30]In addition to *Bib. Ant.* 6-7, this popular tradition is also found in *Gen. Rab.* 38.13; 44.13; *b. Pesaḥ.* 118a; *Deut. Rab.* 2.29; *Cant. Rab.* 1.55; 8.9; *Midr. Teh.* 118.36-38. Winston mentions *Gen. Rab.* 38.6 and *S. 'Olam Rab.* 1, both of which make Abraham a contemporary of the Tower episode, but do not mention the fire (214). The midrash is retold in Ginzberg, *Legends*, 1.198-203. G. Vermes discusses the tradition in some length (*Scripture and Tradition*, 85-90). See also G. W. E. Nickelsburg, "Good and Bad Leaders in Pseudo-Philo's *Liber Antiquitatum Biblicarum*," *Ideal Figures in Ancient Israel* (eds. J. J. Collins and G. W. E. Nickelsburg; SBLSCS 12; Chico, CA: Scholars Press, 1980) 51-52.

> "This [Wis 10:5] would seem to imply that Abraham was present at the building of the tower, *but more likely* the connection is due to the fact that the story of Abraham begins soon after that of the tower of Babel."[31]

Reider treats Abraham's presence at the tower building and the juxtaposition of the two narratives as mutually exclusive. Rather, it is precisely the fact that the two stories follow so closely upon one another that allowed early interpreters to make Abraham a contemporary of the Tower narrative (see, too, C. A. Evans's comment in n. 33 below). Ps-Philo explicitly connects the Tower bricks with Abraham's deliverance.

> And they took him [=Abraham] and built a furnace and lit it. And they threw bricks burned with fire into the furnace. And then the leader Joktan with great emotion *took Abram and threw him along with the bricks* into the fiery furnace. But God caused a great earthquake, and the fire gushing out of the furnace leaped forth in flames and sparks of flame. And it burned all those standing around in sight of the furnace....But there was not the least injury to Abram from the burning of the fire (6:16-17).[32]

The fire in which the bricks were made is the same fire from which Abraham is delivered. This is the identity of אור כשׂדים.

Making Abraham a contemporary of the Tower of Babel might also have served to answer another question in regard to Abraham, namely, what it was that Abraham did to deserve God's favor and promised rewards in the first place (Gen 12:1-3). Abraham's introduction in Genesis 12 as a worthy recipient of God's attention is somewhat abrupt. Why was he, of all people, singled out in Gen 12:1 to become the father of a great nation and a source of blessing to "all the peoples of the earth?" What had he done to merit such special consideration? This particular exegetical tradition provides an answer: Abraham had previously earned God's favor in the Tower of Babel incident. He had resisted the idolatrous effort to build the tower. This is why God delivered him from the "fire," or, to use Ps-Solomon's words, wisdom "kept him blameless before God."[33]

---

[31]Reider, 133-34; my emphasis. Heinisch seems to share Reider's view (199). Winston, however, acknowledges Ps-Solomon's participation in this particular exegetical tradition (214).

[32]Charlesworth, *Pseudepigrapha*, 2.312; my emphasis. See also *Bib. Ant.* 6:5 and 32:1.

[33]G. Vermes holds that this midrash did not originate from the Ur/fire pun, but from reading Gen 15:7 in light of Daniel's fiery ordeal in Daniel 3, citing *Gen. Rab.* 44.13 as proof (*Scripture and Tradition*, 89). This is certainly a possible interpretation, but it does not adequately explain how this tradition would have arisen in the first place. What motive would there have been for reading Gen 15:7 in light of Daniel 3? Could it have been the

There is one other aspect of Wis 10:5 that likewise shows Ps-Solomon's presentation of Abraham to be influenced by ancient exegetical traditions. Ps-Solomon mentions *nations* conspiring to cast Abraham into the fire. Who were these nations and why is there more than one? At first glance at least, the Tower narrative would seem to suggest that the inhabitants of the earth were *united* until after they were scattered, i.e., they were of "one tongue and one language" (שָׂפָה אֶחָת וּדְבָרִים אֲחָדִים). Thus, there would have been no "nations" to conspire to cast Abraham into the fire, as Ps-Solomon says, but only one nation. Nevertheless, Ps-Philo's *Bib. Ant.* 6:1, also implies the plural.

> Then *all those who had been separated* and were inhabiting the earth *gathered* and dwelt together. And migrating from the east, they found a plain in the land of Babylon; and settling there, each one said to his neighbor, "Behold it will happen that we will be scattered every man from his brother and in the last days we will be fighting one another.[34]

Evidently there were independent peoples who had been scattered after the Flood and who then came east and settled together in Babylon. The effect of God's punishment after the aborted attempt to build the Tower was presumably to re-scatter the peoples. Likewise, Jos. *Ant.*, 1.157 speaks of Abraham's resistance to idolatry while in Babylon, which led "the Chaldaeans and *the other peoples of Mesopotamia*" to oppose him. Ps-Solomon's "nations" seems to be another reflex of this tradition.

---

veiled reference to fire in Gen 15:7? Would early interpreters have read Ur as fire *in order* to portray Abraham as a kind of Daniel? This is unconvincing. Rather, it seems that the Abraham/fire connection is motivated primarily by factors closer to the Abraham narrative itself. Rather than seeing the Gen 15:7/Daniel 3 connection as the primary motivating factor in tradition, with the Babylon connection being a later flourish, it is more profitable to look to the early chapters of Genesis for a more immediate solution. Placing Abraham in Babel specifically is the result of the "fire" connection between Gen 15:7 and 11:3. The analogy of Abraham's ordeal and that of Daniel is not the point of origin of the tradition, but a later, and not unexpected, elaboration. See also the comment of C. A. Evans: "The point of departure is the story in Genesis, specifically, the meaning of the word 'Ur' (fire) and the assumption that the story of the tower of Babel in chap. 11 precedes the call of Abraham in chap. 12 for a reason. Pseudo-Philo's imaginative retelling is an attempt to explain these factors. Daniel 3 assists him in this attempt, but is not itself the object of his interpretive retelling" ("Luke and the Rewritten Bible: Aspects of Lukan Hagiography," *The Pseudepigrapha and Early Biblical Interpretation* [JSPSup 14/SSEJC 2; eds. J. H. Charlesworth and C. A. Evans; Sheffield: JSOT, 1993] 198). See also F. W. Farrar, *The Wisdom of Solomon* (Apocrypha; ed. H. Wace; London: J. Murray, 1888) 480.
[34]Charlesworth, *Pseudepigrapha*, 2.310; my emphasis.

The likely biblical motivation for emphasizing a plurality of nations working together to build the Tower is the list of nations in Genesis 10, which lists the descendants of Noah's three sons, Japheth, Ham, and Shem. Although the genealogy likely describes the geographic location of the peoples after the Tower incident, particularly since these peoples are said to speak different languages (10:4, 20, 31), it would have been quite natural for early interpreters to read what we call "chapters 10 and 11" consecutively. Gen 10:32 provides a summary statement to the table of nations: the nations (גוים) descended from Noah's sons were spread throughout the earth after the Flood. These then were the very same peoples who apparently *came together* and settled in Shinar (11:2) and began their ill-fated building project. Even though the reference to a common language in 11:1 for all peoples of the earth would seem to preclude having a multiplicity of nations present in the Tower narrative, there nevertheless came into existence an interpretive tradition that sought some connection between chap. 10, especially v. 32, and chap. 11. In fact, the curious plural ודברים אחדים in 11:1 might have provided a clue that further justified seeing a plurality of nations in the Tower narrative. This phrase might have implied to early interpreters that their "many" languages were made one, only to be confused in 11:9. Whatever the motive for the tradition, however, it is clear that "nations" in Wis 10:5 is one witness to that tradition. It is neither an isolated nor a creative remark on Ps-Solomon's part.

Lot

A second example of Ps-Solomon's use of early exegetical traditions comes in what he has to say about the destruction of the city of Sodom. In the Genesis account there seems to be some suspense over what exactly the sin of Sodom is. Sodom is mentioned first in Gen 13:11-13 as Lot's choice for a homestead. Already here the Sodomites are described as wicked sinners, but the text does not say what their sin is. Similarly, God says in Gen 18:20 that Sodom's sin is grievous, but we are still not told what it is. Thus, although the Sodomites' sinfulness is actually mentioned twice, no clear indication is given of what the Sodomites had done wrong. To be sure, one explanation is derived from the broader context of the narrative itself: the sin was the sexual practices of the Sodomites detailed in Gen 19:1-29.[35] But a passage in Ezekiel presents another understanding of the

---

[35]A clear justification for this understanding is the reference to the outcry (צעקה) against the Sodomites mentioned in 18:21 (זעקה in 18:20), which is repeated in 19:13 in the

sin of Sodom. Ezek 16:49-50 specifically defines Sodom's sin as follows: "This was the sin of Sodom, your sister. She and her sisters were arrogant, overfed, carelessly secure. They did not help the poor and needy. They were haughty and did detestable things before me."[36] Although Ezekiel 16 as a whole is strongly permeated with sexual language, i.e. adultery, the definition of Sodom's sin is not. Ezekiel's allusion to Sodom here makes no overt mention of the Sodomites' sexual misconduct, only their mistreatment of others, which is all the more surprising since the sexual imagery of chapter 16 would have lent itself well to highlighting Sodom's sexual behavior.

The reasons for such an understanding of the Sodom episode in Ezekiel seem clear enough. For one thing, according to Genesis 14, Abraham had successfully recovered the booty that the forces of Kedorlaomer had wrested from Sodom and Gomorrah (14:11-16). Abraham's army single-handedly defeated Kedorlaomer's coalition, which, we are told, prompted a show of thanks from the king of Sodom (v. 17). The king then offered Abraham a reward for his help, which he honorably refused citing an oath he had taken to YHWH (vv. 22-24). Yet, several chapters later, how do the Sodomites show their appreciation? By mistreating Lot, Abraham's nephew.

This theme of mistreatment of outsiders can also be seen in the Sodomites' attempted sexual conduct toward Lot's visitors in Genesis 19. These strangers, two angels, arrive in Sodom. When Lot sees them, he respectfully bows and insists that they stay with him rather than risk a night in the town square (vv. 1-3). Lot's hospitality is to be contrasted to the behavior of the other residents of Sodom. All the men from every part of the city, young and old, surround the house and demand that Lot surrender these visitors to them (vv. 4-5). Lot refuses and the Sodomites prepare to take the visitors by force (vv. 6-9), at which point the angels intervene by striking the Sodomites with blindness (v. 11). The Sodomites' depraved mistreatment of vulnerable, defenseless (from their vantage point)

---

context of sexual misconduct. Gen 19:5-8 also makes explicit the sexual nature of their wickedness. This same explanation may be found, for example, in *Jub* 16:5-6; *T. Levi* 14:6-8; *T. Benj.* 9:1; Jude 7.

[36] See also Zeph 2:9-10 and Isa 1:9-10 (especially when compared to Isa 1:17), which allude to a similar understanding of the sin of Sodom.

visitors[37] stands in stark contrast to Lot's care and concern for their safety.[38]

Ps-Solomon's understanding of Sodom's sin is very similar to what we find in Ezek 16:49-50. The story of Sodom and Gomorrah is mentioned twice in the Book of Wisdom: 10:6-8 and 19:13-17. Although the precise nature of the unrighteous activity of the Sodomites is ambiguous in 10:6-8, it is explicit in 19:14: "Others [=the Sodomites] had refused to receive strangers...." This verse is part of a larger pericope, 19:13-17, where Ps-Solomon condemns the Egyptians' mistreatment of their Israelite guests. It was Joseph, after all, who had been *invited* by Pharaoh to settle his family in Egypt (Gen 45:17-20). The Israelites' eventual enslavement is, therefore, a grievous offense, a show of inhospitality. Or to use Ps-Solomon's language, Egypt committed "wicked acts" (πονηρίαις, v. 13c) by practicing "a more bitter hatred of strangers" (χαλεπωτέραν μισοξενίαν, v. 13d). The Egyptian "hosts" are chided for first welcoming their guests, but then turning around and afflicting them (vv. 14-16; see also Philo, *V. Mos.* 1.36-142). Their punishment was the plague of darkness:

> They were stricken with blindness, *as were those at the door of the righteous man* (ὥσπερ ἐκεῖνοι ἐπὶ ταῖς τοῦ δικαίου θύραις, v. 17a-b).[39]

---

[37]These vulnerable visitors may be the "poor and needy" spoken of in Ezek 16:49.

[38]This also suggests that the two interpretations of Sodom's sin, sexual misconduct and inhospitality, are not mutually exclusive. It may be that the Sodomites' inhospitality is demonstrated through their sexual misconduct. Also relevant here is the story of the Levite and his concubine in Judges 19, which seems to pick up on this theme of "inhospitality" in the Sodom episode. Here, too, a friendly resident encourages the visitors to come inside to safety rather than spend a night in the city square. As with Genesis 19, the men of the town surround the house and demonstrate their inhospitality by demanding that the visitor be handed over to them for sexual purposes. Their deliverance comes, however, not in the form of divine intervention, but by the Levite offering his concubine in his place. On the relationship between Genesis 19 and Judges 19, see S. Lasine, "Guest and Host in Judges 19: Lot's Hospitality in an Inverted World," *JSOT* 29 (1984) 37-59; V. H. Matthews, "Hospitality and Hostility in Gen 19 and Judg 19," *BTB* 22 (1992) 3-11; S. Niditch, "The 'Sodomite' Theme in Judges 19-20: Family, Community, and Social Disintegration," *CBQ* 44 (1982) 365-78; A. M. Tapp, "An Ideology of Expendability: Virgin Daughter Sacrifice in Gen 19:1-11, Judg 11:30-39 and 19:22-26," *Anti-Covenant: Counter-Reading Women's Lives in the Hebrew Bible* (ed. M. Bal; JSOTSup 81; Sheffield: Almond, 1989) 157-74; C. Westermann, *Genesis 12-36: A Commentary* [trans. J. J. Scullion; Minneapolis: Augsburg Publishing House, 1985] 297-79; W. W. Fields, *Sodom and Gomorrah: History and Motif in Biblical Narrative* (JSOTSup 231; Sheffield: Sheffield Academic Press, 1997).

[39]See Gen 19:11.

This "righteous man" in Wis 19:17b is none other than hospitable Lot, and those stricken with blindness were his oppressors, the citizens of Sodom. Both the Sodomites and the Egyptians were "stricken with blindness," the latter in the plague of darkness. Ps-Solomon thus uses the story of Sodom and Gomorrah to strengthen his condemnation of Egyptian *inhospitality*, and hence, shows us his understanding of the sin of Sodom and Gomorrah.[40]

Ps-Solomon is not the lone example of this interpretation. Other ancient interpreters similarly view the Sodomites' sin as inhospitality, dislike of foreigners, and arrogance, e.g., Jos., *Ant.* 1.194 and Matt 10:11-15 (par. Luke 10:8-12),[41] both near contemporaries of Ps-Solomon, and *Pirqe R. El.* 25. Did these sources learn this tradition from the Wisdom of Solomon? This is very unlikely. Rather, Ps-Solomon's comment is more likely merely one early, and relatively brief, witness to an exegetical tradition—and one would think a fairly widespread tradition—not of his own making. Against this background, his condemnation of Egypt's and Sodom's friendly reception and then mistreatment of their guests is perfectly understandable.

Jacob

A third example concerns an apparent military conflict in which Jacob was engaged. We read in 10:12:

---

[40]The parallels between the Exodus and the Sodom episode certainly invite drawing interpretive connections between the two. Both involve an initial friendly relationship with the king followed by mistreatment at the hands of others. Both Lot and the Israelites are delivered through divine intervention, which is followed by their respective periods of "wilderness wandering" and eventual settlement in a new home.

[41]In Matt 10:11-15, Jesus instructs the twelve, that if any town or village they enter does not receive them, they are to shake the dust from their feet: "Truly I say to you, it will be more tolerable for Sodom and Gomorrah on the day of judgment than for that town" (Matt 10:15). There would be no reason for the Sodom and Gomorrah story to be used as an object lesson for inhospitality if inhospitality was not seen as the sin of Sodom and Gomorrah. Sir 16:8 and 3 Macc 2:5 may also reflect this motif: both condemn the Sodomites for their "arrogance" (ὑπερηφανία). See also Rev 11:8 where Sodom is mentioned in the context of a city's inhabitants' refusal to bury the bodies of the "two witnesses." Interestingly, Rev 11:8 refers to the city in question figuratively as "Sodom and Egypt," thus drawing a connection between the two as does Ps-Solomon. Apparently for the writer of the Apocalypse, both Sodom and Egypt are worthy paradigms for the mistreatment of the two strangers in Rev 11:7-10. Heb 13:1-2 also seems to refer to the Sodom episode in the context of entertaining strangers.

> She [=wisdom, cf. 10:9] guarded him from his enemies (ἐχθρῶν) and
> kept him safe from those who lay in wait for him (ἐνεδρευόντων). She
> gave him victory in a hard contest that he might know that godliness is more
> powerful than anything.

Two related questions arise. First, where in the biblical narrative is such a conflict between Jacob and "those who lay in wait for him" described? Second, who specifically are these *enemies* who seem to set some sort of ambush for him? Neither such a conflict nor a multiplicity of enemies seem to be mentioned in the biblical account of Jacob's life.

Although it could be suggested that the "hard contest" mentioned in v. 12c refers specifically to Jacob's wrestling match at Peniel (Gen 32:22-32), this is not the case with v. 12a-b. The plurals ἐχθρῶν and ἐνεδρευόντων are not easily reconciled to the incident at Peniel. A more likely explanation is that Wis 10:12 reflects an exegetical tradition such as that represented in *Jubilees* 37-38. There, Esau's sons are said to chide him for not asserting his strength in taking back his birthright (37:1-8). They take it upon themselves to hire mercenaries from Moab, Ammon, Philistia, Edom, the Hurrians, and the Kittim to wage war against Jacob (37:9-10).[42] Jacob responds by defeating these forces decisively (38:1-14). Perhaps these mercenaries are Ps-Solomon's *enemies* from whom Jacob was protected.[43] None of this, of course, is reflected in Genesis where Esau *alone* is said merely to *plan* vengeance on Jacob (27:41). Furthermore, in Gen 32:4-7, Jacob sends messengers to Esau in Edom in the hope of being reconciled to his brother. Although Jacob anticipates a battle (32:7-9), Esau arrives "with four hundred men" (Gen 33:1) and the two brothers meet and then part amicably (Gen 33:4-16). If anything, the biblical Esau and Jacob seem determined to avoid conflict. The narrative in *Jubilees*, on the other hand, not only reports a battle between the brothers, but mentions specifically in 38:2 that Jacob killed Esau with an arrow through his right breast.[44]

---

[42]The "ambush" of Wis 10:12b ("those who lay in wait for him") may be reflected in *Jub* 37:14: "Jacob did not know that they were coming against him."

[43]It could be argued that Jacob's victory in battle is the "hard contest" wisdom won for him and through which he learned the benefits of "godliness" in v. 12c-d, but the Peniel incident in Gen 32:22-32 is the more likely referent. Wis 10:12a-b and c-d, then, describe two separate events in Jacob's life.

[44]Goodrick sees no mention of "liers in wait" in *Jubilees* (233). One could suggest that the "enemies" of Wis 10:12 refer to Laban and Esau, but this is unlikely, since Laban's actions (Gen 31:22-55) can hardly be considered surreptitious. Moreover, this would necessitate separating 10:12a from 12b. It seems more convincing to read 10:12a-b as speaking of one

The origins of such an exegetical tradition may have been triggered by two related factors. First, although no war is mentioned in the Jacob narrative, the possibility of war is strongly suggested. After all, Esau has four hundred men with him when he comes to Jacob. Is this merely for moral support? Was not his whole reason for collecting such a force presumably to avenge himself? Moreover, Esau has already shown his impulsive character in selling his birthright. Might he not lash out at Jacob at any time? In fact, Esau had already promised that he would kill Jacob for tricking him (Gen 27:41). Would one expect such a vengeful character, having been so provoked, to have a sudden change of heart when finally given the chance to confront his nemesis, now greatly outnumbered? In this light, the fact that Esau and Jacob did *not* fight is striking—so striking, perhaps, that early interpreters might have been tempted to read between the lines what "really" happened. Second, what must also be kept in mind in this regard is the tendency in Second Temple literature to portray biblical figures as ideal types.[45] Ps-Solomon's descriptions of Noah, Abraham, Lot, Jacob, Joseph, the Israelites, and Moses in Wis 10:1-21 as unambiguously righteous characters is an example of this tendency. There is no mention, for example, of Abraham's doubt concerning God's promise to give him a son in his old age (cf. Gen 17:17-18), nor is there any attempt to justify Jacob's disingenuousness with respect to his brother's birthright (Gen 27:1-40). So, too, early interpreters were not so much concerned to draw out the many shades of Esau's moral

---

incident. Goodrick also mentions Cornely's suggestion that the Canaanites could be among these enemies (Gen 34:30), and adds that any and all of these cases are legitimate options (233; see also Deane, 166). Heinisch thinks the plural simply refers to Laban's relatives in Gen 31:23, 32, and 37 (206), but this would not explain the ambush and the ensuing battle. Perhaps another possibility for the plural is found in a tradition recorded by Ginzberg, where Esau and his son Eliphaz (cf. Gen 36:4) along with ten relatives are said to pursue Jacob after he fled from home to Haran (*Legends of the Jews*, 1.345-49; 5.288-89). Larcher mentions both *Jubilees* and the tradition cited in Ginzberg but rejects them, arguing as Goodrick does that the biblical account is sufficient motivation for Ps-Solomon's comment (2.633). F. W. Farrar mentions several options, including the midrash discussed here, but does not seem to have a preference (*The Wisdom of Solomon*, 482).

[45]See, for example, J. J. Collins and G. W. E. Nickelsburg, *Ideal Figures in Ancient Israel: Profiles and Paradigms* (SBLSCS 12; Chico, CA: Scholars Press, 1980), and M. E. Stone, "Ideal Figures and Social Context: Priest and Sage in the Early Second Temple Age," *Ancient Israelite Religion: Essays in Honor of Frank Moore Cross* (eds. P. D. Miller, P. D. Hanson, and S. D. McBride; Philadelphia: Fortress, 1987) 575-86. The relevance of this issue for understanding the Wisdom of Solomon will be discussed a bit more fully in Part III, esp. pp. 147-52.

character (e.g., was he a wicked brother or an innocent victim of Jacob's cunning?). Rather, he was singularly wicked—so wicked, in fact, that he came to be a symbolic representation of a variety of Israel's "enemies."[46] Manufacturing a war between Esau and Jacob based on these biblical hints served this broader purpose.

A tradition of a battle between Jacob and Esau might also have been justified by early interpreters in light of Obadiah's prophecy. Obadiah is a prophecy against Edom for the hostility and arrogance it displays towards Judah in Judah's losing struggle against the Babylonians. The prophecy, although referring to nations, takes on a "personal" flavor throughout: Edom, not surprisingly, is called Esau (vv. 6, 8, 9, 18 [2x], 19, and 21) and Judah is called Jacob (vv. 10, 17, and 18). Esau is chided for its violence (חמס) against Jacob (v. 10) and for waiting at the crossroads to cut down survivors (ולא־תעמד על־הפרק להכרית את־פליטיו; v. 14). Although the historical referent seems to be Edom's hostile posture toward Judahite refugees attempting to escape Babylonian aggression, one can easily imagine early interpreters seeing in this prophecy concerning "Esau" and "Jacob" some indication of a conflict surrounding not the two *nations* but the two *brothers*, i.e., a description of what brother Esau had at one time done to brother Jacob: he waited for Jacob at the crossroads (in an ambush?) and cut down these escapees (from Laban's wrath) as they came by. And where better in the Genesis narrative to place such an event than where open conflict between the two brothers seems certain of happening? Hence, this passage in Obadiah along with the hints of warfare suggested in the Jacob and Esau narrative itself could be seen as possible biblical motives for a tradition that refers to some military conflict between Jacob and Esau. In any event, whatever the biblical motives might have been, it is clear that a tradition of a war between Esau and Jacob existed, was even documented as far back as *Jubilees*, and that this tradition is reflected, however briefly, in Wis 10:12.

---

[46]Esau came to represent political forces opposed to Israel (as already suggested in Gen 25:23), namely Rome (Jos., *Ant.* 1.257; *Gen. Rab.* 65.19; *Tg. Ps.-J.* to Gen 25). Esau also came to represent idolatry (*Gen. Rab.* 63.6) and disinterest in studying Tora (*Jub.* 19:13-15).

Joseph

A fourth example concerns Ps-Solomon's presentation of Joseph in 10:14.

> She [=wisdom] descended with him into the dungeon and did not abandon him in prison until she brought to him the scepter of a kingdom and authority over his masters (τυραννούτων). She showed *his accusers* (τοὺς μωμησαμένους αὐτόν) to be false and gave him eternal glory (δόξαν αἰώνιον).

Who are these accusers? Joseph's brothers do mistreat him (Gen 37:1-36), but nowhere are they said to accuse him of anything. Moreover, the focus of 10:13-14 is clearly the sin from which Joseph was delivered (v. 13b, ἐξ ἁμαρτίας ἐρρύσατο αὐτόν), which is the temptation of Potiphar's wife, and it is in this context that the identity of Joseph's accusers should be sought.[47] In this episode, Pharaoh's wife is the only one who can be said to have accused Joseph of anything. It was, despite Joseph's temporary imprisonment, *her* accusation[48] that wisdom "showed to be false," as evidenced by Joseph's subsequent rise to power. So what of the plural in Wis 10:14? This should be understood in the context of a particular exegetical tradition in which Potiphar's wife and the members of her household were supposedly the objects of Joseph's sexual advances. Such a tradition is clear in Philo's *De Iosepho* 51, where Potiphar's wife is speaking to her husband:

> For not content with taking merely the *women who were his fellow-servants*, so utterly lewd and lascivious has he shown himself, he has attempted to violate me by force, me his mistress.

Apparently, according to Philo's depiction of Mrs. Potiphar's words, Joseph is accused of having had a long track record of making sexual advances on her servants before he even attempted such a thing with her. This accusation, made doubly reprehensible by extending the lie to include the women of the household, is what wisdom proved false.

Such an understanding of multiple accusers could have been justified on the basis of Gen 39:14: "She called to the men of her household (לְאַנְשֵׁי בֵיתָהּ) and said to them, 'He brought to *us* (לָנוּ) a Hebrew man to mock *us* (בָּנוּ).'" Although there is some ambiguity whether "us" refers to the men

---

[47]For the following see Kugel, *In Potiphar's House*, 25-48.

[48]In this regard see also *Jub.* 39:10: "And that woman saw that he would not lie with her and she falsely accused him before his master" (Charlesworth, *Pseudepigrapha*, 2.129).

of the household specifically or the whole household, it seems likely that the female servants were at least included in this remark, especially since Joseph's sexual advances would only really "make sport" of them. More importantly, however, Mrs. Potiphar's use of the singular בי when speaking to her husband in v. 17 is curious in light of the plural בנו when addressing her household in v. 14. Since she alone is the alleged object of Joseph's lust, the singular is precisely what one would expect, and it is the plural in v. 14 that would need explaining. It is reasonable to see how early interpreters might have attached some exegetical significance to בנו, particularly in light of the singular in v. 17, and this is what seems to be reflected in Ps-Philo's comment on Gen 39:14.[49] Mention of Joseph's accusers in Wis 10:14 appears to be another example of this exegetical tradition.

Flood

A fifth and final example concerns the cause of the Flood. As he does for the Sodom episode discussed above, Ps-Solomon mentions the Flood twice, but here we have clearly two different versions of the same story. A perennial problem in interpreting the Flood narrative is the question of who is to blame for the deluge. What would have caused God to inflict such cataclysmic punishment? One possible answer to this question is to lay the blame at Cain's feet. This makes a certain degree of sense, since Cain is the most prominently wicked character mentioned by name in Genesis up to this point.[50] A fairly well documented interpretive tradition, however, offers another explanation; it holds accountable the "giants" (הנפלים) of Gen 6:4, whose wicked acts are mentioned just before the beginning of the Flood narrative in 6:5, and thus provide an immediate antecedent. Evidence for this tradition may be found in several sources, including 3 Macc 2:4:

---

[49]Furthermore, Kugel notes that this tradition of multiple accusers may be reflected in *Gen. Rab.* 87.8 and 88.1. It is Mrs. Potiphar's announcement to her household in Gen 39:14 that "put" Joseph "into the mouths of all of them" (ותתן בפי כלם), meaning that *everyone* joined in the accusation (*In Potiphar's House*, 45-48).

[50]At the same time, however, if Cain is indeed the culprit, one might ask why there would have been such a long wait between his wicked deed and the Flood? The line from Adam to Noah in Genesis 5 is said to include ten generations and span several hundred years. *M. 'Abot* 5.2, for example, attributes this long delay to God's patience. *'Abot R. Nat.* 32 attributes the delay to the righteousness of such figures as Methuselah.

You destroyed those who acted wickedly (ἀδικίαν ποιήσαντας) before you, among whom were the giants (γίγαντες) who trusted in their strength and arrogance (ῥώμῃ καὶ θράσει), bringing upon them boundless water.[51]

Although far from explicit, there is warrant in the biblical text itself for just such a tradition that ties together Gen 6:1-4 and the Flood narrative. First and foremost, the simple fact that the story of the "sons of God" in 6:1-4 immediately precedes the Flood narrative would certainly have signaled, at least to early interpreters, that some causal link existed between them.[52] The problem, however, with seeing a causal relationship between the two is the fact that the perpetrators of 6:1-4 seem to be divine beings of some sort, the בני־האלהים.[53] These beings apparently run rampant, choosing whichever בנות האדם they please. In light of this, it is somewhat curious that YHWH's contention is not with these divine beings. Rather, it is with the earth's human inhabitants that he takes issue (vv. 3 and 5). Verse 5 in particular is difficult to square with the notion that the divine beings were responsible for the flood. That "every inclination of the thoughts his heart was only evil all the time" seems to speak of a broader corruption than simply the events of vv. 1-4.[54]

---

[51]Other examples of this tradition include Sir 16:7; Bar 3:26-28; *1 Enoch* 6:2; 7:1-6; 9:9; *T. Reub.* 5:7; *Jub.* 5:1-11. See also J. P. Lewis, *A Study of the Interpretation of Noah and the Flood in Jewish and Christian Literature* (Leiden: E. J. Brill, 1968) 17-19; Winston, 267; Larcher, 3.797. G. T. Sheppard discusses Bar 3:26-28 at length in *Wisdom as a Hermeneutical Construct: A Study of the Sapientializing of the Old Testament* (BZAT 151; Berlin: de Gruyter, 1980) 85-90.

[52]A similar phenomenon was seen above with respect to Abraham and the Tower narrative. This link here in the Flood narrative may even have been intentional on the part of the author/redactor of the story. N. Sarna, for example, suggests that the use of רב in 6:1 and רבה in v. 5 further signals the causal relationship between the two: the increase of the world's population corresponds to the increase of wickedness upon the earth (*Genesis* [JPS; Philadelphia: Jewish Publication Society, 1989] 47).

[53]The precise identity of these "sons of God" is, like so much in this passage, difficult to pin down, but some sort of divine beings is likely, since they are juxtaposed to the "daughters of man." G. Wenham offers a helpful summary of the various scholarly opinions throughout the history of interpretation that have gained some following at one time or another: angelic beings, royalty (antediluvian rulers), and traditional Sethites (*Genesis 1-15* [WBC 1; Waco: Word, 1987] 139-41). See also C. Westermann who includes a fourth category, divine, non-angelic beings, which would reflect an early polytheism (*Genesis 1-11: A Commentary* [trans. J. J. Scullion; Minneapolis: Augsburg Publishing House, 1984] 371-73). According to Westermann, the view that the "sons of God" are some sort of divine beings is now the consensus position.

[54]G. von Rad, however, speaks of "demonic invasion" by which the human inhabitants of the earth were rendered thoroughly corrupt, thus justifying somewhat God's blame of the

Perhaps the cause of the Flood may be found specifically in the "Nephalim" of 6:4, who may or may not be equated with the sons of God in vv. 2 and 4.[55] Again, this is an attractive solution, since they are mentioned immediately before the narration of the Flood in vv. 5ff., and, hence, might be understood to provide its immediate cause. These Nephalim may also be human figures, if Num 13:33 is allowed to influence the matter, and as such provide some human responsibility for the Flood. In any event, Gen 6:1-4 is ambiguous, and this fact certainly would engender multiple explanations for the cause of the Flood. Blaming Cain seems to fit well with 6:3 and 5, which speaks of humanity's culpability, but the giants of 6:4 provide a more immediate antecedent.

Whatever the "correct" explanation may be, it is far more important for the present study to note that both explanations for the cause of the Flood are represented in the Wisdom of Solomon. In 10:4, the culprit is Cain: "When the earth was flooded because of *him*," (referring to Cain who is the subject of v. 3). On the other hand, the "giants" tradition is reflected in Wis 14:6:

> For even in the beginning, when *arrogant*[56] *giants* (ὑπερηφάντων γιγάντων) were perishing, the hope of the world took refuge on a raft, and steered by your hand left to the world a seed of a [new] generation.

Ps-Solomon thus gives two different explanations for the cause of the flood: Cain in 10:5 and the giants in 14:6.

Biblical Interpretation in Wisdom 10-19

Ps-Solomon's comments on the cause of the Flood raise an issue that is worthy of further reflection and may help us in our understanding of the role that these traditions play for him in general in his retelling of Scripture. That Ps-Solomon offers two different explanations for the Flood does not mean these are necessarily mutually exclusive (i.e., Cain may have been the basis of the trouble which was exacerbated by the

---

humans rather than the "sons of God" (*Genesis: A Commentary* [OTL; Philadelphia: Westminster, 1972] 115).

[55]The relationship between the Nephalim and the sons of God is not clear. Wenham argues that the two ought to be equated (*Genesis 1-15*, 142-43).

[56]The giants' arrogance is likely a reference to their presumption in taking whichever human wives they chose (ויקחו להם נשים מכל אשר בחרו, 6:2).

giants). Nevertheless, the explanations are different. Why would this be the case? Could it be that Ps-Solomon was himself unsure of the cause of the Flood and tried out alternative explanations? Perhaps, but the *Sitz-im-Leben* of his work, encouragement to a beleaguered people (see below, Part III, p. 139-42 and 145-47), makes such an academic explanation quite unlikely. The presence of these two alternate explanations in the Book of Wisdom suggests a more subtle explanation. It is my opinion that Ps-Solomon's incorporation of these traditions is not the result of a deliberate choice to represent alternate explanations for the cause of the Flood. It is a characteristic of ancient retellings of Scripture that the exegetical traditions incorporated into these retellings are not clearly (if at all) marked off from the biblical texts. The line between text and comment was often blurred, so much so that the two often went hand in hand. This is what we find so often in Second Temple midrashic texts, that biblical events are retold again and again by different authors with these same interpretive embellishments. Too much should not be made of this one example of the Flood, but the presence of these two explanations in the Wisdom of Solomon raises the distinct possibility that this early interpreter was not *generating* his own comments on the biblical narrative. Rather than being engaged in a deliberate exposition of the text, Ps-Solomon was simply "talking about the Bible" in the only way he knew how: by including in his retelling of the Bible exegetical traditions that by his time had come to be intimately associated with the Bible itself.[57] In this sense, many of Ps-Solomon's statements about the Bible are valuable witnesses not so much to how he himself "handled" Scripture, i.e., to his own exegetical method, but to exegetical traditions that must have been current in his day and which influenced his *understanding* of Scripture.

The importance of this last observation may also help us to appreciate the breadth and influence these exegetical traditions had not only for Ps-Solomon but in the Second Temple world as a whole. Ps-Solomon, an Alexandrian Jew, was apparently quite conversant with *Palestinian* exegetical traditions, not so much in the sense that he was aware of them and employed them, but that they had permeated his repertoire of biblical knowledge. Moreover, he represented these traditions in "shorthand" form. Some of these traditions, as we have seen, already existed in fuller versions in earlier (e.g., *Jubilees*) and roughly contemporaneous (Philo,

---

[57]This is what J. L. Kugel calls the "legendizing" of midrash ("Two Introductions to Midrash," *Prooftexts* 3 [1983] 131-55, esp. 151. Reprinted in *Midrash and Literature* [eds. G. H. Hartman and S. Budick; New Haven: Yale University Press, 1986] 77-103).

Josephus) sources. Yet fuller versions of other traditions are extant only in later rabbinic sources. It is quite unlikely that these later, elaborate rabbinic versions were based upon Ps-Solomon's elliptical statements. Simply by virtue of their brevity, we can conclude that Ps-Solomon's shorthand comments are not the point of origin for these traditions. Rather, both the fuller rabbinic versions and the earlier abbreviated version found in the Wisdom of Solomon are witnesses to exegetical activity that preceded both of them.[58] This conclusion is given further credence when one considers the fact that our author wrote in Greek.[59] The fact that he was able to incorporate *Hebrew* exegetical traditions speaks volumes for the antiquity of these traditions. That a Greek writer living in Alexandria could allude to Palestinian exegetical traditions with such brevity, almost as an afterthought, and that these traditions had become so connected with the biblical text as to become part of the "retelling" of the Bible, certainly attests to the widespread dissemination of these traditions well before the 1st century AD.[60] Winston makes a similar observation.

---

[58]See also J. Weingreen's analogous thesis that the Tannaim "were not the originators of the expositional process associated with them; they were heirs to an ancient, well-established tradition, traces of which are manifest in the writings of the Hebrew Old Testament" (*From Bible to Mishna: The Continuity of Tradition* [Manchester: Manchester University Press, 1976] ix). Weingreen is referring specifically to Deuteronomy's "proto-mishnaic" character as seen in its handling of the law in Exodus.

[59]It is nearly universally accepted that the Book of Wisdom was written originally in Greek and is not a translation. Some notable exceptions to this dominant view have been: C. E. Purinton ("Translation Greek in the Wisdom of Solomon," *JBL* 47 [1928] 276-304) and D. S. Margoliouth ("Was the Book of Wisdom Written in Hebrew?" *JRAS* 6 [1890] 263-97), both of whom have argued for a Hebrew original. More recently, F. Zimmermann has argued for an Aramaic *Vorlage* ("The Book of Wisdom: Its Language and Character." *JQR* 57 [1966] 1-27 and [1967] 101-35). A succinct summary of advocates of these positions may be found in Winston (17, n. 16), with more detailed treatments in B. J. Lillie ("History of the Scholarship," 108-48) and W. P. Berwick ("The Way of Salvation in the Book of Wisdom" [Ph.D. diss.; Boston University, 1957] 36-41). Even if there may be a remote possibility of a Semitic *Vorlage* to the Book of Wisdom (see, for example, Winston's list of Hebraisms [15, n. 2]), it is best to conclude with Winston that these hypothetical documents would not have been "simply translated by him but rather served as the raw material for a new literary production" (18). Hence, irrespective of what may have been in the background, the Wisdom of Solomon is a composition of Greek origin. For discussions on the language and style of the Greek of the Book of Wisdom and its affinities with Greek literature, see Winston (15-16, nn. 4-14) and Reese (*Hellenistic Influence*, 1-31).

[60]I am not arguing here for a sharp distinction between so-called Palestinian vs. Hellenistic Judaism. Rather, the fact that exegetical traditions that are based on the Hebrew text

...it must be remembered that it is unlikely that either Philo or the author of Wisd knew Hebrew, and whatever knowledge of Hebrew sources they acquired must have been through secondary channels.[61]

He points out correctly that the clear presence of Palestinian traditions in both Philo and the Wisdom of Solomon indicates that these traditions had already penetrated into Alexandria during that time. Yet the manner in which Winston states the issue deflects somewhat the impact that the presence of these Palestinian traditions in the Wisdom of Solomon should have on our understanding of Ps-Solomon's retelling of Scripture. It is precisely the fact that Ps-Solomon probably did not know Hebrew that raises the question of how he came to know these traditions in the first place, and, more importantly, how his audience could have been sufficiently familiar with them so as to understand Ps-Solomon's brief allusions. Ps-Solomon's knowledge of these traditions through "secondary channels" is a vital piece of information that brings us closer to an understanding of the state of biblical interpretation during his time.

Despite this example, however, the commentaries by Larcher and Winston are generally keen to interact with early interpretive traditions (although even these two are not noticeably interested in discussing the biblical motives for the traditions). Overall, however, there is a marked tendency in the scholarly literature to overlook and, in some extreme cases even denigrate, chaps. 10-19 as a whole. Unfortunately, Ps-Solomon's comments are all-too-often relegated to his overactive imagination or simply ignored. Although I will give examples of such reactions at appropriate junctures, two of them may be cited here as representative of a fair amount of scholarly opinion. J. Reider, in his commentary, introduces chap. 10 as follows:

> This and the following chapters tell of the beneficent action of Wisdom in Israelitish history, and since they also show the dire effect of idolatry upon a nation they constitute a serious attempt at a philosophy of history....It should be noted that in interpreting Israelitish history in this way the writer uses *considerable license* and employs extra-biblical sources, if not *sheer imagination*.[62]

---

have made their way into a Greek-speaking Jewish milieu actually argues against any such sharp distinction.

[61] Winston, 62-63.

[62] 132 (my emphasis). See also Reider's description of chaps. 11-19 as characterized by "labored diction and dragging periods" (3) and his citation of Grimm's negative comments regarding the latter chapters as laden with "fantastic adornments and

Reider's comment raises at least one important issue: whether Ps-Solomon was employing "considerable license" and "sheer imagination" is something that must be considered in the context of ancient conventions, not modern. However fanciful these traditions might appear to us, our focus of attention ought to be on placing Ps-Solomon's comments in the context of the exegetical-hermeneutical world in which he lived rather than imposing our own time-bound interpretive expectations upon an ancient writer.[63] Furthermore, it should not be assumed that Ps-Solomon was necessarily aware of any "sources" to his comments. It should not be assumed that his comments point to his conscious dependence on what others have said about Scripture. (This seems to be the implication of Reider's statement that Ps-Solomon "employs extra-biblical sources.") Moreover, neither should we assume that his comments represent the fruit of his own exegetical labors. Rather, his intriguing comments on Scripture are windows into the way in which he, living at one particular point in the timeline of the history of interpretation, understood the biblical text in question.

A second reaction, although admittedly extreme, is from B. M. Metzger and expresses his view of chaps. 10-19 as a whole.

> This prayer [chap. 9] is followed by a meditation upon the activity of wisdom in Israel's history. So marked are the change in style and the deterioration in form and content of the remaining part of the book that many scholars believe these chapters to be the work of a different author from the one who attained the literary heights of the first part of the book. It may well be, however, that pseudo-Solomon discovered what many another author has discovered, namely, that the sublimest inspiration does not abide forever, and that in place of noble thoughts mere commonplaces and bathos can also come from one's pen. Whatever the explanation, it must be acknowledged that whoever was responsible for the last half of the book unfortunately kept on writing long after he had anything fresh to say. The

---

exaggerations" (28; Grimm, 7).

[63] As an aside, it would also be worth exploring whether the "extra-biblical sources" Reider mentions were necessarily written (as might be implied by Reider's comment) or whether they represent oral interpretive traditions. Reider does not seem to deal adequately with the possibility that Ps-Solomon engaged in biblical interpretation that was common in his day by employing existing exegetical traditions that were in all likelihood first oral. As Kugel puts it: "[T]hese explanations, known in Hebrew as *midrash* ("interpretation"), were apparently passed on orally for some time, communicated from scholar to scholar, from teacher to student, or from preacher to listener" (*In Potiphar's House*, 2). It is the continuity of interpretive traditions from biblical times to the rabbinic period that Weingreen argues is implied by the term "oral Tora" (*From Bible to Mishna*, 8).

rhetoric of this portion often degenerates into bombast, and there is a marked lack of spontaneity.[64]

Metzger's comment concerns Ps-Solomon's style in chaps. 10-19, and hence, to be fair, is not directed at the types of questions that are the concern of this study. But, still, is there not more to the latter portion of the Book of Wisdom? Does not Metzger's observation draw the reader's attention away from what would otherwise be a fruitful avenue of inquiry? When the topic turns to biblical interpretation in the Wisdom of Solomon, chaps. 10-19 are anything but commonplace. Rather, they are a mine of valuable information concerning the state of biblical interpretation in antiquity. Since the focus of this study is to place Ps-Solomon's comments in their exegetical milieu, it is desirable to see these comments, in some form, in other writings, i.e., a "lack of spontaneity," as it were, on Ps-Solomon's part. Chapters 10-19 may have "deteriorated in form and content" (which, I would argue, is itself a debatable point), but the allusions to existing interpretive traditions contained therein should not be overlooked in the process. There is more at work in the second half of the Book of Wisdom than meets Metzger's eye. And although the near dismissal of these chapters in Metzger's comment would prove too extreme for most, the relative dearth of detailed work done on chaps. 10-19 gives one reason to wonder whether assessments such as this are not at least given implicit consent. Much work has been done on the opening chapters of the book, particularly the issue of immortality,[65] but detailed work on the

---

[64]B. M. Metzger, *An Introduction to the Apocrypha* (New York: Oxford University Press, 1957) 70.

[65]A brief sampling of such works include: P. Beauchamp, "Le salut corporal des justes et la conclusion du livre de la Sagesse," *Bib* 45 (1964) 491-526; H. Bückers, *Die Unsterblichkeitslehre des Weisheitsbuches* (Münster: Aschendorffschen Verlagsbuchhandlung, 1938); M. Delcor, "L'immortalité de l'âme dans le Livre de la Sagesse et dans les documents de Qumrân," *NRT* 77 (1955) 614-30; P. Grelot, "L'eschatologie des Esséniens et le livre d' Hénoch," *RevQ* 1 (1958) 113-31; M. Kolarcik, *The Ambiguity of Death*; M.-J. Lagrange, "Le Livre de la Sagesse, sa doctrine des fins dernières," *RB* 4 (1907) 85-104; G. W. E. Nickelsburg, Jr., *Resurrection, Immortality and Eternal Life in Intertestamental Judaism* (HTS 26; Cambridge: Harvard University Press, 1972) esp. 48-92; R. Schütz, *Les idées eschatologiques du Livre de la Sagesse* (Paris-Strasbourg: P. Guenther, 1935); R. J. Taylor, "The Eschatological Meaning of Life and Death in the Book of Wisdom," *ETL* 42 (1966) 72-137; J. P. Weisengoff, "Death and Immortality in the Book of Wisdom," *CBQ* 3 (1941) 104-33; W. Weber, "Der Auferstehungsglaube im Eschatologischen Buche der Weisheit Salomos," *ZWT* 54 (1912) 205-39, "Die Seelenlehre der Weisheit Salomos," *ZWT* 51 (1909) 314-32, "Die Unsterblichkeit der Weisheit Salomo's," *ZWT* 48 (1905) 409-44.

presence of interpretive traditions in the Wisdom of Solomon has received no systematic treatment.

It is with this in view that I proceed with a study of two representative passages in this latter portion of the Wisdom of Solomon, 10:15-21 and 19:1-9. Aside from considerations of space, my reasons for choosing these particular passages are twofold. (1) Both deal with the departure from Egypt, which provides a thematic unity to this study. Furthermore, in selecting two passages from opposite ends of the second part of the book,[66] I would hope to obviate a possible objection, i.e., that I have carefully selected a single pericope that is replete with exegetical traditions and left other less compliant passages out of the discussion. Although one might expect to find evidence of such traditions in Ps-Solomon's "catalog of heroes" in chap. 10, this would not be the first impression one would carry away from chap. 19. And yet, as we shall see, 19:1-9 is as replete with exegetical activity as 10:15-21. (2) As J. M. Reese and others have argued, the Exodus in general is important for understanding not only chaps. 10-19, but chaps. 1-9 as well.[67] Hence, although chaps. 1-9 do not enter into the discussion here to any great extent, a clearer understanding of chaps. 10-19 may provide some insight into Ps-Solomon's use of the Exodus theme throughout the book.

My approach is to isolate, in the order in which they appear in these pericopes, particular comments on Scripture made by Ps-Solomon that do not appear to be easily justified on the basis of a surface reading of the Exodus narrative. I have isolated nineteen such comments that I feel are particularly interesting and worthy of further study. With each of these comments I have asked myself the same two questions. (1) Are there any other sources of relative antiquity, either earlier than, contemporary with, or later than Ps-Solomon, that say the same thing or something similar? (2) Is there anything in the biblical text that could have motivated this exegetical tradition? My answer to the first question is typically, though not always, "yes." Where a comment of Ps-Solomon's finds no concrete parallel, it is possible that Ps-Solomon may well be acting here as an

---

[66]The fact that the departure from Egypt forms a frame around the second half of the book is itself an indication of its thematic importance.

[67]The recontextualization of the Exodus in chaps. 1-9 has been touched upon by some, but, apart from Reese's list of "flashbacks," has received no systematic treatment (*Hellenistic Influence*, 122-40). As mentioned above, however, Reese's focus is to establish the unity of the book on the basis of duplication of words and phrases in both parts of it. That the afterlife in chaps. 1-9 is seen as an "Exodus" which would provide a thematic unity is suggested by Reese at several junctures but is not developed further.

innovative exegete. This is not necessarily so, however. It may just as well be the case that he is the only extant witness to this particular tradition. In view, however, of the density of these documented traditions in the Wisdom of Solomon, the latter is indeed the more likely solution, but I am quite content to leave the matter open. My answer to the second question is likewise typically, but not always, "yes." Where I judge a particular biblical motive to be obvious, I state it as such. Where the matter is more ambiguous, I offer several options in an attempt to be more faithful to the subtle nature of the evidence. In any event, despite the subtlety involved in discerning the biblical motives for the interpretive traditions that underlie Ps-Solomon's comments, his understanding of the Exodus in 10:15-21 and 19:1-9 is clearly at home in the world of Second Temple biblical interpretation, and it is to a detailed study of his comments on Exodus that we now turn.

Part II

*Ps-Solomon's Retelling of the Exodus
In Wis 10:15-21 and 19:1-9*

As we have already glimpsed briefly, the Wisdom of Solomon is a work of varied character. Chapters 1-6 are primarily concerned with the topic of immortality. Chapters 7-9 are a speech by "Solomon" wherein our anonymous author extols wisdom and recounts his quest for her. With chap. 10, Ps-Solomon turns specifically to Scripture and a review of divine wisdom's acts of deliverance throughout Israelite history, some of which were discussed in Part I: vv. 1-14 recount the stories of Adam (vv. 1-2), Cain (vv. 3-4), Noah (v. 4), Abraham (v. 5), Lot (vv. 6-8), Jacob (vv. 9-12) and Joseph (vv. 13-14). What follows in vv. 15-21 is a succinct overview of Israel's Egyptian captivity in general, with specific attention paid to the actual departure from Egypt (the way to the sea, the crossing of the sea, and the Song at the Sea). This passage not only is a continuation of Ps-Solomon's review of history, but also serves to introduce the Exodus theme, which, along with the wilderness period, is the primary subject of the remainder of the book.[1] The theme of the departure from Egypt in particular is picked up once again in 19:1-9, where the focus is on the

---

[1] Hence, 10:15-21 is important not only for the purpose of this study, but for understanding the book as a whole, for it links the historical survey of 10:1-14 to what follows, and thereby acts as a bridge between the two parts of the book. See comments in Part III. See also J. M. Reese, *Hellenistic Influence*, 144-45; A. Schmitt, "Struktur, Herkunft und Bedeutung der Beispielreihe in Weish 10," *BZ* (1977) 1-22, esp. 4-6; U. Offerhaus, *Komposition und Intention*, 95-97, 119; U. Schwenck-Bressler, *Sapientia Salomonis*, 45-46, 57-58. E. C. Webster, building on the work of A. G. Wright, understands all of 10:1-12:2 to function as a transition ("Structural Unity in the Book of Wisdom," *East Asia Journal of Theology* 4 [1986] 102-3).

flight from Egypt, the Egyptians' pursuit, and the crossing of the sea.[2]

In the following pages, I will undertake to examine in detail the exegetical content of 10:15-21 and 19:1-9, giving full weight, where relevant, to the interpretive traditions that find there way in to Ps-Solomon's retelling of the Exodus. Hence, my aim will not be to offer a line by line commentary as such, but to highlight, in the order in which they appear, the particular exegetical traditions that form the backdrop to Ps-Solomon's comments, and to attempt to explain the exegetical process that Ps-Solomon and these traditions represent.

---

[2]A thematic outline of 10:15-19:22 is as follows:

1. *Exodus*: 10:15-21; 19:1-9
2. *Wilderness*: 11:1-14; 19:10-12
3. *Plagues*:
       a) 11:15-20 (animals)
               11:21-12:2: God's strength and mercy
               12:3-11: Canaan shown mercy [Conquest]
               12:12-22: moral: God does as he pleases
       b) 12:23-27 (animals)
               13:1-9: nature worship is "excusable"
               13:10-15:17: man-made idols (wood and clay)
                   [14:1-7: the wood of Noah's ark contrasted to the wood of idols]
       c) 19:13-21 (darkness)
4. *Egypt and the plagues contrasted to Israel and the wilderness:*
       a) 15:18-16:4 and 19:10-12: Egypt is plagued by animals, but Israel receives quail in the desert. [16:5-14: but when Israel is plagued by animals in the desert, they are quickly delivered.]
       b) 16:15-29: Egypt is plagued by heavenly elements (rains, hail, storms), but Israel receives manna.
       c) 17:1-18:4: Egypt is plagued by darkness, but Israel has the pillar to guide them through the desert
       d) 18:5-25: Egypt is plagued by death of the firstborn. Israel, too, is plagued by death in the desert, but only for a short while. (It is interesting to note that in his effort to maintain the Plague/Wilderness contrast, Ps-Solomon does not contrast the death of the Egyptian firstborn to the deliverance of Israel's firstborn from Pharaoh's decree as he does in 19:4-5.)

1. Egypt Had "Kings" during the Plagues (10:16b)[3]

Verse 16 begins with wisdom said to have "entered" Moses, here appearing not by name but by the epithet "servant of the Lord" (v. 16a). The fact that it is wisdom who is said to enter Moses comes as no surprise, for Ps-Solomon gives wisdom an active role throughout chap. 10: she protected and delivered Adam (10:1), steered the ark through the flood (10:4), protected Abraham and gave him strength to follow God's command to sacrifice Isaac (10:5), rescued Lot (10:6), guided, prospered and protected Jacob (10:10-12), and delivered Joseph (10:13-14). It is thus fully expected that wisdom would have some hand in Israel's delivery from Egypt. Verse 15 differs from vv. 1-14, however, in that wisdom here is said to "enter" Moses, through whom *she* (not Moses) "withstood dread kings" by means of the plagues. Wisdom is not so intimate with any of the other figures in chap. 10. Why then is she said to enter Moses? Ps-Solomon's comment most likely reflects a particular understanding of the burning bush incident in Exodus 3-4. It is there that Moses was first confronted by God and became a "changed man," so to speak. At this divine encounter, Moses was both commissioned and empowered to deliver the Israelites from Egypt. It is the significance of this encounter that separates Moses from the other figures in chap. 10, and this is described by Ps-Solomon as wisdom "entering" Moses. Exod 4:16 and 7:1 may be particularly relevant. It is in these passages that Moses is, according to one reading, "elevated" to divine status, being called אֱלֹהִים.[4] Moreover, this dose of divine power in both Wis 10:16a and Exod 7:1 is followed immediately by the plagues, a sequence that we also see in Sir 45:2-3 (see below) and *V. Mos.* 1.155-58. Also, the fact that Moses is called עֶבֶד (LXX θεράπων) in Exod 4:10, in the context of the Horeb theophany, may explain θεράποντος κυρίου of

---

[3] 10:15 (Israel as a "holy people and blameless race") does not represent a particular exegesis of the Exodus, but the "black and white" categories that are a characteristic of Wisdom literature. The importance of 10:15 (and 19:1a) for our understanding of the Wisdom of Solomon as a whole is treated in the appendix.

[4] A fuller discussion of Moses as divine can be found in the exhaustive treatment of Moses traditions in W. Meeks, *The Prophet-King: Moses Traditions and the Johannine Christology* (Leiden: E. J. Brill, 1967) 103-6. B. L. Mack deals with this theme as it pertains to Moses' ascent to Sinai ("Imitatio Mosis: Patterns of Cosmology and Soteriology in the Hellenistic Synagogue," *Studia Philonica* 1 [1972] 27-55). Philo, in *V. Mos.* 1.158, speaks of Moses' elevation to divine status in this way: "Again, was not the joy of his partnership with the Father and Maker of all magnified also by the honour of being deemed worthy to bear the same title? For he was named god and king of the whole nation...."

Wis 10:16a. Thus, wisdom entering Moses seems to comment on the burning bush incident.

It is, however, v. 16b that is of more specific exegetical interest here. We read *She* [=wisdom] *withstood dread kings with wonders and signs* (καὶ ἀντέστη βασιλεῦσιν φοβεροῖς ἐν τέρασιν καὶ σημείοις). The plural "kings" is noteworthy, since the reference appears to be to the one Pharaoh of the plagues.[5] Several solutions have been proposed, the most popular of which is the "allusive plural...by which one person is alluded to in the plural number."[6] This is not only the commonly held position, but in many respects the most straightforward and reasonable solution. The use of a plural form when referring to a singular is common throughout Greek literature[7] including the NT.[8] Most importantly, it is a phenomenon that

---

[5] See also G. Ziener, *Begriffssprache*, 131.

[6] The definition is Winston's (219). Referring to Wis 10:16b, Grimm (202), Heinisch (210), and Larcher (2.641) do not use the term "allusive," but "plural of majesty." The plural of majesty is a specific category of the allusive plural (Smyth, §1007). See also F. W. Farrar, *The Wisdom of Solomon*, 483.

[7] Winston (219) cites Smyth, §1007 and BDF, §141. Although I do not question the existence of the allusive plural in general, the examples cited by Smyth and Winston can be better explained otherwise. For example, *Eumenides* 100, cited by Smyth, reads, "I [Clytemnestra's ghost] suffer [παθοῦσα] from my dearest ones [φιλτάτων]." Smyth understands the plural to refer to Clytemnestra's killer Orestes, but this is not supported by the context. The use of the participle suggests that the action is taking place in the speaker's present, i.e., Clytemnestra's ghostly state. It is in the afterlife that she is lamenting the reproach of those she had killed while alive. This is clear in lines 95-99. The φίλοι she thus refers to in line 100, therfore, is not her killer Orestes but those whom she had killed, her husband Agamemnon and his mistress Cassandra. The plural is not allusive but actual. But, of course, this does not mean that the allusive plural does not enjoy widespread attestation. It is a very common grammatical phenomenon throughout the breath of Greek and Hellenisitic literature. The point made here is simply that not every unexpected plural is necessarily allusive.

[8] Moulton, 3.25-28; Zerwick, *Biblical Greek* (Scripta Pontificii Instituti Biblici 114; Rome: Pontifical Biblical Institute, 1963) 3. Winston cites Matt 2:20 as a NT example of the allusive plural (as does Moulton, 3.7, 25). This particular example, however, like *Eumenides* 100 cited in the previous note, is not convincing. I am in full agreement with W. D. Davies and D. C. Allison, that Matt 2:19-21, which speaks of Jesus' return from Egypt after the death of Herod, is a deliberate echo of LXX Exod 4:19-20, which speaks of Moses' return to Egypt after the death of Pharaoh (*The Gospel According to Saint Matthew* [ICC; Edinburgh: T & T Clark, 1988] 1.217). The verbal correspondence between Matt 2:20 and LXX Exod 4:19 is clear:

Exod 4:19: Τεθνήκασιν γὰρ πάντες οἱ ζητοῦντές σου τὴν ψυξήν
For all those seeking your life have died.

Matt 2:20: Τεθνήκασιν γὰρ οἱ ζητοῦντες τὴν ψυξήν τοῦ παιδίου
For those seeking the life of the child have died.

occurs in the Wisdom of Solomon. For example, Wis 9:4a, 9:12c, and 18:15a speak of "thrones" where one throne is clearly in view. Likewise, in 10:3b, we see Cain's "fratricidal rage" (ἀδελφοκτόνοις θυμοῖς); in 10:5c it is Abraham's compassion (σπλάγχνοις) for Isaac; in 10:14c it is Joseph's rise to power (σκῆπτρα βασιλείας). These plurals are certainly not to be understood literally: Cain does not succumb to fratricidal rage more than once; Abraham does not have "compassions" for his son. The plurals in Wis 10:3b and 5c most likely indicate the intensity of Cain's rage and Abraham's compassion. The "thrones" of 9:4a, 9:12c, and 18:15a,[9] and the plural concerning Joseph in 10:14c[10] are probably plurals of majesty or perhaps "elliptical" plurals, where "thrones" would refer not to a multiplicity of thrones, but royal authority and everything that goes along with it. Hence, it seems perfectly reasonable to understand "kings" in 10:16b in the same way.

Although the allusive plural should be given weight in explaining "kings" and other unexpected plurals in the Wisdom of Solomon, there are at least three points worth considering that broaden the discussion somewhat. First, Ps-Solomon is not consistent in his use of the allusive plural. For example, although we have "thrones" in 9:4a and 9:12c, we read "throne" in close proximity (ἀπὸ θρόνου δόξης σου, 9:10b). Of course, one would have no reason to expect Ps-Solomon to employ the allusive plural in every possible instance. But likewise, neither is there any reason to assume that every unexpected plural is necessarily allusive. Other possibilities must be explored before arriving at a conclusion. Second, as I have shown in Part I, there are at least three plurals elsewhere in chap. 10 that are best understood as examples of interpretive traditions rather than allusive plurals. The plural "nations" that were in "wicked

---

Matthew alludes to Exod 4:19 in an effort to identify Christ's flight from Herod with Moses' flight from Pharaoh. Matthew's use of the plural thus reflects his theology, not his grammar. But again, this is not to give the impression that the allusive plural is not a common phenomenon in the NT. See the many legitimate instances cited in BDF, §141-42; Moutlon, 3.25-28.

[9]See also the comments by Winston (202) and Larcher (2.570). Similarly, P. W. Skehan considers θρόνων and σκήπτρων in 7:8 to be examples of the frequent occurrence of grammatical plurals as "logical singulars according to well-known Greek usage" ("Notes on the Text of the Book of Wisdom, *Traditio* 3 [1945] 11, reprinted in *Studies in Israelite Poetry and Wisdom* [Washington, D.C.: Catholic Biblical Association of America, 1971] 132-36).

[10]This appraisal of Pharaoh's strength functions, for Heinisch (210) and Larcher (2.641), to emphasize wisdom's superior strength. The irony is evident: the author gives Pharaoh great might only to denigrate him further by wisdom's might.

agreement" against Abraham (10:5, pp. 23-24) is clearly not allusive, since there could not be *one* nation in *agreement* with itself. Rather, these nations were those of the Tower episode, as Jos. *Ant.*, 1.157 (and perhaps *Bib. Ant.* 6:1) likewise attests. Jacob's "enemies" (10:12, pp. 27-30) are Esau and his mercenary army (cf. *Jubilees* 37-38). Joseph's "accusers" (10:14, pp. 31-32) are not his brothers. Neither does "accusers" simply refer to Potiphar's wife, but to the women of her household, an interpretation that explains the curious plural of Gen 39:14 and which is also reflected in Philo's *De Iosepho* 51. Hence, there ought to be no great surprise if a similar exegetical explanation could be shown to account for "kings" in v. 16. (This also applies to the plural "dumb" [κωφῶν] in 10:21a to be discussed below under #8).

Third, and most important for our understanding of "kings" in Wis 10:16b, is the fact that there are other texts that mention "kings" in conjunction with the plagues. This is significant, since it raises the possibility that more than mere literary convention is at work. Ps 105 (104):26-36 is an example that will make clear what is at stake.[11] Verse 30 mentions the plague of frogs that "went up to the bedrooms of *their kings*" (מלכיהם/βασιλέων αὐτῶν). Of course, whether Ps-Solomon had this problem in mind, or even whether it is ultimately behind the tradition that he reproduces, is impossible to tell.[12] Still, the wording of this psalm should at the very least bring into the discussion the possibility that Ps-Solomon's "kings" is not an example of the allusive plural, but dependent on a biblical text that either he or at least the particular exegetical tradition of which he is a part adduced to comment on the plagues. Sir 45:2-3 is even more significant in leading us to this conclusion.

---

[11]Throughout this study, wherever the numbering of a psalm differs between the MT and LXX, the MT number will be given first and the LXX in parentheses. If only the LXX psalm is cited, it will be marked as such. If any psalm is simply cited without any specific designation, it refers either to the MT alone or to both MT and LXX where the numbers are the same.

[12]Skehan suggests that Ps 76 (75):13 ("he is feared by the kings of the earth," למלכי־ארץ/τοῖς βασιλεῦσι τῆς γῆς) is behind Ps-Solomon's comment ("Borrowings from the Psalms in the Book of Wisdom," *CBQ* 10 [1948] 390, reprinted in Skehan, *Studies*, 155). Psalm 105 (104), however, is a much more likely candidate, since the connection between kings and the Exodus, especially the plagues, is explicit. Psalm 76 (75) is more a general statement of YHWH's confrontations with non-Israelite rulers. There is nothing that connects Psalm 76 [75] to the Exodus.

He [=God] made him [=Moses] equal in glory to the holy ones [ἁγίων][13] and magnified him in the fears of his enemies. By his words he caused signs [σημεῖα] to cease[14] and glorified him in the presence of *kings* [βασιλέων].

That Ben Sira also has "kings" during the plagues is striking and gives one pause to wonder whether the grammatical explanation offered by many commentators is quite as certain, or at least as exclusive, as is often assumed.[15] In sum, we have in Ps 105 (104):30, Sir 45:3b, and Wis 10:16b clear reference to "kings" of Egypt who were subject to the plagues. Despite, then, the ubiquity of the allusive plural in Greek literature and its presence elsewhere in the Book of Wisdom, Ps-Solomon's "kings" does not seem to me to reflect a literary convention. The mention of "kings" in these three texts and the plurals "nations," "enemies," and "accusors" in chap. 10 suggest that, here, too, Ps-Solomon's comment is part of an interpretive tradition.

It remains, however, to ask who these "kings" actually were. No definitive conclusion can be reached, but some suggestions are worth investigating. Both Artapanus (in Eusebius, *Pr. Ev.* 9.27.7-10) and Josephus (*Ant.* 2.238-53) relay a tradition of a young Moses taking charge

---

[13]This seems to be Ben Sira's way of handling Moses' elevation to some sort of divine status in Exod 4:16 and 7:1 discussed above. אלהים is understood as angels.

[14]This comment refers to the cessation of the plagues at Moses' command in Exod 8:13, 31; 9:33; 10:18-19.

[15]The plural is the reading in the Greek text of Ben Sira's grandson and the Peshitta (although the reading in Codex Ambrosianus does not have the plural pointing). Two Sahidic manuscripts (55, 254) have the singular βασιλέως. The Hebrew text from the Cairo Geniza (manuscript B) also has the singular מלך. See R. Smend, *Die Weisheit des Jesus Sirach* (Berlin: Georg Reimer, 1906) 427, and *Griechisch-Syrisch-Hebräischer Index zur Weisheit des Jesus Sirach* (Berlin: Georg Reimer, 1907) 35; N. Peters, *Der jüngst Wiederaufgefundene hebräische Text des Buches Ecclesiasticus* (Freiburg: Herdersche Verlagshandlung, 1902) 235-36; D. Barthélemy and O. Rickenbacher, *Konkordanz zum Hebräischen Sirach, mit Syrisch-Hebräischem Index* (Göttingen: Vandenhoeck & Ruprecht, 1973) 224; Z. Ben-Ḥayyim, ed., *The Book of Ben Sira: Text, Concordance and an Analysis of Vocabulary* (Jerusalem: The Academy of the Hebrew Language and the Shrine of the Book, 1973) 200; P. C. Beentjes, *The Book of Ben Sira in Hebrew: A Text Edition of all Extant Hebrew Manuscripts and a Synopsis of All Parallel Hebrew Ben Sira Texts* (VTSup 68; Leiden: E. J. Brill, 1997) 79. On the basis of *lectio difficilior*, the plural is certainly to be preferred, but this is by no means conclusive. The simplest text-critical explanation is that the Greek plural represents a different Hebrew *Vorlage* from that which is represented in the Cairo Geniza text. In any event, βασιλέων is not an isolated aberration, but one of at least three examples that have "kings" present at the plagues.

of Pharaoh's army and leading a campaign against the invading Ethiopians, and this may help explain the plural "kings."[16]   But this tradition has little to do with Ps-Solomon's "kings."   For one thing, we may presume that there is only one Ethiopian king involved, since there is only one campaign against the Ethiopians.   Second, the context of Wis 10:16b is the plagues. The account of the campaign against the Ethiopians, however, has nothing to do with the plagues in Egypt; this episode would seem to take place prior to Moses' flight from Egypt (Exod 2:11-15).   Not only do the respective contexts make this distinction clear, but the manner in which Moses secures this victory against the Ethiopians is more a testimony to his own ingenuity than the divine intervention of the plagues that is assumed in Wis 10:16.[17]   Hence, "kings" does not refer to the Ethiopian campaign. We may also rule out for the same reason a related and equally hypothetical possibility, Israel's intimidation of Edom, Moab, and Canaan after the crossing of the sea mentioned in Exod 15:15-16 (cf. Ps 136:17-20).[18] Throughout 10:15-21 and 19:1-9, Ps-Solomon seems to maintain a strict adherence to the chronology of the Exodus narrative.[19]   Exod 15:15-16

---

[16]This possibility is mentioned by F. W. Farrar, *The Wisdom of Solomon*, 483.

[17]According to Josephus (a bit fuller than Artapanus' account), Moses accepts command of the army to repel the invading enemy.   Yet the route he takes to engage the battle is overrun by serpents.   To counteract this plague, Moses brings with him baskets full of ibises, which Josephus tells us are "the serpent's deadliest enemy."   This maneuver Josephus calls "a marvelous stratagem" (στρατήγημα θαυμαστόν) and "a wonderful proof of his sagacity" (συνέσεως θαυμαστὴν ἐπίδειξιν).   There is nothing particularly miraculous about Moses' victory over the Ethiopians.   Wisdom's deliverance, on the other hand, is accompanied by "wonders and signs" (τέρασιν καὶ σημείοις).   Τέρας in the Wisdom of Solomon is consistently used in contexts of divine intervention (See also Ziener, *Begriffssprache*, 148-49).   The word is used in Wis 17:15 regarding the plague of darkness as well as Exod 4:21; 7:3 (where it is paired with σημεῖον, as it is in Wis 10:16b); 7:9; 11:9, 10; LXX Pss 77:43 and 104:27, all of which refer to the plagues, and Exod 15:11, which refers to the miracle at the sea in general (see also Wis 19:8 and τέρατα). See also W. Meeks, who discusses the emphasis on signs and wonders of Moses in non-rabbinic Jewish sources (*The Prophet-King*, 162-63).

[18]This seems to be Schmitt's view: "Entweder schließt dieser Plural auch Könige außerhalb Ägyptens ein, mit denen Mose während des Wüstenzugs in Konflikt gerät, oder aber er steht in Bezug auf eine einzige Person (sc. Pharao) verallgemeinernd" (96).   Schwenk-Bressler suggests that Exodus 17 (presumably Joshua's battle against the Amalekites) is the biblical referent for "kings" (*Sapientia Salomonis*, 98).

[19]The sequence in Wis 10:15-21 and the corresponding events in Exodus are as follows:

Wisdom 10	Exodus
16b	7:14-12:30 (plagues)
17a	12:31-36 (plundering the Egyptians)
17b-d	13:17-22 (way to the sea)

refers to the events after the crossing of the sea, and, hence, does not fit the chronological sequence of the passage.

Perhaps a more obvious solution is simply the fact that, according to the biblical narrative in Exodus, there was more than one Pharaoh alive during Moses' lifetime. The first Pharaoh attempted to control the Israelite population, first by enslaving them (1:9-14), then by ordering the midwives to kill all male children at birth (1:15-21), and finally in an all-out assault by having all male children thrown into the Nile (1:22). It is from this Pharaoh's edict that Moses escaped (2:1-10). During Moses' stay in Midian (2:11-4:17), this first Pharaoh died (2:23) and was (presumably) replaced by another. It was to this Pharaoh that YHWH commanded Moses to return to lead the Israelites out of Egypt (3:10, see also 4:19). The fact that there were two kings would account for the plural.[20]

This solution to the "kings" of Wis 10:16b has merit, but it runs into one significant roadblock. Once again, Ps-Solomon seems clear in indicating that the dread kings whom wisdom withstood were kings of the plagues. In other words, since Ps-Solomon's "kings" refers to the time of the plagues, identifying one of these kings as the Pharaoh who gave the decrees in Exodus 1 and who died in Exod 2:23, *before* the onset of the plagues, will not really help. We have, thus, the same problem as

---

| 18-20a | 14:1-31 (crossing the sea) |
| 20b-21 | 15:1-21 (Song at the Sea). |

Keeping this sequence in mind will help clarify what the biblical referent is for Ps-Solomon's comments throughout 10:15-21 and 19:1-9.

[20]If Ps-Solomon's "kings" is meant to account for this multiplicity of kings, it is possible that Wis 10:16b is an early witness to an interpretive tradition documented fully only later. There is a concern expressed in some rabbinic texts that the Pharaoh of Exod 1:8-22, i.e., the Pharaoh who issued the decree to drown the male children in the Nile, be the same Pharaoh as the one of the plagues (for a fuller discussion of this interpretive tradition see J. Cohen, *The Origins and Evolution of the Moses Nativity Story* [Studies in the History of Religions 58; Leiden: E. J. Brill, 1993] 78-79, n. 26.). The reason for such a tradition, despite the clear statement to the contrary in Exod 2:23 of the first Pharaoh's death, is to justify God's measure-for-measure punishment of Pharaoh. It is a question of theodicy: why would God punish the second Pharaoh for something the first Pharaoh did? The answer: there were not two Pharaohs but only one, and his "death" in 2:23 merely refers to leprosy, i.e., as if he were dead. (See *Exod. Rab.* 1.34 and *Tg. Ps.-J.* to Exod 2:23. See also Ginzberg's paraphrase of this tradition [*Legends*, 5.412-13, n. 101]. Completely unrelated to this is the well known rabbinic controversy recorded in *b. Soṭa* 11a, that the new king of Exod 1:8 is really no new king at all, but rather indicates a change in policy of the one Pharaoh who reigned during both Joseph's and Moses' lifetime. J. Cohen points out that the LXX rendering of "new" is ἕτερος [other] and may reflect an early stage of this controversy [*Origins and Evolution*, 79]).

with the Ethiopian campaign solution mentioned above. For the same reason, neither will Exod 4:19 provide a solution to the problem: "For all those who sought your life have died" (כי־מתו כל־האנשים המבקשים את־נפשך, τεθνήκασιν γὰρ πάντες οἱ ζητοῦντές σου τὴν ψυχήν). The point of 4:19 is to show that these enemies of Moses had died and so cleared the way for Moses' return. They had already died before the onset of the plagues, and hence were not those afflicted by the "wonders and signs" spoken of in Wis 10:16b. Furthermore, 4:19 does not specify who these enemies are; by itself it does not imply a multiplicity of kings.

We are therefore cast back upon Ps 105 (104):30, whose mention of "kings" seems to be the only sure source for the plural in Sir 45:3 and Wis 10:16b. But if the latter two were, directly or indirectly, citing this psalm in saying "kings," how might they have understood its plural? Perhaps Ben Sira and Ps-Solomon understood the psalm's "kings" as referring to Pharaoh and his servants or officials. This offers certain advantages. After all, throughout the plagues narrative, Moses and Aaron are said to confront Pharaoh *and his court* (Exod 7:11, 20-22; 8:7, 18, 21-24, 29-31; 9:11, 20, 30, 34; 10:1, 6-7; 11:8; 12:30; see also 14:5). In other words, it is not just Pharaoh who is the audience of Moses' proclamation, but his officials as well; the two seem to go hand in hand. In this regard, Exod 7:8-10; 8:20-24, and 10:1 are particularly interesting. In all three instances, YHWH's command is that Pharaoh specifically be confronted with the threat of the plague in question, yet it is Pharaoh *and his officials* who together wind up bearing the punishment. Moreover, this state of affairs is reflected succinctly in Ps 135 (134):9: "He sent signs and wonders (LXX σημεῖα καὶ τέρατα) into your midst, O Egypt, against Pharaoh and all his servants (ἐν πᾶσι τοῖς δούλοις αὐτοῦ/בכל־עבדיו)."[21] Perhaps the expressions in Psalm 105 (104) and 135 (134) were understood to be equivalent. In other words, "kings" in Psalm 105 (104), Sira 45, and Wisdom 10 could refer not only to the king himself but to his officials and advisors as well. In any case, it does seem likely that Ps-Solomon's "kings," particularly in light of the identical statement by Ben Sira, is more than mere literary convention, and very plausibly reflects an exegetical tradition based on Pss 105 (104) and/or 135 (134).

---

[21]See also *V. Mos.* 1.15: τοῖς ἐν τέλει τῶν Αἰγυπτίων.

2. Israelites Received "Payment" for Their Period of Slavery (10:17a)

In 10:17a, Ps-Solomon reproduces an exegetical tradition that is fairly well attested in later sources. This tradition concerns Exod 12:35-36 (also 3:21-22 and 11:2-3), where the Israelites are said to plunder (בצל/σκυλεύω)[22] the Egyptians, and maintains that the plundering was quite justified, a payment for years of unpaid servitude. Hence, we read in v. 17a: *She rewarded holy ones for their labors* (ἀπέδωκεν ὁσίοις μισθὸν κόπων αὐτῶν). This interpretive tradition is quite early, appearing in *Jub* 48:18,[23] Philo's *V. Mos.* 1.141,[24] and Ezekiel the Tragedian's *Exagoge* 162-66.[25] Winston comments that the many instances of this tradition,

> clearly imply that the Israelite borrowing of gold and silver vessels from the Egyptians has been a special target of the polemical and anti-Semitic literature of the Greco-Roman age and that Jewish writers found it necessary to provide some sort of apologetic defense.[26]

---

[22]The piel of בצל with the accusative in both biblical and mishnaic Hebrew refers to plundering or stripping. In Hellenistic literature, σκυλεύω carries specific connotations of despoiling slain enemies, a point that will become relevant below under #4 (pp. 66ff.).

[23]"And on the fourteenth day we bound him [=Prince Mastema] so that he might not accuse the children of Israel on the day when they were requesting vessels and clothing from the men of Egypt—vessels of silver, and vessels of gold, and vessels of bronze—so that they might plunder the Egyptians *in exchange for the servitude* which they subjected them to by force" (Charlesworth, *Pseudepigrapha*, 2.140; my emphasis).

[24]"For they took out with them much spoil, which they carried partly on their backs, partly laid on their beasts of burden. And they did this not in avarice, or, as their accusers might say, in covetousness of what belonged to others. No, indeed. In the first place, they were but receiving a *bare wage* [μισθόν] for all their time of service" (my emphasis).

[25]"But when you are about to leave, I will make the Egyptians well-disposed to you and each of your women will receive from her neighbor vessels and raiment of all kinds, gold, silver and garments, so that the Egyptians shall *render payment* [μισθὸν ἀποδῶσιν] for all the work the Jews have done" (H. Jacobson, *The Exagoge of Ezekiel* [Cambridge: Cambridge University Press, 1983] 60-61; my emphasis). Jacobson argues for a date in the second half of the second century BC for the *Exagoge*, making it roughly contemporary with *Jubilees* (11). In a footnote, he raises the question of whether Wis 10:17 exhibits the same tradition found in the *Exagoge* (209, n. 18). I think, rather, that this is beyond reasonable doubt.

[26]Winston, 220. A similar view seems to be espoused by A. Marmorstein ("The Background of the Haggadah." *HUCA* 6 [1929] 165-66). The apologetic motive is especially clear in *V. Mos.* 1.140-42.

Winston's observation is certainly correct, although it is still a question whether anti-Jewish polemic is the ultimate point of origin for this tradition or whether Exod 12:35-36 simply posed a moral difficulty within Judaism itself.[27] In any event, it is clear that many ancient interpreters found the Exodus passage problematic and sought to justify Israel's actions by claiming that it was "payment for services rendered."[28] Ps-Solomon's passing comment in Wis 10:17a is another, and fairly straightforward, witness to this exegetical tradition.

Some commentators seem to be concerned with the form this payment took. Goodrick, following Grimm, considers that the reward must refer to "deliverance in general," since material booty is "too worldly."[29] Goodrick's point is well taken with respect to the troubling nature of Exod 12:35-36, but he fails to appreciate how the "payment for services rendered" tradition eases the difficulty. Israel's actions are justified not by relegating the nature of the reward to something non-material, which could only be done by completely ignoring the meaning of this tradition everywhere else, including the biblical texts, but precisely by making the *material* reward the *just* recompense for generations of material depravity.[30] *Mek. Pisha* 13.126-29, commenting on Exod 12:35, approaches the problem differently. This tradition finds the mention of gold, silver, *and clothing* among the booty significant. The order in which

---

[27]*Jubilees* and *Exagoge*, for example, include this tradition, but neither work elsewhere seems particularly dedicated to responding to anti-Jewish polemic. Still, the matter should be left open.

[28]Larcher correctly points out that this notion in Wis 10:17a is implied in the verb ἀποδίδωμι, meaning "render, reward, recompense" (2.641; also BAGD, LS).

[29]Goodrick, 236; Grimm, 203.

[30]*V. Mos.* 1.140-42 is quite explicit in this regard. See also Winston's comments (219-20) and Reider's (138). Reider also cites *b. Sanh.* 91a, which speaks of a lawsuit brought by the Egyptians before Alexander the Great requesting they be compensated for what Israel took when leaving Egypt centuries before. Alexander answers that they would first have to pay the Israelites for their period of bondage. See also *Memar Marqah* 1.10 (J. MacDonald, *Memar Marqah: The Teaching of Marqah* [BZAW 84; Berlin: Alfred Töpelmann, 1963] 2.37-38 [Aram. 1.24-25]; Z. Ben-Ḥayyim, *Tibat Marqe: A Collection of Samaritan Midrashim* [Jerusalem, 1988] 95). (As mentioned in the preface, all references to the *Memar Marqah* will be given according to the handy divisions in MacDonald's bilingual edition, including the appropriate page numbers for both his Aramaic text [vol. 1] and his translation [vol. 2]. I have chosen to cite primarily MacDonald's edition despite the fact that Ben-Ḥayyim's volume is not only a superior edition but uses the more original title of the work *Tibat Marqe*. The references to MacDonald's edition, however, will be followed by the appropriate pages in Ben-Ḥayyim's edition. Any Aramaic will be reproduced from Ben-Ḥayyim's edition.)

these items are given indicates that "garments were much dearer to them than silver or gold חביבה עליהם יותר הכסף ומן הזהב]."[31] Preferring clothing over precious metals would at least appear to put the Israelites' actions in a more positive light, but in no way does it diminish the fact that the booty was material.[32]

Irrespective of the fact that Ps-Solomon does not indicate the exact nature of the plunder, there is no doubt that the "payment for services rendered" tradition lies behind his comment. Its more elaborate retelling in Philo (roughly contemporaneous), *Jubilees*, *Exagoge* (both older), and the *Mekilta* (later) attests to its popularity. What is particularly important for this study, however, is the terse form in which Ps-Solomon alludes to this tradition. Such terseness is typical of our interpreter, as is seen throughout this study, and argues strongly for this tradition's antiquity and popularity; the "shorthand" manner in which Ps-Solomon's alludes to this tradition shows how very much a part of his thinking this tradition was. In fact, we may even take this one step further: Ps-Solomon's terse allusion to this tradition may reflect not his appropriation of a tradition, but his own understanding of the biblical event, and understanding that has been shaped by the interpretive world of which he was a part. It may even also suggest the degree to which his readers were familiar with this tradition, so familiar that just an abbreviated reference was all that was needed. This is one particularly clear example of an existing corpus of exegetical traditions of which Ps-Solomon made use in his retelling of the Exodus.

---

[31] All references to the *Mekilta* are according to the divisions in Lauterbach's edition of the *Mekilta de-Rabbi Ishmael* unless otherwise noted. Where relevant, the text from the edition by H. S. Horovitz and I. A. Rabin is also reproduced (*Mechilta D'Rabbi Ismael*. Jerusalem: Bamberger & Wahrman, 1960).

[32] Ginzberg, echoing both the *Mekilta* and Philo, says that the Israelites did not plunder "to gratify love of riches," but to make up for their years of abject slavery (*Legends*, 2.372, and especially 5.436, n. 233). See also the discussion by D. Daube who understands the material plunder to be modeled on the slave law of Deut 15:13: "When you release him from you, do not send him off empty-handed" (*The Exodus Pattern in the Bible* [Westport, CT: Greenwood, 1979] 55-61). It is perhaps worth mentioning Wis 10:11 in this regard, where wisdom is said to make Jacob rich in the face of Laban's coveteousness. Apparently, one way in which wisdom demonstrates her aid to God's people is through material reward.

3. The Pillar of Cloud Was for the Purpose of "Protecting/Sheltering" the Israelites (10:17c)

Before discussing the pillar of cloud specifically, a preliminary issue concerns 10:17b: *She guided them in a wondrous way* (ὡδήγησεν αὐτοὺς ἐν ὁδῷ θαυμαστῇ). Many commentators consider the "wondrous way" to be a reference to the miracles during the forty years in the wilderness.[33] This certainly makes sense in view of God's miraculous provision for his people in Exodus 16 (manna and quail) and 17 (water from the rock). Reading "wondrous way" as referring to the wilderness period is perhaps further justified by reading v. 17c-d (pillars of cloud and of fire) as likewise referring to the miraculous guidance in the desert (described, for example, in Num 14:14). But, as we have seen above, Ps-Solomon seems to adhere closely to the chronology in Exodus. Hence, equating the "wondrous way" with the forty years in the desert is problematic in view of the chronology of Wis 10:16-21, since the departure from Egypt does not occur until v. 18. The mention of the pillars in v. 17c-d refers to the Exodus event (Exod 13:22; 14:19-20). The "wondrous way," then, is something that occurs before the crossing of the sea, i.e., in conjunction with the Israelites' way to the sea upon leaving Egypt.[34]

If this is how "wondrous way" is to be understood, a possible biblical basis for Ps-Solomon's comment may be Exod 13:17-18:

> When Pharaoh had released the people, God did not lead them on the way through Philistine country, even though it was shorter, for God thought, "Lest the people change their mind when they see war and turn back to Egypt." So God led the people by the desert road [toward] the Reed Sea. And the Israelites went up from Egypt in battle array.

The Israelites took the *unexpected* route to the sea. The strength of posing this passage as the biblical motive for Ps-Solomon's "wondrous way" is the use of ὡδήγησεν in both Wis 10:17b and LXX Exod 13:17 (MT נחם; see also LXX Pss 77:14 and 105:9). This is how Larcher, for example,

---

[33]Goodrick, 236; Heinisch, 210; Reider, 138-39; Clarke, 99; Geyer, 71.

[34]This opinion is also held by Larcher (2.642) and Reider (139). *Mek. Besh.* 1.57-59, however, commenting on Exod 13:18, speaks of the Wilderness period: the purpose for taking the route they did was to experience the miracles of manna and water from the rock. The following lines (59-60), however, concur with what we read in Wis 10:17b: "'By the way,' indicates that it was for the purpose of tiring them." Likewise, lines 67-69 explain that the purpose for the route taken was to emphasize the miracle of the dividing of the sea, citing Ps 106:9 and 22.

understands θαυμαστῇ and concludes that the proper transla*ion of θαυμαστῇ in this context should not be "wondrous" but "astonishing" or "strange,"[35] i.e., unexpected. Although this would appear to account for Ps-Solomon's statement, it does seem to stretch the semantic range of θαυμαστός a bit too far, and therefore another solution should be sought. It is better to understand ὁδῷ θαυμαστῇ in conjunction with v. 17c-d: the "wonder" refers to the pillars that accompanied the Israelites on the way to the sea (Exod 13:20-22).[36] *V. Mos.* 1.29 may be an echo of such an understanding, calling the pillar a "prodigy" (τεράστιον) and a "mighty work of nature" (μεγαλούργημα τῆς φύσεως), "the like of which none can remember to have been seen in the past" (ὃ μηδεὶς πω μέμνηται πάλαι γεγονός). Philo, then, refers to the miraculous *manner* in which YHWH brought the Israelites to the sea. This, too, is what is described by Ps-Solomon as "wondrous way." He then elaborates on the pillar of cloud and of fire in v. 17c-d, which brings us to the third of Ps-Solomon's comments on the Exodus to be discussed in this study.

Ps-Solomon describes the pillar of cloud in 10:17c as follows: *She became for them a shelter by day* (καὶ ἐγένετο αὐτοῖς εἰς σκέπην ἡμέρας). There are two elements of Ps-Solomon's description that differ noticeably from the biblical description. First of all, it is not the presence of the Angel of God (Exod 14:19) or YHWH himself (13:21; 14:24) that is associated with the pillar of cloud, but it is wisdom. As we have seen earlier, this is not surprising, since wisdom is given credit for the plagues in v. 16, not YHWH as in the biblical account ("She entered Moses and resisted dread kings ⟋with wonders and signs"); and below it is again wisdom, not YHWH, who is to some extent identified with a "flame of stars" (pillar of fire, v. 17d), who led the Israelites through the Red Sea (v. 18), who drowned the Egyptians (v. 19), and who gave voice to the dumb and infants (v. 21). Throughout 10:1-11:1, wisdom is the active

---

[35]2.642; see also 3.1054. Schwenk-Bressler is of the same opinion (*Sapientia Salomonis*, 99). He posits reading θαυμαστῇ as "seltsam," but does not offer support for such a translation.

[36]Larcher suggests (but does not adopt) this view on grammatical grounds: "...l'asyndète initiale indique que la portée de 17b est explicitée en 17c-d..." (2.642). The reason Larcher does not adopt this argument is that he feels this would necessitate reading the "wondrous way" as referring to the desert, which would disrupt the chronology of the passage. I agree with Larcher that the chronology of the passage should remain intact, but reading "wondrous way" would not automatically refer to the desert. In this context, v. 17c-d, which follows καί, *describes* the wondrous way of v. 17b, which is the route to the sea. (For the epexegetical use of καί see BDF, §442; Moulton, 3.335; Smyth, §2881-84.)

agent in delivering God's people—from Adam to the wilderness period. Hence, wisdom's association with the pillar of cloud, rather than YHWH or the Angel of God, is fully expected.[37]

The second point of difference here between the Wisdom of Solomon and the account in Exodus is that wisdom not only is said to have "guided them in a marvelous way" (v. 17b), which is clear from the biblical text, but is described as a σκέπη (v. 17c). It is difficult to know precisely what Ps-Solomon intends by this. The word can mean both "covering" or "protection." With respect to the former, both the noun (σκέπη) and the verb (σκεπάζω) may be understood spatially, i.e. in the sense of "covering."[38] But there is also ample evidence for both the noun and the verb used abstractly, as some form of protection, for example in battle.[39] Both of these meanings would make sense in the context of Exodus 14, but can more precision be obtained in determining what our author meant by σκέπη?

---

[37]Although it is clear that wisdom is closely associated with the cloud, I have some question whether, according to Wis 10:17c, wisdom is to be *identified* with the pillar of cloud or merely thought to be *in* the cloud, as are YHWH and the Angel of God in the Exodus. The use of γίνομαι + εἰς elsewhere in the Wisdom of Solomon would seem to argue for the former (2:14; 14:11, 21; see also Larcher, 2.642; cf. also the idiom היה + ל meaning "to become," e.g. Exod 4:3 where Aaron's staff becomes a snake [ויהי לנחש] or 9:24 which recounts Egypt's becoming a nation [היתה לגוי]). Hence, wisdom *became* the cloud by day. Yet, γίνομαι + εἰς can also indicate a change of location (see BAGD, 159, 4c and examples), i.e., "wisdom *came to* the cloud by day." This latter translation of the idiom is contrary to the conventional translation of Wis 10:17c and, hence, I am somewhat hesitant to press this. Yet, "wisdom came to the cloud" may fit more in the context of 10:1-11:1, where wisdom acts as the divine agent rather than being personified in any earthly phenomenon. It is perhaps easier to see Ps-Solomon identifying wisdom with the role that YHWH/the Angel of God played in the cloud rather than the cloud itself. In any case, the precise nature of the association of wisdom and the cloud should not be pressed either way, and I am more than content to stay with the conventional translation.

[38]For σκέπη as a physical covering, see Exod 26:7; Judg 9:15; Job 21:28; 24:8; 37:8; LXX Pss 16:8; 35:7; 60:4; 62:7; 90:1; 104:39; 120:5; Sir 14:26; 29:22; 34:16; Hos 4:13; 14:18; Isa 4:6; 16:13; 25:4; 49:2; Ezek 31:3, 12, 17; Ep Jer 68; 1 Macc 9:38. For σκεπάζω meaning "to cover," see Exod 33:22; Num 9:20; Deut 32:11; LXX Pss 16:8; 26:5; 60:4; 90:4; Sir 14:27; 51:16; 1 Macc 6:37. This sense is similar to Wis 19:7, where the cloud is also mentioned: "The cloud was seen overshadowing (σκιάζουσα) the camp."

[39]The use of σκέπη as "protection" is less frequent than "covering," but well attested nevertheless: Esth 4:14; Sir 6:29; Isa 16:4 (?); 30:3; 2 Macc 5:9; 13:17; 3 Macc 5:6. Also noteworthy is σκεπαστής, which occurs only in the abstract sense: Exod 15:2; Deut 32:38; LXX Ps 70:6; Sir 51:2; 3 Macc 6:9. Σκεπάζω as "to protect" is very common: Exod 2:2; 12:13, 27; 40:3, 21; Deut 13:8; 1 Sam 23:26; 26:1, 24; LXX Pss 30:20; 63:2; Sir 22:25; 28:19; Zeph 2:3; Isa 30:2; 1 Macc 3:3; 11:16; 2 Macc 10:30; 3 Macc 3:27, 29.

It is easy enough to see how σκέπη in 10:17c could be understood as "protection." It could be argued that an ancient interpreter's purpose for expanding the biblical text by calling the cloud a "protection" is to emphasize its role in protecting Israel at the sea from the advancing Egyptian army (14:19-20). The cloud did not merely guide them on the way by day (13:21-22), but, at one particular point in the journey from Egypt (14:19-20), the cloud stopped guiding and, placing itself between the two camps, began protecting. Philo (*V. Mos.* 1.178) puts it this way:

> And, when they were about to begin the passage, a most extraordinary sign occurred. The guiding cloud [ἡ ὁδηγὸς νεφέλη], which at other times stood in front, turned round to the back of the multitude to form its rearguard, and thus posted between the pursuers and pursued regulated the course of the latter and drove them before it under safe protection [σωτηρίως καὶ ἀσφαλῶς].

Tg. Ps.-J. to 14:19 also emphasizes the cloud's protective activity, saying that the cloud "received" (מקביל), i.e., intercepted, the arrows and stones that the Egyptians were hurling at them. This is echoed in *Mek. Besh.* 5.43-50 (מקבלין) and in a parable in 5.15-36 (commenting on Exod 14:19): in protecting the Israelites, the cloud did what any father would have done to protect his son when attacked by robbers or wolves, or oppressed by the scorching sun. Finally, both *Tg. Ps.-J.* and *Tg. Neof.* elaborate the end of Exod 14:20. The two camps were kept apart to keep them from *engaging in battle* (למסדרא סדרי קרבא), thus further highlighting the cloud's protective role.[40]

Both the semantic range of σκέπη and the activity of the cloud in Exodus 14 allow for the meaning of "protection," a meaning that is attested in several ancient sources. But there is also ample evidence of a tradition that understands the cloud's function spatially, as a "covering" over the Israelites. There is, to begin with, Ps 105 (104):39, which I would suggest is the likely source of Wis 10:17c, since it too refers to the cloud *at the sea* as a covering: "he spread out a cloud as a covering" (διεπέτασεν νεφέλην εἰς σκέπην αὐτοῖς).[41] Moreover, Exod 14:24 says that YHWH "looked

---

[40]This midrash in the Targums is a gloss on the root קרב in Exod 14:20: ולא קרב זה אל זה כל הלילה. Rather than understanding the root as "to come near" (a rather mundane point, for what would be the point of keeping the camps from "approaching" each other?), the Targums took the perfectly reasonable step in understanding the meaning of this root according to its homonym, "to wage war."

[41]In addition to this psalm, Goodrick cites Sir 34:16 (where YHWH is called a "shelter [σκέπη] from a hot wind") and says that Wis 10:17c is "clearly explained" by these two

down" (שָׁקַף) from the pillar of fire and cloud, which implies that the cloud is located above the Israelites as a covering in some sense. We also have Exod 40:34-38 and Isa 4:5-6, where the cloud is said to cover the tent. Both of these passages describe the cloud in a manner reminiscent of the pillar in Exodus 13-14.[42] These passages all seem to assign to the pillar of cloud a "covering" function.

In addition to these biblical passages, the cloud as a covering is also found in a number of rabbinic sources. *Midr. Teh.* 105.134-35, commenting on Ps 105:39, connects Psalm 105 with Exod 40:38. Both *Cant. Rab.* 1.44 and *Num. Rab.* 21.22 comment as well on Exod 13:21-22 and connect it to Isa 4:5 and 6, hence giving the cloud a covering function. In *Mek. Besh.* 1.178-92, we read that there was not merely one cloud but seven all around the Israelites: one on each of their four sides, one beneath, one above, and one leading the way.[43] In 1 Cor 10:1, Paul refers to the

---

passages (236). I find it very unlikely, however, that Sir 34:16 can be adduced as a direct cause for Ps-Solomon's comment. It is too vague to be connected with any certainty to Wis 10:17c.

[42]Isa 4:5-6 says: "Then YHWH will create over all of Mount Zion and over its assembly a *cloud by day and smoke and a glow of flaming fire at night*; indeed, over all the glory there will be a canopy. [This] *shelter will be a shade from the heat by day*, and a refuge and hiding place from storm and rain." The cloud in Exod 40:34-38 is said to be visible during the day as was in Exodus 13-14. The "cloud as a covering" tradition seems to indicate the concrete manifestation of God's presence with his people (Exod 40:34-38; Num 12:4ff.; 17:7; Isa 4:5 and 6). God's presence in the pillar of cloud and fire is explicit in Exod 14:24 ("YHWH looked down from the pillar of fire and cloud [בעמוד אש ענן] to the Egyptian army"). A similar notion may be found in Rev 7:15: "...he who sits on the throne will spread his tent (σκηνώσει) over them." In John 1:14, the presence of the *logos* on earth is expressed in similar language: "The word became flesh and 'tented' [ἐσκήνωσεν] among them." Y. Amir considers Wis 10:17c an example of the concretization of "an abstract entity of metaphysical speculation" ("The Figure of Death in the 'Book of Wisdom,'" *JJS* [1979] 156). See also G. Ziener who sees in the cloud "die Gegenwart der Weisheit" (*Begriffssprache*, 130).

[43]W. S. Towner discusses this tradition and the various versions of it that appear throughout rabbinic literature (*The Rabbinic "Enumeration of Scriptural Examples": A Study of a Rabbinic Pattern of Discourse with Special Reference to* Mekilta D'R. Ishmael [SPB 22; Leiden: E. J. Brill, 1973] 155-61). He concludes from his form-critical investigation that the list of seven clouds is "selected by means of criteria no longer completely clear to us " (157; see also 160). Towner's conclusion is balanced, particularly in light of the fact that the lists of seven vary considerably. Nevertheless, it is not overreaching to say that this tradition, at least in part, seems to be accounting for the various locations of the cloud in Exodus 13 and 14: guiding them in front (13:22), protecting them from behind (14:19), and hovering above (14:24). But I agree with Towner that, although the number seven enjoys support in a variety of sources, the precise impetus for this number is not immediately clear. See also *Bib. Ant.* 23:10 where God is

Israelites as "under the cloud" (ὑπὸ τὴν νεφέλην) as they passed through the sea.

Memar Marqah 1.10, commenting on Exod 12:37, is another witness to this tradition, but raises a particular issue not treated in the other sources mentioned above. It speaks of "the cloud above them and the fire before them" (ענה עליהון ואשתה קמין).[44] This remark seems to imply that the cloud and the fire were active at the same time, something that reflects the ambiguity of the Exodus narrative itself. Exod 13:21-22 reads:

> YHWH would walk before them by day in a pillar of cloud to guide them [לנחתם] on the way, and at night in a pillar of fire to give them light [להאיר להם] so that they might travel [ללכת] day and night. The pillar of cloud by day and the pillar of fire at night did not depart [לא־ימש] from before them.

This passage seems to make a clear distinction between the daytime function of the cloud and the nighttime function of the fire. 14:20, however, specifies that the pillar of cloud was active at night (כל־הלילה) as well. Furthermore, upon closer examination, 13:21-22 does not necessarily justify restricting the pillar of cloud to only a daytime function. In fact, there is a way of reading this passage, documented in some rabbinic texts, that seems to imply the opposite. The purpose of the pillar of cloud was *to guide* them (לנחתם) by day. At night, the pillar of fire was given *to give them light* (להאיר להם) *in order to travel* (ללכת) day and night (v. 21; cf. also Ps 78:14 and Neh 9:12). The two pillars performed two different functions. This would not necessarily mean that the cloud ceased at night (after all, the Israelites still needed guidance), but only that the fire appeared at night in addition to the cloud in order to allow the cloud to do its job. This is reflected in *Mek. Besh.* 1.234-38, which comments on Exod 13:22:

> This scriptural passage says that while the pillar of cloud was still there [קים היה], a pillar of fire began to gleam [צמח]. Another interpretation:....This passage suggests that you can learn from the Torah what the proper custom on the eve of the Sabbath should be. The pillar of

---

said to have set a cloud beneath the feet of the Israelites so as to bring them through the sea (*et substravi sub pedibus eorum nubem*; see also H. Jacobson, *A Commentary on Pseudo-Philo's Liber Antiquitatum Biblicarum*, 2.723).

[44]MacDonald, 2.38 (Aram. 1.25); Ben-Ḥayyim, 97.

fire should begin to shine [צמח] while the pillar of the cloud is still present
[קיים יהיה].[45]

Apparently, the *Mekilta* understands לֹא־יָמִישׁ of Exod 13:22 to refer to both the cloud and the fire: neither one departed. This at the very least implies that there was a period of overlap between the appearance of the two pillars, which is also suggested by Exod 14:24, where YHWH looks down from *both* pillars (בעמוד אש וענן) in the *morning* watch (בְּאַשְׁמֹרֶת הַבֹּקֶר). This also seems to indicate that there was a period of overlap as the pillars "changed guard." Even more interesting, however, is 14:19-20, where the cloud's nocturnal duty is of longer duration: it is active keeping the two camps apart *all night* (כָּל־הַלָּיְלָה). Apparently, the pillar of cloud, at least on this one occasion, was present alongside the pillar of fire not just at the time of transition, but throughout the entire night.

In any event, the obvious point should not be lost, that an exegetical tradition that interprets the pillar of cloud's function at the sea as a "covering" is widely documented. Perhaps it is best not to press the distinction between the cloud's protective and covering functions. Yet, in the final analysis, "covering" may be preferable for understanding Wis 10:17c, since the *protective* function of the cloud, according to Exod 14:20, is said to occur at night (more specifically, *one* night). For Wis 10:17c, however, the σκέπη was during the day; hence "covering" is a better translation.

Although it is not related specifically to the exegetical motif of the pillar of cloud as a "protection/covering," Ps-Solomon's description of the pillar of fire in 10:17d bears mentioning. He refers to it as *a flame of stars at night* (φλόγα ἄστρων τὴν νύκτα). To my knowledge, Ps-Solomon is alone in describing the pillar of fire in this way. Even so, this description is probably best explained, at least in part, on the basis of ancient Near Eastern influence. Both Georgi[46] and Reese[47] connect "flame of stars" to the Isis myth, which is itself part of a broader mythological motif. One aspect of this motif is that the resurrected deity takes his/her place among the heavenly bodies.[48] Weinfeld places this motif in its fuller

---

[45]See also *b. Shab.* 23b. Rashi holds the opposite view, that the two pillars did not overlap.

[46]439.

[47]Reese, *Hellenistic Influence*, 48. Reese argues at length (36-50) for the influence of the Hellenized Isis cult on Ps-Solomon's depiction of wisdom.

[48]H. Frankfurt, *Kingship and the Gods* (Chicago: University of Chicago Press, 1948) 195. See also B. E. Shafer, ed., *Religion in Ancient Egypt: Gods, Myths, and Personal*

ancient Near Eastern context by giving several examples of stars shooting off course to defeat the enemy.[49] He understands the pillar of fire and cloud in Exod 14:24-25 as "divine attendants," a notion that he says has parallels in Ugaritic literature.[50]

What has not received sufficient emphasis, however, is a factor that ties this mythological motif more closely to Ps-Solomon's comment specifically. For understanding the flame of stars as "divine attendants" comes into even sharper focus when we consider not only its ancient Near Eastern context, but the prevalence of this theme in both biblical literature and early interpretive traditions: angels are often identified as "stars."[51] Moreover, an angel is certainly an active participant in the Exodus. In the pillar of cloud and fire, we find not only YHWH's presence (13:21 and 14:24), but the Angel of God's presence (מַלְאַךְ הָאֱלֹהִים; 14:19). Furthermore, there is an interpretive tradition that has the angelic host take

---

Practice (Ithaca: Cornell University Press, 1991) 38. J. S. Kloppenburg ("Isis and Sophia in the Book of Wisdom" *HTR* 75/1 [1982] 57-84) has contributed a clear assessment of the Isis-Sophia confrontation in the Wisdom of Solomon, and in the process evaluated the previous work of J. M. Reese and B. L. Mack (*Logos und Sophia: Untersuchungen zur Weisheitstheologie im hellenistischen Judentum* [Göttingen: Vandenhoeck & Ruprecht, 1973]). He concludes that Sophia throughout the Wisdom of Solomon is presented with characteristics similar to Isis in order to offset "the immediate and powerful challenge of this popular cult" (67). Kloppenburg does not, however, connect the "flame of stars" to the Isis myth. See also H. Ringgren, *Word and Wisdom: Studies in the Hypostatisation of Divine Qualities and Functions in the Ancient Near East* (Lund: H. Ohlssons, 1947) 147.

[49] M. Weinfeld, "'They Fought from Heaven'—Divine Intervention in War in Ancient Israel," ErIsr 14 (1978) 23-30 (Hebrew, English summary).

[50] Weinfeld refers specifically to the ʿnn ilm and ʾišt ʾištm. See C. H. Gordon, *Ugaritic Textbook*. (AnOr 38; Rome: Pontifical Biblical Institute, 1965) 197 (text 137).

[51] Some relevant passages in the Hebrew Bible are Job 38:7; Ps 147:4 (?; cf. Isa 40:26); Amos 5:26; Isa 14:12. The theme is common in the apocalyptic imagery of Revelation (1:10; 8:10 [Wormwood]; 9:1; 12:4 [cf. Dan 8:10]; cf. 22:16 [Christ as the "bright Morning Star"]). There is also *1 Enoch* 21-22, which speaks of the punishment of the "fallen stars." A passage perhaps most closely resembling Wis 10:17d is *Bib. Ant.* 32:17. This is a comment on Deborah's victory against Sisera (Judg 5:20), a victory that Ps-Philo clearly compares to God's deliverance of the Israelites out of Egypt: "And let the sea and its abyss be a witness, because not only has God dried it up before our fathers, but also he has diverted the *stars* from their positions and attacked our enemies." The reading *astra* (stars), however, poses some difficulty. Although likely original, there are witnesses that read *castra* (army), in which case *Bib. Ant.* 32:17 would be irrelevant in this context. The entire matter is discussed more fully in H. Jacobson, *Commentary*, 2.896-97. Jacobson argues that *castra* could easily be a corruption from *astra*, but still prefers *castra* to *astra*. See also P. Schäfer, *Rivalität zwischen Engeln und Menschen: Untersuchungen zur rabbinischen Engelvorstellung* (SJ 8; Berlin: de Gruyter, 1975) 23-26.

an active role in gaining Israel's departure from Egypt and the Egyptians' defeat in the sea. This tradition is evident in some later rabbinic texts, notably *Pesiq. R.* 21, *Num. Rab.* 8.3, and *'Abot R. Nat.* A 27,[52] but its antiquity is supported by its appearance in *Mek. Besh* 3.97-99, which, commenting on Exod 14:13, says,

> At that moment Moses prayed and the Lord caused them to see squadrons and squadrons of ministering angels [תורמיות תורמיות של מלאכי השרת] standing before them....[53]

Thus, the activity of angels at the sea plus the common biblical and extra-biblical connection of angels with stars may have led to Ps-Solomon's mention of "stars" as constituting the pillar of fire.

Having said this, however, we should not lose sight of the simple fact that, although the identification of angels with stars is a feature found in a number of sources, as is the presence of angels at the Red Sea, Ps-Solomon is alone in referring to the pillar of fire as a "flame of stars" specifically. This raises some question as to what extent the angel/stars identification will help us in understanding Ps-Solomon's description of the pillar of fire. Rather than being an exegetical motif that accounts for certain concrete elements in the biblical text, "flame of stars" is probably an example of Ps-Solomon rationalizing a supernatural phenomenon. Below under #15 (pp. 112ff.), where the crossing of the sea is a "new creation" (Wis 19:6), we will see more clearly Ps-Solomon's motive for wanting to explain certain phenomena in ways that do not violate natural law. It is enough to mention here that the pillar of fire might have called for such an interpretation in a way that the pillar of cloud would not have. A cloud is a perfectly common part of one's everyday experience, and, since clouds are generally located "up" somewhere, we can see the logic of referring to the pillar of cloud as a σκέπη, in keeping with popular tradition. The pillar of fire, however, is truly an amazing phenomenon and is not so easily explained. In this respect, the motive for Ps-Solomon's description of the fire may be

---

[52]Of these three midrashim, only the first implies the potential of angelic aid, since God reprimands the angels for attempting to help—as if God would need assistance (see Ginzberg, *Legends*, 3.26). The other two midrashim are similar to each other. They both attribute the defeat of the Egyptians to an angel, drawing upon Ps 18:11; Cant 1:9; Isa 37:24, 36 (see Ginzberg, *Legends*, 3.14).

[53]See also *Mek. Besh.* 7.40-43, which comments on Exod 14:24: "He delivered them [=the Egyptians] into the hands of youthful angels [מלאכים נערים],...into the hands of cruel angels [מלאכים אכורים]."

his attempt to bring this curious biblical phenomena into line with what he (and his readers) understood, and would accept, about the universe in which they lived. Since the purpose of the pillar of fire was to guide the Israelites at night, it is a perfectly natural step to refer to the fire by means of the lights that are normally used for guidance in nighttime travel — stars. Hence, what may form the proper backdrop for Ps-Solomon's comment is not an interpretive tradition based on elements in the biblical text itself, but rather a problem created when the worlds of the text and Greek philosophy collide.[54]

We cannot conclude this discussion without considering another useful perspective, offered by the context of the Book of Wisdom as whole, from which to view the "flame of stars" in 10:17d. The phrase φλόγα ἄστρων appears elsewhere only in 17:5: "brilliant flames of stars" (ἄστρων ἔκλαμπροι φλόγες). The context of this latter passage is the ninth plague. Ps-Solomon says that the Egyptians were completely in the dark with no source of light available to them, neither fire nor "brilliant flames of stars." The verbal correspondence between 17:5 and 10:17d is striking and serves to intensify the contrast between God's punishment of the Egyptians and his care for the Israelites. In 17:5, the "flame of stars" is of no avail to the Egyptians *to give them light*, unlike God's care for his people in 10:17d, where he lighted their way by a "flame of stars" when they crossed the sea. The plague of darkness was so oppressive that not even the stars, which are normally associated with the night, were able to provide light for the Egyptians. Yet, as is so typical in the Wisdom of Solomon, the very manner by which God's punishment was brought upon the Egyptians was also used to deliver his people: wisdom provides a "flame of stars" at night.[55]   Ps-Solomon's understanding of light and

---

[54]As mentioned above, such an approach on Ps-Solomon's part is seen also in Wis 19:6 (see below, #15). Winston discusses that passage in more detail ("The Book of Wisdom's Theory of Cosmogony," *HR* 11/2 [1971] 185-202). He adduces a wealth of evidence that supports the notion that Ps-Solomon accepted the prevailing Greek philosophical notion that creation was not out of nothing but from pre-existing "formless material" (cf. Wis 11:17; ἀμόρφου ὕλης). Thus, the miracles associated with the Exodus are explained not on the basis of God violating the physical laws of the universe, but of the various physical elements exchanging their properties. See, for example, Wis 16:15-29, where creation is said to serve God by "changing into all forms" (v. 25) and 19:18-21, where the elements are said to "change places with one another" (v. 18). According to Winston, Ps-Solomon's commtiment to prevailing Greek notions of creation can also be seen in his clear avoidance of the concept of *creatio ex nihilo* in 19:6 (Ibid., 194).

[55]The principle of *talion* is a recurring theme in the Wisdom of Solomon. See 11:5-9; 16:5-10; 18:8, and Winston, 232-33. This particular view of divine justice, that God uses

darkness in 17:20-18:4 cements the connection between the punishment of the Egyptians in the ninth plague and the pillar of fire. Concerning the ninth plague, 17:21 reads: "over those [=the Egyptians] alone the heavy weight of darkness was spread" (μόνοις δε ἐκείνοις ἐπετέτατο βαρεῖα νύξ, 17:21a). Yet, "for your [God's] holy ones there was a very great light" (Τοῖς δε ὁσίοις σου μέγιστον ἦν φῶς, 18:1a). And what was that light? "A flaming pillar of fire, a guide for an unknown journey" (πυριφλεγῆ στῦλον ὁδηγὸν μὲν ἀγνώστου ὁδοιπορίας, 18:3a-b). Thus, the darkness the Egyptians[56] experienced in the ninth plague is contrasted to the light given to the Israelites on their journey from slavery.[57]

4. The Sea "Cast Up" the Egyptians so as to Allow the Israelites to "Plunder" Them (10:19b-20a)

Winston and others have noted that Ps-Solomon's comment in 10:19b-20a is an unmistakable witness to a popular exegetical tradition.[58] He says that the Red Sea *cast them* [=the Egyptians] *up from the bottomless depth. Therefore the righteous plundered the ungodly* (καὶ ἐκ βάθους ἀβύσσου ἀνέβρασεν αὐτούς. διὰ τοῦτο δίκαιοι ἐσκύλευσαν ἀσεβεῖς). To say that the Egyptians were "cast up" from the sea is intended, at least in part, to explain how the Egyptians could be plainly seen on the shore by the Israelites (14:30) while elsewhere they are said to have "sunk like a stone"

---

the same means to deliver the Israelites and to punish the Egyptians, is explicit in 19:5.

[56]17:21a clearly implies that the Israelites did not undergo the period of darkness, a fact that serves to intensify the contrast between the two peoples.

[57]It is tempting to connect this statement further with Gen 1:17-18, especially in light of Ps-Solomon's interaction with the creation theme elsewhere. M. Gilbert, for example, argues at length for creation imagery throughout the Wisdom of Solomon ("La Relecture de Gn 1-3 dans le Livre de la Sagesse," *La Création dans l'Orient Ancien* [LD 127; eds. P. Beauchamp et al.; Paris: Éditions du Cerf, 1987] 323-44), as does W. Vogels ("The God Who Creates is the God Who Saves: The Book of Wisdom's Reversal of the Biblical Pattern," *Église et Théologie* 22 [1991] 315-35). Gilbert, however, does not connect Wis 10:17b to Gen 1:17-18. Ps-Solomon's understanding of creation's role in delivering the Israelites and punishing the Egyptians is spelled out clearly in 16:24 and 19:6. In light of this, we may understand the function of the clouds in Exodus 13-14 to be analogous to the creation of light (sun, moon and stars) and the separation of day and night, light from darkness, in Gen 1:17-18. This would add another dimension to our understanding of the relationship between 17:5 and 10:17: they are both examples of creation "serving its maker" (16:24) for the benefit of God's people and for the punishment of their enemy.

[58]Winston, 221. See *V. Mos.* 2.255, *Mek. Besh.* 7.94-108, and nn. 60 and 61 below (p. 67).

(Exod 15:5).[59]   For the Egyptians to be seen on the shore in 14:30, early interpreters reasoned that the sea must have cast them up again after they had drowned.[60]   Many commentators on the Wisdom of Solomon mention *T. Ps.-J.* to Exod 15:12 in this context, which tells of the sea and the land each refusing to accept the Egyptian dead lest God's wrath be upon them. [61] Only after God swore to the land that there would be no repercussions did it swallow the dead. This interpretation is meant to reconcile Exod 15:12, which states that the *earth* swallowed them up, and Exod 14:28; 15:1, 4, 5, and 10, where the Egyptians were consigned to a watery grave.   The order of events according to this tradition is: (1) the sea swallowed the Egyptians (Exod 14:28; 15:1, 4, 5, 10); (2) the sea, not wanting to incur God's wrath, cast them up onto the shore for all to see (the result of which is described in Exod 14:30); (3) after being reassured that it would not be punished, the earth swallowed them up (Exod 15:12).

This precise form of the tradition, however, is not reflected in Wis 10:19b-20a. Although Ps-Solomon certainly does have the Egyptians dead on the shore, visible for all to see, the specific purpose for which they were cast up is different. It is not merely so that the Egyptians might be seen by the Israelites or to obviate God's punishment. Rather, Wis 10:19b-20a says that the sea cast them up, "*therefore* (διὰ τοῦτο) the righteous plundered the ungodly." In other words, the sea cast up the Egyptians *so that* the Israelites could plunder them. What "plundering" does Ps-Solomon have in mind? It is certainly not the "reward" mentioned in v. 17a (commenting on Exod 12:35-36), but some act of plundering that *followed* the closing up of the sea over the Egyptians. Such an act of plundering is mentioned in *Mek. Besh.* 7.94-108 (see also Jos., *Ant.* 2.349). The *Mekilta* comments on Exod 14:30 and gives four reasons why Israel is said to see the Egyptians מֵת[62] on the shore: (1) to prove to the Israelites that the Egyptians did not

---

[59]A similar fate is described in Exod 14:28, which has the Egyptians *covered* (כסה/καλύπτω) by water, in Exod 15:1 and 4, where God *hurled* them (רמה, ירה/ῥίπτω) into the sea and they were *drowned* (טבע/καταποντίζω, 15:4), and in 15:10, where they are likewise said to have *sunk* (צלל/δύω).

[60]See also *b. Pesaḥ.* 118b; *b. 'Arak.* 15a; *Mek. Shir.* 9.7-15; *Midr. Teh.* 22.39-42. Although there is no verbal correspondence, Israel's enemies in the Hebrew Bible are sometimes treated in a similar manner. See, for example, Lev 18:25-28, where the Canaanites are said to be vomited (קיא, cf. LXX προσοχθίζω "be angry") out of the land.

[61]See Reider, 139; Clarke, 72; Winston, 221; Grimm, 203; Goodrick, 327; Larcher, 2:644-45; Deane, 167; *Pirqe R. El.* 42; *b. Pesaḥ.* 118b.

[62]The syntax of Exod 14:30 leaves this verse open to several possible interpretations, a factor that the *Mekilta* seems to exploit: וירא ישראל אתהמצרים מת על־שפת הים. The form מֵת can be a verb (3ms perfect or ms participle) or an adjective. The perfect would necessitate,

escape;[63] (2) to prove to the Egyptians that the Israelites had not drowned;[64] (3) to enable the Israelites to take the spoil (וכדי שיקחו הבזה את ישראל), which the *Mekilta* says was "silver and gold [כסף וזהב], and precious stones and pearls [ואבנים טובות ומרגליות]"; (4) to enable the Israelites to reprove the enemy. Ps-Solomon's comment certainly seems in line with the third reason given by the *Mekilta* (the other three reasons are not reflected at all in Wis 10:19b-20a). He says that the Egyptians drowned (κατακλύω) in the sea and then washed up on shore to be plundered. We may safely conclude, then, that Ps-Solomon's comment, in referring specifically to the element of plundering, is early evidence of a tradition similar to that cited in the *Mekilta*.

One final point to be considered here is the precise identity of the plunder taken at the sea. Here the difference between the *Mekilta* and Josephus (*Ant.*, 2.349) is important. The *Mekilta* says that the spoils gathered from the Egyptian dead were riches, probably because it interprets this act of plundering in light of the previous instance in Exod 12:35-36, where the nature of the spoils is explicit. For Josephus, however, plundering the Egyptians explains how the Israelites got their weapons; Josephus' comment provides an explanation for how the Israelites could be subsequently armed for battle en route to Canaan (Exod 17:8-16; Num 20:14-21; 21:1-3, 10-35; 31:1-54).[65] Ps-Solomon, however, does not specifically identify the nature of the spoils. Is he thinking of arms or riches? On the one hand, both Ps-Solomon and the *Mekilta* are explicit in saying that the Egyptians themselves were cast up (the antecedent of

---

"Israel saw *that* the Egyptians *had died* on the shore of the sea," which the syntax of this verse does not allow. Reading it as a participle yields, "Israel saw the Egyptians *dying* on the shore" (reflected in the third reason given by the *Mekilta*). The adjective would be "the Egyptians *dead* on the shore."

[63] See also, for example, *V. Mos.* 2.255; *Memar Marqah* 2.7.

[64] This interpretation reads מֵת as a participle, indicating that the Egyptians were still alive to witness the Israelites' deliverance.

[65] This problem is obviated also by reading חמשים as "armed." Josephus, therefore, stands in a tradition that reads חמשים in Exod 13:18 not as "armed," as others do, since this would already explain how Israel got her weapons, but "fifth," indicating that one out of five left Egypt. See *Mek. Besh.* 1.7-85. LXX Exod 13:18 reads, "The Israelites went up from Egypt in the fifth generation" (πέμπτῃ δὲ γενεᾷ ἀνέβησαν οἱ υἱοὶ Ἰσραὴλ ἐκ γῆς Αἰγύπτου). On the various translations of חמשים, see I. Drazin, *Targum Onkelos to Exodus: An English Translation of the Text with Analysis and Commentary (Based on the A. Sperber and A. Berliner Editions)* (Hoboken: Ktav, 1989) 137, n. 22. See also S. E. Loewenstamm, *The Evolution of the Exodus Tradition* (Jerusalem: Magnes, 1992) 225-32.

αὐτοὺς being τοὺς ἐχθροὺς of v. 19a),[66] whereas Josephus says that only their *weapons* (τὰ ὅπλα τῶν Αἰγυπτίων), not their bodies, were cast up. Might we say, then, that Ps-Solomon's comment is tied more closely to the *Mekilta* than Josephus, and hence, he too has riches in mind? This is not necessarily so. One could posit, quite hypothetically, some sort of conflation of the two traditions: Ps-Solomon may be saying that the *bodies* that were cast up (*Mekilta*) were *stripped* of armor and weapons (Josephus). Such a solution is reasonable on etymological grounds, since both the verb σκυλεύω and the noun τὰ σκῦλα regularly refer specifically to armor and weapons.[67] Josephus says the Israelites "collected" (συναγαγών) the Egyptian weapons, since, as we have seen above, for him there were no bodies on shore to strip. Ps-Solomon's use of σκυλεύω within the broad context of Hellenistic usage strongly suggests that he understands the Israelites to have stripped the weapons (Josephus) from the Egyptians (*Mekilta*) either dead or dying on the shore. There could be elements of both traditions—the spoil as weapons and as riches— represented in Wis 10:20a.[68]

Reese, however, raises a strong argument to the contrary. The proper understanding of σκυλεύω in Wis 10:20a, he asserts, should not be determined by its use in Hellenistic literature in general, but by its use in the biblical text that Ps-Solomon is interpreting.[69] LXX Exod 12:36 also has ἐσκύλευσαν (MT נצל), where the referent is unambiguously non-military spoils. Although Larcher considers this an "improper" use of the verb in Exod 12:36,[70] it does not necessarily follow that Ps-Solomon may not have been influenced by it. It is best, therefore, to be cautious here where our author does not offer clues for us to arrive at a more definitive

---

[66]Goodrick briefly entertains the unlikely possibility that ἀνέβρασεν could have meant "bring up" (cf. Lat., Syr., and Arab.), and thus αὐτοὺς could refer to the Israelites (237). But this does violence to the context as well as the meaning of the verb elsewhere, as Goodrick himself is quick to point out. See also Winston, 221; Reider, 139.

[67]BAGD, LS, also Larcher, 2.645.

[68]Commentators who understand the spoils to be weapons are Grimm, 203; Schmitt, 97; Goodrick, 237-38; Heinisch, 211. See also Schwenk-Bressler, *Sapientia Salomonis*, 103-4. I am not suggesting that Ps-Solomon consciously combined the two accounts of Josephus and the *Mekilta*, only that these traditions that are represented separately in Josephus and the *Mekilta* may also appear together in the Wisdom of Solomon. Because of the inherent difficulties in dating not only the written sources, but the traditions themselves represented in the written sources, one can hardly justify saying anything more specific.

[69]112-13.

[70]2.645. The "spoils as riches" tradition is also found in *Mek. Pisha* 13.142-49. See also Ginzberg, *Legends*, 3.27 and 30; 6.9 and 11, nn. 48 and 55.

solution. What is clear, however, is that, for Ps-Solomon, the Israelites in some sense plundered the Egyptians after the sea cast them up onto the shore, and in saying so, he shows that some form of this exegetical tradition guided his exposition of Scripture. And, as we have seen above under #2, it is the brevity of this allusion that argues for the antiquity and popularity of this tradition in his day.

5. The Red Sea Was a "Bottomless Depth" (10:19b)

Ps-Solomon refers to the sea where the Egyptians were drowned as a "bottomless depth" (ἐκ βάθους ἀβύσσου),[71] an identification which seems to reflect well-attested biblical usage.[72] What may have led to this identification seems to be, at least in part, the reference to the Red Sea as תהמת in Exod 15:5 and 8. Furthermore, the LXX routinely translates both the singular (תהם) and the plural (תהמת)[73] as ἄβυσσος, a factor which may have had some influence on Ps-Solomon's choice of ἐκ βάθους ἀβύσσου to describe the Red Sea.[74] The identification of the Red Sea with

---

[71]Reese maintains that ἄβυσσος should be understood in the classical sense of "bottomless" (*Hellenistic Influence*, 4). Winston also suggests the classical sense, but allows for the substantive "abyss," which is common in the LXX (221). Grimm's translation reflects the substantive use: "deep abyss" (203). Several commentators translate ἐκ βάθους ἀβύσσου as "out of the depths of the abyss." See Reider, 139; Winston, 221; Goodrick, 237; Georgi, 439; Larcher, 2.639.

[72]See, for example, LXX Ps 105:9 ("He rebuked the Red Sea and it dried up; he led them [ὡδήγησεν] through the depths [ἐν ἀβύσσῳ, MT תהמת] as through a desert"); Isa 51:10 ("Was it not you who dried up the sea, the waters of the great deep [ὕδωρ ἀβύσσου πλῆθος], who made a road [ὁδὸν] in the depth [βάθη] of the sea so that the redeemed might cross over?"); Isa 63:12-13 ("Who sent his glorious arm of power to be at Moses' right hand? Who divided the waters [ὕδωρ] before them to gain for himself everlasting renown? Who led them through the depths [ἀβύσσου]?").

[73]The plural form of the MT may have played a part in inspiring the tradition in *Mek. Shir.* 5.1-24, where *both* the upper depth and the lower depth contribute to the Egyptians' demise.

[74]The singular תהם occurs twenty-one times in the MT, seventeen of which are rendered ἄβυσσος in the LXX. Of these seventeen, twelve refer to the primordial waters of creation, i.e., תהם of Gen 1:2 (Gen 1:2; 7:11; 8:2; Ezek 31:4, 15 (2); Amos 7:4; LXX Pss 35:6; 41:7; 103:6; Job 28:14; 38:16); four refer to the sea in general apart from a specific creation context (Ezek 26:19; Job 38:30; Jonah 2:6; Hab 3:10 [although creation myth language is employed throughout chap. 3]); and one, Isa 51:10 quoted above, refers to the Red Sea. The plural form occurs fifteen times in the MT and ten times it is rendered ἄβυσσος in the LXX. Of these ten, six refer to the primordial waters (LXX Pss 32:7; 76:16; 134:6; 148:7; Prov 3:20; 8:24); three refer to the Red Sea (LXX Pss 76:16 [perhaps

the deep suggests that even in the biblical period there was some connection between the waters of creation (see, e.g., תהום in Gen 1:2) and the parting of the sea: as God gathered the waters together and dry land appeared in Gen 1:9, God separated the waters of the Red Sea to reveal the dry land so that the Israelites could walk through. A juxtaposition of creation and the Exodus is what seems to be implied not only in the passages cited above (n. 74), but also in Exod 15:16 where Israel is said to have been "created" somehow in conjunction with the crossing of the sea.[75] Elsewhere, in both biblical and extra-biblical literature, other acts of deliverance are seen as Exodus-type events, and are described by employing Exodus and creation language.[76] It is likely that Wis 10:19b, too, reflects some understanding

---

primordial waters]; 105:9; Isa 63:13); and one refers to the sea in general (LXX Ps 106:26). The data may be more conveniently considered in the following table.

	Primordial Waters	*Sea*	*Red Sea*
תהום translated ἄβυσσος in the LXX	Gen 1:2; 7:11; 8:2; Ezek 31:4, 15 (2); Amos 7:4; LXX Pss 35:6; 41:7; 103:6; Job 28:14; 38:16	Ezek 26:19; Job 38:30; Jonah 2:6; Hab 3:10	Isa 51:10
תהמה translated ἄβυσσος in the LXX	LXX Pss 32:7; 76:16; 134:6; 148:7; Prov 3:20; 8:24	LXX Ps 106:26	LXX Pss 76:16 (?); 105:9; Isa 63:13

[75]For Exod 15:16, I read עם זו קנית as "a people you created." The root קנה can also mean "buy," "acquire," or "beget," but with God as the subject, the meaning "create" is likely. See Gen 14:19, 22; Ps 139:13; Prov 8:22. The entire issue is discussed in P. Humbert, "'Qânâ'' en Hébreu Biblique," *Festschrift Alfred Berthold* (Tübingen: J.C.B. Mohr [Paul Siebeck], 1950) 259-66. Several extra-biblical texts from the ANE also seem to support such an understanding of קנה. See, for example, P. D. Miller, Jr., "El, The Creator of Earth," *BASOR* 239 (1980) 43-46; F. M. Cross, *Canaanite Myth and Hebrew Epic: Essays in the History of the Religion of Israel* (Cambridge: Harvard University Press, 1973) 15-16; 50-51; J. Hoftijzer and K. Jongeling, *Dictionary of North-West Semitic Inscriptions* (Handbuch der Orientalistik 21; Leiden: E. J. Brill, 1995) 2.1015-16.

[76]One biblical example is the deliverance from Babylon in Isa 44:24-27. Ps-Philo employs creation/Exodus language to speak of Deborah's victory against Sisera: "It will be *like the night when God killed the firstborn of the Egyptians* [*Erit similis nocti cum Deus percussit primogenita Egiptiorum*] on account of his own firstborn. And then I will cease my hymn, for the time is readied for his last judgments. For I will sing a hymn to him in the *renewal of creation* [*innovatione creature*]. And the people will remember his saving power, and this will be a testimony for it. And *let the sea with its abyss be a witness* [*Et mare testis sit cum abysso suo*], because not only has God dried it up before our fathers, but also he has diverted the stars from their positions and attacked our enemies" (*Bib. Ant* 32:16-17;

of the juxtaposition of Exodus and creation, not only in light of his use of ἄβυσσος to describe the Red Sea, but particularly in light of the presence of this theme in 19:6-7.[77] There Ps-Solomon writes, "all of creation in its own nature was fashioned completely anew" (ὅλη γὰρ ἡ κτίσις ἐν ἰδίῳ γένει πάλιν ἄνωθεν διετυποῦτο, 19:6). What precisely is this "new creation?" It is manifested explicitly in the parting of the Red Sea (19:7a-b) and other alterations of the natural order in connection with the plagues (19:10) and the provision of quail in the desert (19:11-12). That Ps-Solomon clearly sees the events surrounding the Exodus as a new creation certainly suggests that the same understanding is at work, as in 10:18b, where the author refers to the Red Sea as ἄβυσσος.[78] Ps-Solomon's comment here is firmly at home with both biblical and post-biblical modes of expression.[79]

Charlesworth, *Pseudepigrapha*, 2.347; my emphasis). *Memar Marqah* 1.9 is another example of the close relationship between creation and deliverance. Commenting on Exod 12:1-2 and the departure from Egypt ("This month will be for you the beginning of months"), we read: "...the beginning of the months is made like The Beginning (בראשית), which was made the start of creation" (MacDonald, 2.31 [Aram. 1.21]; Ben-Ḥayyim, 87). Both God's creation and his deliverance began on the first day of the first month. See also *Memar Marqah* 2.7 (MacDonald, 2.56 [Aram. 1.37]; Ben-Ḥayyim, 123), where, at the Song at the Sea, creation was renewed, and J. Bowman, "The Exegesis of the Pentateuch among the Samaritans and among the Rabbis," *OTS 8* (ed. P. A. H. DeBoer; Leiden: E. J. Brill, 1950) 248-49. The creation/Exodus theme is prevalent enough in both biblical and extra-biblical literature that a fuller treatment here would take us far afield. See B. W. Anderson, ed., *Creation in the Old Testament* (IRT 6; Philadelphia: Fortress/London: SPCK, 1984); W. J. Dumbrell, *Covenant and Creation: An Old Testament Covenant Theology* (Grand Rapids: Baker, 1993); K. Eberlein, *Gott der Schöpfer—Israels Gott: Eine exegetische-hermeneutische Studie zur theologischen Funktion alttestamentlicher Schöpfungsaussagen* (Beiträge zur Erforschung des Alten Testaments und des antiken Judentums 5. Frankfurt am Main: Peter Lang, 1986).

[77]M. Kolarcik argues for the importance of the creation theme throughout the Wisdom of Solomon, particularly the parallelism of creation and salvation, including especially the Exodus ("Creation and Salvation in the Book of Wisdom," *Creation in the Biblical Traditions* [eds. R. J. Clifford and J. J. Collins; CBQMS 24; Washington, D.C.: Catholic Biblical Association of America, 1992] 97-107).

[78]See also the clear juxtaposition of creation imagery and God's deliverance of the godly to their final "exodus" (Wis 3:2; 7:6), eternal life, in 5:15-23. There the Lord is said to "arm all creation to repel his [=the righteous] enemies."

[79]Larcher suggests that Wis 10:19b is an example of a comment based ultimately on an *awareness* of the Hebrew, since the LXX does not have ἄβυσσος in Exod 15:5 and 8, but βυθός in 15:5 and κύματα in 15:8 (*Études*, 88). He assumes that Exod 15:5, 8 are *directly* responsible for Ps-Solomon's description of the Red Sea, but this is at best problematic, if not highly unlikely. The equation of the Red Sea and the deep is simply too common a phenomenon to locate Ps-Solomon's scriptural motive in one specific passage. The more

Another matter of interest here is one we have already seen above with respect to the "flame of stars" (under #3; 10:17d). Wis 19:6ff. seems to reflect not only some form of the creation/Exodus theme, but a concern to make the notion of miracles more palatable to his readers.[80] This is why he says, "all of creation in its own nature was fashioned completely anew." The reason a new creation was necessary was that, under the natural laws of the "old" creation, waters do not divide (19:7), the earth does not yield gnats, nor the rivers frogs (v. 10), nor do quail come up from the sea (v. 12). Yet, since this is precisely what happened to the Exodus generation, Ps-Solomon felt constrained to present these facts in some other way. Such a philosophical explanation of Ps-Solomon's reference to creation in the context of the Exodus does not necessarily militate against his participation in the popular biblical and post-biblical creation/Exodus theme; his philosophical sensibilities might simply have served to give added substance to the theme. We will return to this topic below under #15 (pp. 112ff.). The point is worth mentioning here, if anything, to remind us of how complex the matter of Ps-Solomon's intreraction with Scripture is, and how concerned he was to bring the message of the sacred text to bear on his Hellenistic audience.

6. Israelites Sang "To Your Holy Name" (10:20b)

Ps-Solomon says in 10:20b: *they hymned, O Lord, your holy name* (καὶ ὕμνησαν, κύριε, τὸ ὄνομα τὸ ἅγιόν σου).[81] Some commentators suggest

---

likely explanation, and one that is demonstrated throughout this study, is that Ps-Solomon is simply part of an exegetical tradition that, in this case, is ultimately of Hebrew origin.

[80] According to Winston, "The author employs a Greek philisophical principle in order to make the notion of miracles more plausible. The Presocratics had already taught the material interchange of the elements....By the Hellenistic age it was a commonplace of Greek philosophy that the stuff of which the world was made is *apoios hyle*, and that therefore the elements were mutually interchangeable....The Stoics, in their attempt to explicate divination and the various miracle stories it involved, made especial use of this principle to show that the gods could accomplish anything without violating the laws of nature..." (Winston, 324-25). This interchange of elements, then, implies for Ps-Solomon a new creation (Ibid., 331). See also Gregg, 182, and M. Dell 'Omo, "Creazione, Storia Della Salvezza e Destino Dell' Uomo," *RevistB* 37 (1989) 317-27.

[81] The Greek does not specify how many songs were sung. Hence, the translation "They sang hymns" is not warranted and should be rejected. The plural "hymns" is offered by Reese, 108, 113; Reider, 139; Goodrick, 238; and the RSV. Clarke reads "sang the glories" (68). It is tempting, however, to retain this plural translation, since it allows one to

that v. 20b should be read in light of Isa 12:5 (ὑμνήσατε τὸ ὄνομα κυρίου).[82] It is interesting to note this similarity, but nothing is really gained by citing it with regard to Ps-Solomon's comment. For one thing, Isa 12:5 does not say "holy name," but "the name of YHWH." This is not splitting hairs. It is difficult to see what value there is in adducing Isa 12:5 as the source of Ps-Solomon's comment when "holy name" is missing. This is even more true in view of the fact that "holy name" (קֹדֶשׁ שֵׁם) is a fairly common expression in the Hebrew Bible,[83] a fact that argues strongly against attributing Ps-Solomon's comment to any one verse that is not otherwise connected to the Exodus.[84]   Exod 15:1 provides a more immediate motive: "Moses and the Israelites sang this song *to YHWH.* [LXX τῷ θεῷ] They said, 'I will sing *to YHWH'* [LXX τῷ κυρίῳ]." YHWH is, of course, the holy name. Since Exod 15:1 introduces the Song at the Sea, just as Wis 10:20b introduces Ps-Solomon's comments on the Song at the Sea (vv. 20c-21b, see below), it seems that Ps-Solomon's "your holy name" is simply a reflection of what the biblical text itself explicitly mentions. The presence in the LXX of τῷ θεῷ rather than τῷ κυρίῳ in the first part of 15:1 where the MT has ליהוה, brings an added dimension to the discussion, particularly if we posit the possibility that the LXX had some influence in Ps-Solomon's thinking (either deliberately or not).[85] The second mention of YHWH in 15:1 comes in a clause that looks like the actual beginning of the song: ויאמרו לאמר אשירה ליהוה. Since the *name* of YHWH is actually incorporated as the initial element of the hymn, this

read the verse in light of the fact that two songs seemed to have been sung at the sea: that which Moses and the ישראל בני sang (15:1b-18) and that which Miriam and "all the women" (כל־הנשים) sang (15:21) (see, for example, Philo, *V. Mos.* 1.180 and *Mek. Shir.* 10.89-91 [see also Ginzberg, *Legends*, 3.36]). Nevertheless, in light of the fact that Ps-Solomon gives no indication of how many hymns were sung, Winston's translation is among those more faithful to the Greek: "They hymned your holy name, O Lord" (219). Others who have the same or similar translation are Ziener, 68; Schmitt, 96; Larcher, 2.639; Georgi, 440; Heinisch, 208.

[82] See Grimm, 204; Deane, 167; Heinisch, 211 (who also cites Sir 39:35 as a parallel: "Now sing [ὑμνήσατε] with all your heart and voice and bless the name of the Lord [τὸ ὄνομα κυρίου]").

[83] See Lev 22:32; 1 Chr 16:10, 35; Pss 30:5; 105:3; 111:9; Isa 29:23; 57:15; Ezek 36:20. See also Luke 1:49. The related phrase קדשׁ זכר is found in Pss 30:5 and 97:12.

[84] P. W. Skehan, for example, implies that Ps-Solomon's comment is a conscious application of Ps 105 (104):3: ἐπαινεῖσθε ἐν τῷ ὀνόματι τῷ ἁγίῳ αὐτοῦ; "glory in his holy name" ("Borrowings from the Psalms," 390, reprinted in *Studies*, 155). It is, however, highly unnlikely that Ps-Solomon has this verse in mind.

[85] LXX has τῷ θεῷ. Some witnesses to the LXX omit τῷ θεῷ altogether but none reads τῷ κυρίῳ, which would correspond to the Hebrew text ליהוה.

clause specifically is what Ps-Solomon may be underscoring by saying "they hymned your holy name."

7. The Israelites Sang "With One Accord" at the Sea (10:20c)

At first glance, 10:20c as a whole does not appear to be of particular exegetical interest: *They praised with one accord your champion might* (τήν τε ὑπέρμαχόν σου χεῖρα ἤνεσαν ὁμοθυμαδόν). The Song at the Sea was indeed a song of praise for God's deliverance, but ὁμοθυμαδόν raises some suspicion. It seems like an insignificant flourish, but this is precisely the point. Since the word or its Hebrew equivalent is not explicit in the biblical text, and since it does not add to the discussion, one wonders why Ps-Solomon would bother to say it. The reason is that ὁμοθυμαδόν represents an exegetical tradition aimed at solving a particular "problem" reflected in the MT, and the manner in which this problem is solved finds ample parallels elsewhere.

Exod 15:1 introduces the Song at the Sea: אז ישיר־משה ובני ישראל, "Then Moses and the Israelites sang." The subject is plural but the verb is singular (ישיר). Might this lack of subject/verb agreement have led early interpreters to envision the plural subject as somehow "one" to correspond to the singular verb, and hence inspire a comment like "they sang with one accord?" Taken in isolation, however, this is not the likely motivation for Ps-Solomon's comment, since lack of subject-verb agreement, is not uncommon in the Hebrew Bible.[86] Hence, it could rightly be questioned whether such a common occurrence would have motivated an "explanation" by early interpreters. But there is another grammatical problem more difficult to circumvent. The verse continues, ויאמרו לאמר, "*They* said (saying)." This clause introduces the Song at the Sea, which is a song to be sung by "Moses and the Israelites." And, as expected, the verb is plural: ויאמרו. But what did *they* say? The song itself begins with a singular

---

[86] A close parallel to Exod 15:1 within the book of Exodus is Exod 10:3: "Moses and Aaron came (יבא) to Pharaoh and said (ויאמרו)...." Exod 15:1, along with many other passages in the Hebrew Bible, display a specific case of incongruence, namely a singular verb preceded by a compound subject (A + B, etc.). See GKC, §146f. The matter of incongruence in the Hebrew Bible in general is taken up by J. Levi, *Die Inkongruenz im biblischen Hebräisch* (Wiesbaden: Harrassowitz, 1987). The phenomenon in question is taken up specifically in chap. 8, "Das Prädikat vor Mehrteiligem Subjekt" (Ibid., 43-53). See J. Huehnergard's review of Levi (*Hebrew Studies* 35 [1994] 174-81).

verb: "*I* will sing to YHWH" (אָשִׁירה ליהוה). The use of the singular verb אָשִׁירה when the reader is led to expect the plural would have presented a wonderful opportunity for early interpreters to offer an explanation. This, perhaps even in addition to the juxtaposition of the singular יָשִׁיר to the plural subject משה ובני ישראל, poses an exegetical problem, and Ps-Solomon's "*they* sang with *one* accord" appears to be a documented witness to one manner of handling this difficulty.

It is perhaps worth emphasizing here that our concern is with the exegetical opportunities that early interpreters might have found in such grammatical phenomena. The grammatical "problem" discussed here, as we will see below, is just one example of similar grammatical phenomena that inspired explanations by early interpreters. It is true of course that the use of the singular is hardly a problem for modern conventions (for example, hymns in the singular sung collectively), nor is it a problem within the Hebrew Bible itself (for example, the collective "I" used in the Psalms).[87] This fact, however, should not obstruct our view to the world of early biblical interpretation, where it is precisely grammatical or syntactical issues such as the single/plural problem that spawned such rich exegetical activity. This is not to say, of course, that the use of collective singulars was somehow strange to these ancient interpreters. Rather it offered an opportunity to "engage" the text.

Before proceeding to a discussion of some parallels in rabbinic sources to Ps-Solomon's comment, we should first consider "with one accord" in light of the LXX and Targums. Both the singular יָשִׁיר and the plural יֹאמרו are reflected in the LXX and targumic traditions. The singular אָשִׁירה, however, is plural in the LXX and Targums.

Hebrew	LXX	Tg. Onq.	Tg. Ps.-J.
יָשִׁיר	ᾖσεν	שבח	שבח
יֹאמרו	εἶπαν	אמרו	אמרין
אָשִׁירה	ᾄσωμεν	נשבח[88]	נשבחא[89]

---

[87]See especially B. Childs, who sees the singular in Exod 15:1 as a stylistic feature similar to that used in the Psalms (*Exodus,* 249-50). Other modern explanations are offered by N. Sarna, who says that the singular verb אָשִׁירה can refer only to Moses, but he does not attempt to reconcile this to יֹאמרו (*Exodus,* 77). Likewise, M. Noth calls the song at the sea a "'solo hymn' with a single speaker in the first person...," although this, too, does not account for the plural elements (*Exodus,* 123). J. Hyatt says that the reference is to "Moses, or the person taking Moses' role in the cult, or the personified community" (*Exodus,* 164).

[88]*Tg. Onq.* has a second verb נודי, "we will give thanks."

[89]Like *Tg. Onq., Tg. Ps.-J.* has a second verb (נחדה) but in reverse order. *Tg. Neof.* and

One tentative conclusion to be drawn from these data is that the singular יָשִׁיר apparently did not pose a particular exegetical problem for the translators of the LXX or Targums, since they read the singular as well. Hence, if יָשִׁיר did play a role in Ps-Solomon's interpretation "with one accord," the evidence from the LXX and Targums suggests that that role is arguably a secondary one. This is also suggested by the fact that יָשִׁיר receives some attention in rabbinic sources, but the problem most often discussed is not the verb's number but its tense (past or future), especially as it is affected by אָז.[90] Yet the possibility that the incongruence of singular יָשִׁיר plus the plural subject contributed to Ps-Solomon's exegesis should not be dismissed too quickly. There are at least some rabbinic texts that seem to consider יָשִׁיר worthy of some comment. *Mek. Shir.* 1.11-12 comments on Exod 15:1 ("Moses and the Israelites") saying, "Moses was considered equal to Israel [שְׁקוּל כְּיִשְׂרָאֵל][91] and Israel was considered equal to Moses [שְׁקוּלִין כְּמֹשֶׁה] when uttering the song." It does not seem that the mere fact that Moses and the Israelites are mentioned side by side would account for the *Mekilta's* comment.[92] Rather, it is that "Moses and the Israelites" are the subject of a singular verb. This same tradition is seen in the timeless anecdote found in *Cant. Rab.* 4.2.

> Rabbi was once expounding the Scripture and the congregation became drowsy. He wanted to rouse them so he said: "One woman in Egypt brought forth six hundred thousand at one birth." There was a certain disciple present named R. Ishmael son of R. Jose, who said to him: "Who can that have been?" He replied: "Jochebed who bore Moses, who was considered the equal of six hundred thousand [שְׁקוּל כְּנֶגֶד שִׁשִּׁים רִבּוֹא], the number of all Israel, as it says, 'Then sang Moses and the children of Israel'" (Exod 15:1).

Another possible conclusion may be drawn from the data of the Targums and LXX. Since the MT alone reads the singular אָשִׁירָה "I will sing," and if we grant as above that his ὁμοθυμαδόν reflects the singular

---

Frg. Tg. also have the plural "we will sing."

[90]See *Exod. Rab.* 23.1-4 and *Mek. Shir.* 1.1-10. This tradition is not reflected in Wis 10:20c.

[91]See J. Goldin's translation "on par with" (*The Song at the Sea*, 67). The edition by Horovitz and Rabin has מֹשֶׁה שְׁקוּל כְּנֶגֶד כָּל יִשְׂרָאֵל (116).

[92]Larcher attributes "with one accord" to this juxtaposition of "Moses and the Israelites" in Exod 15:1, but both he (2.646-47) and Reider (139) cite the "choral" tradition discussed below (see, too, n. 94) to substantiate their comments. I argue below that this tradition does not adequately explain Ps-Solomon's comment.

אִשִּׁירָה, it seems that Ps-Solomon might in this case have been familiar with
an exegetical tradition based specifically on a Hebrew textual tradition.[93]
The difficulty with this conclusion, however, is that there is no Hebrew
exegetical tradition that clearly treats the אִשִּׁירָה problem of 15:1 in the
same way. The typical (and ubiquitous) explanation in rabbinic literature
is that the song was antiphonal: Moses sang first (hence the use of the first
person in 15:1) and the Israelites responded by repeating the same words.[94]
Some commentators see a reflex of this tradition in Ps-Solomon's
ὁμοθυμαδόν.[95] Despite the ubiquity of this tradition, however, it is very
unlikely that ὁμοθυμαδόν refers to alternating choruses. Throughout the
LXX, ὁμοθυμαδόν is used in the sense of simultaneous activity, not of two
parties (in this case choirs) alternating their activity.[96]   Rather, Ps-
Solomon's use of ὁμοθυμαδόν seems to be a clear statement to the
contrary: they all sang at the same time.

   Winston approaches the problem by citing a number of Hellenistic
sources, by which he seems to imply that Ps-Solomon's ὁμοθυμαδόν should
be understood as a literary convention.[97]   Although this solution has merit,

---

[93] P. Grelot mentions this possibility as well, albeit in passing ("Sagesse 10,21 et le Targum
de l'Exode," *Bib* 42 [1961] 49).

[94] J. Goldin mentions that the doubling of the verb (וַיֹּאמְרוּ לֵאמֹר) "suggests to the sages that
some kind of responsive...recitation took place when the Shirah was recited" (*The Song at
the Sea*, 77).   For other ways in which לֵאמֹר is handled, see J. L. Kugel, *In Potiphar's
House: The Interpretive Life of Biblical Texts* (San Francisco: Harper Collins, 1990)
47-48.   The tradition of alternating choirs is found in *Mek. Shir.* 1.87-99; *b. Soṭa* 27b,
30b; *m. Soṭa* 5.4; *Exod. Rab* 23.9; *Memar Marqah* 2.7; *V. Mos.* 1.180 (cf. Ginzberg,
Legends, 3.34, 6.12, n. 63).   See also Sarna, *Exodus*, 76; Goldin, *Song at the Sea*,
77-79.   Israel repeating the *singular*, however, still leaves us with the problem of
incongruence. According to *Memar Marqah* 2.7, Moses and the Israelites alternated the
verses of the song.   An overview of the different types of antiphony attributed to Moses
and the Israelites here may be found in, J. L. Kugel, *The Idea of Biblical Poetry:
Parallelism and Its History* (New Haven: Yale University Press, 1981) 116-19.

[95] For example, see Reider, 139; Larcher, 2.646.

[96] See Exod 19:8; Job 2:11; 16:11; Jer 5:5; Jdt 4:12; 7:29; 13:17; 15:2, 5, 9.   See also
Acts 15:25.

[97] Winston, 222.   Winston does not elaborate on the connection between Wis 10:20c and
the other uses of ὁμοθυμαδόν he cites.   Reese is more explicit in attributing Ps-Solomon's
use of ὁμοθυμαδόν to Hellenistic influence (*Hellenistic Influence*, 49).   Also worth
mentioning in this regard are three passages in Ps-Philo's *Biblical Antiquities* that describe
other biblical songs as sung in unison: Joshua's song in 21:9, Deborah's song in 32:1, and
perhaps Hannah's song in 51:7.   S. Weitzman argues that the pluralization of biblical songs
in Second Temple literature performs a specific function ("Sing to the Lord a New Song:
The Role of Songs within Biblical Narrative and their Resonance in Early Biblical
Interpretation" [Ph.D. diss., Harvard University, 1993] 144-50).   Citing *Midrash Tehillim*

I am more inclined to the view that "with one accord" in Wis 10:20c is the lone extant witness to an existing exegetical tradition specifically aimed at solving the אשׁירה problem. Although "with one accord" is not found in other ancient works in connection with the Song at the Sea, the *manner* in which the singular אשׁירה seems to be explained in 10:20c represents a fairly common approach in rabbinic texts to explain similar singular/plural problems that occur in the Bible.

Examples of such an approach are legion, but two will illustrate the point sufficiently. *Mek. Besh.* 3.22-25 comments on Exod 14:10. The biblical text reads, והנה מצרים נסע אחריהם, "The Egyptians were marching after them." The *Mekilta* comments,

> It is not really written 'were marching' [נסעים] but 'was marching' [נסע]. This means that the Egyptians all formed squadrons, each marching like one man [כאישׁ אחד].[98]

The unexpected singular is thus explained in a manner analogous to what we find in Wis 10:20c. Another example (among the many) is a comment on Gen 49:6 found in *Gen. Rab.* 99.7. Gen 49:6 reads "For in their anger they slew a man [אישׁ]." "They" refers to Levi and Simeon. The "man" they slew refers to the Shechemites who violated Dinah. The reference to the Shechemites as "a man" is explained in *Gen. Rab* 99.7 as follows:

> Did they then slay but one man? But it says, *And they slew every male* (Gen 34:25)? But were not all of them as one man [כאישׁ אחד] before the Holy One, blessed be He? Thus it says, *Behold* [הן], *the nations are but as*

---

to Psalm 18, Weitzman points out that the singing of songs was thought to exercise "an atoning power that merits divine pardon" (Ibid., 148). The songs then were used as communal expressions of gratitude for divine forgiveness (Ibid., 149). With respect to Ps-Philo's pluralization of biblical songs specifically, Weitzman suggests that these "reconfigurations" serve to democratize the songs (Ibid., 205-6). Weitzman's thesis is attractive and broadens the discussion, but does not nullify the argument presented here. It may be that *early* interpreters (Weitzman's argument seems to be based to a certain extent on *Midrash Tehillim*, which is likely dated generally to the Talmudic period) seized upon certain elements in the biblical text in order to make their homiletical point.

[98]An alternative explanation is found in *Exod. Rab.* 21.5: the singular verb means that *Mizraim* refers not to the nation, but to Egypt's guardian angel. *Exod. Rab.* 21.5 extends this to include another part of Exod 15:1 that exhibits a similar singular/plural problem: "*horse and rider* he has cast into the sea." The singular there means that the horse and rider refer to Egypt's guardian angel. The same midrash is also found in *Exod. Rab.* 23.15 and *Deut. Rab.* 1.22.

a drop of a bucket (Isa 40:15). Now what does 'hen' mean? It is Greek,
meaning one. Thus it says, *And you shall smite the Midianites as one man*
(Judg 6:16). Similarly, *The horse and his rider* [סוס ורכבו] *he has thrown
into the sea* (Exod 15:1), as though they were but one horse and his rider
[כסוס אחד ורוכבו]. [99]

Saying "as one," or something similar, to explain a singular form where
the context demands a plural is a well documented rabbinic phenomenon.[100]
It is not overreaching to suggest that Ps-Solomon's ὁμοθυμαδόν is evidence
of a similar exegetical maneuver.

What increases this possibility is Ps-Solomon's own use of
ὁμοθυμαδόν elsewhere in the Wisdom of Solomon, namely 18:5.
Commenting on the Egyptians drowning in the sea he says,

> You destroyed them *with one accord* [ὁμοθυμαδόν] in violent waters
> [ὕδατι σφοδρῷ].

It seems that Ps-Solomon says "with one accord" here for the same reason
he says it in 10:20c, to account for a singular where there ought to be a
plural. The problem in the biblical text to which Wis 18:5 is responding is
Exod 15:1, the same one addressed in *Gen. Rab.* 99.7 quoted above: "horse
and his rider (סוס ורכבו) you have cast into the sea." Were there only one
horse and one rider? No, but for Ps-Solomon, consistent with the
analogous problem in 10:20c, the singular indicates that God threw them

---

[99]See also J. L. Kugel, "The Story of Dinah in the *Testament of Levi*," *HTR* 85/1 (1992)
12-15. Kugel argues that the curious singular in Gen 49:6 is also responsible for the
tradition represented in *T. Levi* 6.4-5, that Levi and Simeon were responsible for killing
one man each (Simeon killed Hamor and Levi killed Shechem), and, presumably, the rest
of the male populace was killed by the other brothers. Kugel cites Eusebius, *Pr. Ev.*
9.22.10-12 as evidence for this tradition.

[100]Examples could be multiplied. A final example offered here concerns the dispute over
Exod 8:2 ("And the frog came up [ותעל הצפרדע] and covered [ותכס] the land of Egypt")
recorded in *b. Sanh.* 67b: "R. Eleazar said: One frog (צפרדע אחד) bred (השריצה) and filled
(מלאה) the land. This is a matter disputed by Tannaim. R. Akiba said: There was one frog
and it filled (מלאה) all the land of Egypt. But R. Eleazar b. Azariah said to him, 'Akiba,
what do you have to do with *Haggadah*? Stop your talking and devote your self to
'Leprosies' and 'Tents.' One frog croaked for the others, and they came.'" An early
witness to this "one frog" tradition seems to be found in a fragment of Artapanus' work
recorded in Eusebius, *Pr. Ev.* 9.27.32: "Again Moses released *a frog*, through his staff,
and in addition to these things, *locusts and lice*." (Charlesworth, *Pseudepigrapha*, 2.902;
italics his). The date given for Artapanus' work is somewhere between 250-100 BC
(Ibid., 2.890), a fact that certainly suggests the antiquity of this piece of exegesis. See also
Weingreen, *From Bible to Mishna*, 20.

into the sea "as one." The same notion is found in *Mek. Shir.* 2.95-102: "When the Israelites do the will of the Lord, their enemies are before them as but one horse and his rider." All of this shows that, irrespective of the fact that an identical explanation for אשירה is not readily attested, the clear presence of the same type of explanation in other ancient texts, as well as in Wis 18:5, raises the distinct possibility that Ps-Solomon's "with one accord" reflects an exegetical tradition that dealt with the אשירה problem. It seems, then, that "with one accord," is not merely a flourish, but evidence of an exegetical tradition that grappled with the biblical data.[101]

One final comment concerns *your champion might* (τήν τε ὑπέρμαχόν σου χεῖρα) in that same verse. On one level, ὑπέρμαχος χεῖρ ("defending hand"[102] or "champion might"[103]) may reflect יד חזקה, which is a fairly common designation for the Exodus event (Exod 3:19; 6:1 [2x]; 13:9; 32:11). But, perhaps the more specific biblical referent is Exod 14:31: "Israel saw the mighty deed [היד הגדלה/τὴν χεῖρα τὴν μεγάλην] that YHWH had done [אשר עשה יהוה/ἃ ἐποίησεν κύριος] to the Egyptians." Significantly, the mention of God's mighty deed in Exod 14:31 is followed immediately by the Song at the Sea. The deed and song are also juxtaposed in Wis 10:20c: "They *hymned* with one accord your champion *might*."

Furthermore, the nationalisitc and militaristic overtones of ὑπέρμαχος are well attested throughout the broad scope of Hellenistic literature. Even in Wis 16:17, ὑπέρμαχος is used similarly in the context of God's punishment of idolatrous Egypt. There God's hand (χεῖρα, 16:15) is against the Egyptians in the form of fire (evidently the lightning that accompanied the hail, cf. Exod 9:23-24, אש/πῦρ). This fire, unquenchable even in water, shows that even "the universe is the champion of the righteous" (ὑπέρμαχος γὰρ ὁ κόσμος ἐστὶν δικαίων, 16:17). The

---

[101]Not only is "horse and his rider" of Exod 15:1 relevant to this discussion, but Exod 14:25 as well. There, in the context of the Egyptians' retreat at the sea, we read: ויאמר מצרים אנוסה. Another biblical passage that may have helped inspire this exegetical tradition is Isa 43:17: המוציא רכב־וסוס חיל ועזוז יחדו. These same factors may be reflected in Philo's comment, that the Egyptians were destroyed "one and all" (*V. Mos.* 1.180). The only other use of ὁμοθυμαδόν in the Wisdom of Solomon is 18:12, where our author comments on the fact that in the plague of death, the Egyptians died "with one accord, all by one form of death" (ὁμοθυμαδόν δὲ πάντες ἐν ἑνὶ ὀνόματι θανάτου). The relevant biblical passage here may be Exod 11:5: *every* first born throughout *all* of Egypt, whether rich or poor, will die."

[102]Reider, 139.

[103]Winston, 219. Two examples from the Hebrew Bible of "hand" meaning "power" or might" are Prov 18:21 and 2 Kgs 13:5.

LXX provides two further occurrences of such a use of ὑπέρμαχος, both of which refer to God as "champion" of the Jews: 2 Macc 8:36 and 14:34.[104] Josephus, too, referring to the conquest of the land, writes that God was "championing their cause" (ὑπερμαχοῦντος αὐτῶν; Jos., *Ant.* 3.309). There are also several examples of this in classical Greek sources.[105] These uses of ὑπέρμαχος provide a valuable background for understanding Wis 10:20c: YHWH is *fighting* on behalf of his people (cf. Exod 14:14, 25; 15:3). In this sense, Ps-Solomon's use of ὑπέρμαχος χείρ may be understood as a terse summary of what God has been doing in delivering the Israelites from Egypt, specifically waging war against the Egyptians.

8. The "Dumb" Sang at the Sea (10:21a)

That the dumb (κωφῶν) are said to sing at the sea is a most curious statement and, as far as I can see, Ps-Solomon is alone in making such a remark. He seems to be saying that those who sang the Song at the Sea were previously "dumb" before wisdom intervened and made it possible for them to sing. The biblical motive for this statement is most often considered to be Moses' speech difficulty in Exod 4:10 (כבד־פה וכבד לשון; ἰσχνόφωνος καὶ βραδύγλωσσος) and 6:12, 30 (ערל שפתים, ἄλογος).[106] Whatever Moses' particular problem might be, it is clear that he considers it enough of a problem to warrant his release from God's command to confront the king of Egypt. In response, God arranges for Aaron to be Moses' "prophet" to do the speaking for him (Exod 7:1, see also 4:16).

But there are seemingly insurmountable difficulties in adducing this episode as an explanation for Ps-Solomon's comment. First, and most

---

[104]According to Georgi (440) and Reese (*Hellenistic Influence*, 11), ὑπέρμαχος is a divine title. The nationalistic overtones in 2 Maccabees in particular bear some similarity to God's deliverance of the Israelites out of Egypt.

[105]In Sophocles' *Antigone* 194, Creon praises Eteocles' service to the state for having defended Thebes in battle (ὃς πόλεως ὑπερμαχῶν), a judgment echoed in Euripides' *Phoenician Maidens* 1252 (νῦν πόλεως ὑπερμαχεῖς). The warrior imagery is also seen in Plutarch's *Numa* 16 (ὑπερμαχητικός) and *Cato the Younger* 53 (ὑπερμάχομαι). Deane cites Philo's *De Somniis* 2.42 (μεγάλη γε ἡ ὑπέρμαχος χείρ) as a close parallel to Wis 10:20c (168).

[106]This explanation is adopted in varying degrees by Winston, 222; Reider, 139; Geyer, 100; Larcher, 2.647; Deane, 168.

important, Moses' speech problem in Exodus was overcome so that he and Aaron could confront Pharaoh by means of the plagues and ask for the release of the Israelites, not so that he could sing praise to YHWH at the sea. The entire episode of Moses' speech difficulty is, in fact, irrelevant to the identity of the "dumb singers" in 10:21a. It is unclear in what specific sense Moses' mouth could be said to be opened (ἀνοίγω) at the sea in a way that it had not already been opened when he began talking to Pharaoh. Second, even assuming that this episode is relevant, Exodus still does not say that Moses was "dumb." He merely had some difficulty speaking (whatever that difficulty was). Third, "dumb" is plural (κωφῶν); hence, Ps-Solomon is likely speaking of more than one person. Although, once again, it would be possible to understand the plural as an example of an "allusive plural," as some have argued with respect to "kings" in Wis 10:16b (see #1 above, pp. 45ff.), the problem would still remain: who would this one person be whose mouth was opened at the sea? Furthermore, the plural is a problem only if we assume that the referent is Moses and his speech difficulty, but, again, the context of this comment is the Song at the Sea.

Seeing these difficulties, some commentators have offered other solutions. One such attempt is to maintain the connection to Exodus 4 and 6, but to extend the reference to include the Israelites along with Moses, thus accounting for the plural κωφῶν. Reider, for example, says that κωφῶν "clearly" refers to Moses and Exod 4:10, "though the plural includes others besides Moses."[107] Goodrick, following F. W. Farrar,[108] says that Exod 4:10 is "ideally extended to all Israelites."[109] But these approaches do not bring us any closer to solving the problem, for (1) again, it is unclear why one would appeal to an incident in the early portion of the Exodus narrative to explain Ps-Solomon's comment on the Song at the Sea; (2) although the incident accounts for the plural, we still have the same problem as above: Moses is not "dumb" in Exodus 4 or 6; (3) if anything, this problem is not solved but compounded when including all Israel, for just as Exodus does not say that Moses was dumb, it certainly does not say that the Israelites suffered the same disability. In sum, it is still necessary to show in what way the Israelites were dumb, and not merely to state that Moses' situation is "ideally extended" to the Israelites. One commentator, to be sure, does try to explain in what way the

---

[107]Reider, 139.
[108]F. W. Farrar, *The Wisdom of Solomon*, 483-84.
[109]Goodrick, 238.

Israelites were dumb. This is Deane, and he proposes that the Israelites, "who through fear had not dared to sing to God in the house of bondage, now praised Him in a hymn of victory."[110]   Such groping, however, will not go very far in providing a satisfying solution for understanding Ps-Solomon's statement.

Another solution, closer to the mark, is to have κωφῶν refer to the Israelites at the sea (not to Moses and his speech problem), and to understand the word metaphorically.   This approach has the twofold advantage of locating the problem at the Song at the Sea and of taking the plural literally.   The difficulty I see, however, is that in understanding the plural literally, this approach also needs to understand "dumb" metaphorically, since, at the sea, the Israelites were not actually dumb. Grimm argues that "mouth of the dumb" refers to those who were previously ungifted (*Unbegabte*) for rhetoric (*Beredsamkeit*) or composing poetry (*Dichtergabe*),[111] i.e., the Israelites required some special help to compose such a beautiful song as Exodus 15.   Heinisch holds a similar view, explaining both κωφῶν and νηπίων in v. 21b as referring to the Israelites who were "by nature incapable of praising God worthily," i.e., it was *as if* they were dumb.[112]   None of these solutions, however, really does justice to Ps-Solomon's words "opened the mouth of the dumb."   The underlying assumption is that our author does not mean anything of interpretive consequence, that his comment is not really connected to the Song at the Sea in any concrete way.   Since the remark is considered to be a free addition or flourish, not an example of interpretation, a metaphorical explanation is deemed sufficient.

Other solutions offered are those by G. Ziener, E. G. Clarke, and D. Georgi. Ziener understands v. 21 to refer to the rabbinic legend where angels raised the Israelite boys whom Pharaoh had thrown into the river in Exod 1:22.[113]   Although this is certainly relevant for νηπίων in v. 21b (discussed below, #9, pp. 88ff.), it does not help to explain κωφῶν. Clarke[114] and Georgi[115] cite Isa 35:6 as a parallel (τρανὴ ἔσται γλῶσσα

---

[110]Deane, 168.

[111]Grimm, 204. A similar explanation is given by E. C. Bissell (*The Apocrypha of the Old Testament* [New York: Charles Scribner's Sons, 1880] 254).

[112]Heinisch, 211. See also J. Fichtner, *Weisheit Salomos* (HAT 2, Reihe 6; Tübingen, 1938) 42, and E. Osty, *Le Livre de la Sagesse* (La Sainte Bible; Paris: Éditions du Cerf, 1955) 880, n. h.

[113]Ziener, 70. See *Exod. Rab.* 23.8.

[114]Clarke, 72.

[115]Georgi, 440.

μογιλάλων, "those who speak with difficulty will speak clearly" [MT ותרן לשון אלם]), as does Grelot (who also adduces Isa 32:4, "the tongue of stammerers will speak fluently" [ולשון עלגים תמהר לדבר צחות]).[116] Although it is certainly possible that these passages were at one time brought to bear on the Song at the Sea (particularly in view of the wilderness imagery in Isa 35:6b), "stammering" (Isa 32:4) and "difficulty speaking" (Isa 35:6) are quite different from being "dumb."[117] If Isa 35:6 or 32:4 is responsible for Wis 10:21a, why does Ps-Solomon say "dumb," which these passages do not say, rather than "stammering," which they do say?

It seems that yet another solution is in order. I suggest that Ps-Solomon's "wisdom opened the mouth of the dumb" is evidence of an exegetical tradition that dealt with a specific difficulty in the biblical text found in Exod 14:14. Beginning in v. 10, where the Israelites see the Egyptians approaching, they complain to Moses (vv. 10-12). Moses responds that God will deliver them this day from Pharaoh and his army (v. 13). V. 14 reads, "YHWH will fight for you, ואתם תחרישון." Some English versions translate this latter clause somewhat vaguely: "You have only to be still" (NRSV); "You need only to be still" (NIV); "Hold your peace" (NEB); "while you keep silent" (NASB). But it seems that, rather than offering a word of comfort as these English translations imply, Moses is reprimanding the Israelites for their faithlessness despite God's deliverance from Egypt. The phrase should be translated "keep still," or even better "be quiet!"[118] We can imagine the problem this might have created for an early interpreter of sacred Scripture. Moses—the mediator, the deliverer, the author of the Torah—said "be quiet." Yet, several verses later, without having been told that they may resume speaking, these very

---

[116]"Sagesse 10,21," 50. J. Fichtner holds the same opinion ("Der AT-Text der Sapientia Salomonis." *ZAW* 57 [1939] 177). Larcher considers the connection to Isa 35:6 to be "incontestable" (*Études*, 88).

[117]Schwenk-Bressler seems to have similar reservations about adducing Isa 35:6 (*Sapientia Salomonis*, 106, n. 167).

[118]Perhaps the closest biblical parallel to this interpretation of החריש in Exod 14:10 is 2 Kgs 18:36. The Israelites did not respond to the threats of Sennacherib's commander: "The people kept silent [והחרישו]; they did not answer him, because the king had commanded, 'Do not answer him' [לא תעבהו]" Here, as we see in Exod 14:10, the hifil of חרש is used to describe the people's silence in response to their leader's command to be quiet. See also Gen 24:21; 1 Sam 10:27; Jer 38:27. This root consistently denotes the absence of speech.

same people break out in song. How can this be other than by an act of God to open the mouth of the dumb?[119]

The advantage of this explanation over others that have been offered is that it locates Ps-Solomon's comment firmly in something that is happening in the context of the Song at the Sea, which is, after all, the topic of his discussion in Wis 10:20-21. We actually have Israelites (thus accounting for the plural κωφῶν), and they are actually dumb, not simply suffering from a speech impediment or lacking gifts for composing poetry. After Moses tells the people to be quiet, they are obediently quiet for the remainder of chapter 14. Between 14:14 and 15:1, they do not utter a sound—Moses told them not to. One might even imagine a silent mass of humanity passing through the sea. But no sooner do they get to the other side than they open their mouth in song.

As mentioned above, it appears that Ps-Solomon's comment is the lone, extant witness to this tradition. This is no doubt at least part of the reason why there are such varied attempts at understanding the comment. And the absence of any clear parallel certainly militates against arriving at a definitive solution. Nevertheless, there is some evidence that lends support, if indirect, to the solution I have proposed. One such piece of evidence is *Cant. Rab.* 1.49. This midrash understands ואתם תחרישׁון of Exod 14:14 as a strong reprimand, just as in my explanation of Ps-Solomon's comment. The biblical text in view in *Cant. Rab.* 1.49 is Cant 1:9, "I have compared you (דמיתיך), my darling, to a mare harnessed to Pharaoh's chariots." The mention of Pharaoh's chariots provides an obvious motive to associate this passage with the crossing of the sea in Exodus.[120] Our primary focus here is דמיתיך, the piel of דמה. *Cant. Rab.* 1.49, like Wis 10:21a, appears to make a great deal out of a relatively minor point in Exod 14:14; it does so by exploiting the potential ambiguity

---

[119]W. R. Churton gives both Exod 4:10 and 14:10-14 as cross-references to Wis 10:21a (*The Uncanonical and Apocryphal Scriptures* [London: J. Whitaker, 1884] 244). Unfortunately, the nature of his commentary precludes any comment on the relevance of Exod 14:10-14, but he likely had something similar in mind to what I am proposing. Of course, the imperfect could simply be understood as the future (cf. LXX ὑμεῖς σιγήσετε). This, however, would not substantially alter the point. If Moses were simply telling the people what was going to be the case (rather than commanding them to be quiet), their subsequent singing would still require some explanation.

[120]M. H. Pope presents in some detail the exegetical issues concerning Cant 1:9 as well as the major currents in the history of interpretation of this passage (*Song of Songs: A New Translation with Introduction and Commentary* [AB 7c; Garden City: Doubleday, 1977] 336-43).

of the root, which can mean "to compare" or "to be silent," and then applies the passage to Exod 14:14. The midrash reads as follows:

> R. Eliezer said: Israel was like a king's daughter who had been carried away captive, and when her father made ready to ransom her she motioned to her captors, and said to them, 'I am yours and belong to you and will follow you.' Said her father to her: 'What! Do you think I am not able to deliver you? I will silence you [דומה דמיתיך]; be completely silent' [דומי בשתיקה]. So when Israel was camped on the Red Sea *and the Egyptians pursued after them, and overtook them encamping by the sea* (Exod 14:9), the Israelites motioned to the Egyptians out of fear and said to them, 'We belong to you and are yours and will follow you.' Said the Holy One, blessed be He, to them: 'What! Do you think I am not able to deliver you? Be quiet.' The word "I have compared you" [דמיתיך] here means "I made you silent" [שתקתיך]. Hence it is written *The Lord will fight for you, and you shall be quiet* (Exod 14:14).

This midrash exploits the semantic range of the root דמה and comes to a climax in the last few lines, where it explicitly tells us that it understands דמיתיך as "I have made you silent" rather than "I have compared you." It then ties this in to Exod 14:14. Any possible misunderstanding is obviated by the last two sentences of the midrash itself: "The word דמיתיך here means שתקתיך, I made you silent." This midrash reads דמיתיך as "be silent" not simply because the verbal root allows it, but because it is clearly a comment on why Moses says "be quiet" in Exod 14:14. Moses' utterance, in other words, is construed as a reprimand to the Israelites for their rebellion in failing to trust in YHWH's deliverance, just as I have proposed for Wis 10:20c.

A second example supporting my solution to Wis 10:20c is found in *Mek. Besh.* 3.140-49. This is even more telling than *Cant. Rab.* 1.49, because it provides an explicit tie, like Wis 10:20c, between Exod 14:14 and the Song at the Sea.

> Shall the Lord perform miracles and mighty deeds for you and you be standing there silent [ושותקין]? The Israelites then said to Moses: Moses, our teacher, what is there for us to do? And he said to them: You should be exalting, glorifying and praising, uttering a song of praise, adoration and glorification to Him in whose hands are the fortunes of wars,...At that moment the Israelites opened their mouths and recited the song.

The *Mekilta* understands Exod 14:14 as a question: "YHWH will fight for you, *and you are keeping quiet*?!" This is precisely the opposite

interpretation of Exod 14:14 to that found in Wis 10:20c and *Cant. Rab.*
1.49.[121] Nevertheless, this midrash is relevant to our understanding of Ps-
Solomon's comment. Although Ps-Solomon understands Exod 14:14 as a
reprimand ("don't speak") and the *Mekilta* understands it as a question
("why are you not speaking?"), they are both clearly connecting Exod
14:14 with the Song at the Sea. For Ps-Solomon, the reprimand in
Exod 14:14 precludes any possibility of singing, and so divine aid is needed
for the Israelites to open their mouths in song. For the *Mekilta*, Exod
14:14 is not a reprimand, but a question for the purpose of encouraging the
Israelites not to keep silent in the face of their glorious deliverance from
Egypt. As such, the *Mekilta* offers an alternate explanation to Exod 14:14:
by understanding תחרישׁון ואתם as a question, the tension between Exod
14:14 and 15:1 is resolved. In other words, both midrashim offer *opposite*
explanations but for the *same* difficulty posed by Exod 14:14 and 15:1. I
conclude, therefore, that Ps-Solomon's "opened the mouth of the dumb"
represents one solution to the perceived contradiction between Exod 14:14
and the Song at the Sea.

9. "Babes" also Sang at the Sea (10:21b)

There is a popular interpretive tradition that has infants singing at the sea.
This tradition is found in a number of sources, two of which are *Exod.
Rab.* 23.8 and *T. Ps.-J.* to Exod 15:2.[122] I quote *Exod. Rab.* 23.8 at length.

> R. Judah said: Who was praising the Holy One, blessed be He? It was
> those babies whom Pharaoh had sought to cast into the Nile that sang
> praises to the Holy One, blessed be He, whom they recognized [מכירין] at
> the sea. Why was this? Because when Israel was in Egypt and an Israelite
> woman was about to give birth, she would go to the field and deliver there;
> and as soon as the child was born, she would forsake the youth and entrust
> him to the Holy One, blessed be He, saying, 'Lord of the Universe! I have
> done my part; now do Yours.' R. Johanan said: Immediately, the Holy
> One, blessed be He, would descend in his glory (as if it were possible to
> speak thus), cut their navel, and wash and anoint them, for so Ezekiel says,
> *But you were thrown out into the open field in neglect* (16:5), and as it
> is written, *on the day you were born your cord was not cut* (v. 4), and it is

[121] See also *Mek. Besh.* 3.135-36.
[122] This tradition also appears in *Exod. Rab.* 1.12; *t. Soṭa* 11b; *Pirqe R. El.* 42; *Pesiq. Rab.
Kah.* 17.6; *b. Soṭa* 30b; *Tg. Ezek.* 16. See also Ginzberg, *Legends*, 2.257-58 (5.394,
n. 25) and 3.33-34 (6.12-13, nn. 61 and 64).

written, *I clothed you with richly colored fabric* (v. 10) and *I bathed you with water* (v. 9). He placed two pieces of flint in his hand, one of which fed the child with oil and the other with honey, as it says, *He nourished him with honey from a crag* (Deut 32:13). They grew up in the field, for it says, *I made you grow like a plant of the field* (Ezek 16:7); and as soon as they had grown up they would return to their parents' home. When they were asked, 'Who looked after you?' They replied, 'A fine handsome young man came down and attended to all our needs,' as it says, *My beloved is white and ruddy, pre-eminent above ten thousand* (Cant 5:10). When the Israelites came to the Sea, and their children with them, and the latter beheld the Holy One, blessed be He, at the Sea, they said to their parents: 'This is He who did all those things for us when we were in Egypt,' as it says, 'This *is my God, and I will glorify Him* (Exod 15:2).

The relevant portion of *Tg. Ps.-J.* to Exod 15:2 begins about halfway through the verse and reads as follows:

> From their mothers' breasts the children[123] were pointing with their fingers [מחוון באצבעתהון] to their fathers and said, 'This is our God who nourished us with honey from the rock and oil from the field, gave birth to us and left us there, and he sent the angel and he washed us and swaddled us. Now we will praise him, the God of our fathers, we will extol him.'

Ps-Solomon's statement in Wis 10:21b "made the tongues of babes clear" (γλώσσας νηπίων ἔθηκεν τρανάς) appears to be another, albeit succinct, witness to this popular midrash in which infants (according to the Targum they were at their mothers' breasts [חדיי אימהון]) join in the Song at the Sea.[124] The fact that *Exod. Rab.* 23.8 and *T. Ps.-J.* to Exod 15:2 (as well as the other sources) conclude by citing Exod 15:2 clearly indicates that there is something in Exod 15:2 that motivates their comments. What appears to be the specific motivating factor is the demonstrative זה. For these sources listed above, saying "this" was apparently understood to involve an act of pointing (see especially the Targum), as if the babes were physically indicating God's presence.

What is crucial for our understanding of the exegetical thinking behind this midrash is the factor of "recognition" (הכיר) mentioned specifically in *Exod. Rab.* 23.8 and clearly implied in the Targum (see also

---

[123]The British Museum Manuscript 27031 reads עקא, which is an error. The correct reading, which is found in the Vatican Library Frg. Tg. and the Nürnberg Frg. Tg., is עקיא. See M. Maher, *Targum Pseudo-Jonathan: Exodus: Translated with Notes* (The Aramaic Bible 2; Collegeville, Minnesota: The Liturgical Press, 1994) 203, n. 7.

[124]See Winston, 222-23.

Pirqe R. El. 42; *b. Soṭa* 11b).   Infants are said to be the ones who recognized God at the sea, and it is this recognition that gives them the right (so to speak) to point up to the sky and proclaim that *this* was indeed their God.   After all, who else in the Exodus narrative could have *recognized* YHWH other than those to whom he had previously descended, whose navel he had cut, and whom he had washed and anointed?[125]   That the ability to recognize YHWH at the sea was a point of concern for early interpreters is seen also in *Mek. Shir.* 3.28-39.   This midrash also comments on Exod 15:2 but arrives at exactly the opposite conclusion, albeit for the same reason.

> R. Eliezer says: How can you say that a maid-servant saw at the sea what Isaiah and Ezekiel and all the rest of the prophets did not see? It says about them: 'through the prophets have I spoken in parables' (Hos 12:11). And it is also written: 'The heavens were opened and I saw visions of God' (Ezek 1:1). To give a parable for this, to what is it like? A king of flesh and blood enters a province surrounded by a circle of guards. His heroes stand to his right and to his left, soldiers before him and behind him. All the people ask, 'Which one is the king?' because he is of flesh and blood as they are. But, when the Holy One, blessed be He, revealed Himself at the sea, no one needed to ask 'Which one is the king?' But as soon as they saw Him they *recognized* Him [הכירוהו], and *they all* [כלם] opened their mouths and said: 'This is my God and I will glorify him.'

Although the *Mekilta* says that all the people (rather than just the children) recognized YHWH, the concern of this tradition is certainly the issue of how they, or anyone else, would have been able to identify God positively. The question that might have arisen in an early interpreter's mind is: "How is it that someone can point [suggested by זה] to YHWH and make such a statement when YHWH had not yet appeared to anyone but Moses?"   The

---

[125]A curious element to this tradition, and one that I have not seen discussed, is the fact that the babes who were delivered in Exodus 1 could not have been babes in Exodus 15. Too much time elapsed, 80 years in fact, since this is the age given for Moses at the time of the Exodus (Exod 7:7). This problem may be obviated, at least in part, if we assume that the edict was not rescinded and male infants were being thrown into the Nile for the entire 80 years. This view has at least implicit support, since the edict is never actually rescinded in Exodus. In this sense, the babes singing at the sea would be those who had been *most recently* delivered from Pharaoh's decree. If this is so, the "babes at the sea" tradition would be an alternate tradition to the one that states that Pharaoh did rescind his edict after his astrologers told him that Moses had already been born (see *Pirqe. R. El.* 48; *b. Soṭa* 12b; *Jub* 47:3; J. Cohen, *Origins and Evolution*, 5, n. 2; 11; 98-99; H. Gressmann, *Mose und seine Zeit: Ein Kommentar zu den Mose-sagen* [FRLANT 18; Göttingen: Vandenhoeck & Ruprecht, 1913] 1-16).

answer the *Mekilta* gives may be paraphrased thus: "Well, this would be a problem if we were dealing with a human king, but since it was God himself who appeared, there wasn't the slightest doubt in *anyone's* mind who it was!" *Exod. Rab.* 23.8 and others, however, deal with the "recognition" problem differently: "Those who pointed and recognized YHWH at the sea could only be those who had previously beheld him: the babes delivered from Pharaoh's edict." The solutions differ, but the motive for both is the same.

What gave rise to this "delivered babes" tradition? P. Grelot and U. Schwenk-Bressler, for example, attribute Ps-Solomon's comment directly to Ps 8:3 ("From the lips of children and babes you have ordained praise because of your enemies, to silence the foe and avenger").[126] This solution has some merit. Although these infants of Ps 8:3 are not singing, they are engaged in the act of praising, and, hence, could account for the phenomenon of infants singing in Wis 10:21b. Ps 8:3 could also be read so as to place these babes in some contentious situation (the "foe and avenger" are mentioned), and, thus, could be seen as an allusion to the Red Sea incident. Yet, despite these factors, a more likely source for the "delivered babes" tradition is Ezek 16:1-7. The primary reason why this passage is to be preferred over Ps 8:3 is that both *Exod. Rab.* 23.8 and *Tg. Ps-Jonathan* refer to it in connection specifically with the Song at the Sea, whereas Ps 8:3 is not mentioned. Furthermore, the connection between Ezek 16:1-7 and the Exodus is much more evident than what we see in Ps 8:3. Although Ezek 16:1-7 properly understood is an allegory of God's care for unfaithful Jerusalem, it is not too difficult to see how a midrashist might exploit the imagery of this passage (exposed infants delivered by divine intervention) and employ it to describe God's care for the actual infants who were the subjects of Pharaoh's decree—which is precisely what we see in *Exodus Rabbah and Tg. Ps-Jonathan.* To understand the origins of this tradition, the vital factor to keep in mind is not simply the fact that the infants *sang*, but the fact that they were *delivered* from something. It was those who were delivered who then responded appropriately by recognizing God at the sea and singing to him. In light of this, one would have to explain why Ps 8:3, which really refers neither to singing (only *praising*) nor to the Exodus, would have inspired an interpretation of

---

[126]For a full treatment of the various scriptural allusions that are involved in this tradition, see P. Grelot, "Sagesse 10,21," 49-60. He also cites *b. Soṭa* 1.6 (i.e., 11b), which brings together Deut 32:13 and Ezek 16:4-6, and introduces this to the context of Exodus 15 (Ibid., 54). *B. Soṭa* 30b clearly connects Exod 15:2 to Ps 8:3.

singing infants in connection with the *Exodus*. Ezek 16:1-7, however, was introduced into the Exodus narrative, since its imagery could be easily exploited to speak to the deliverance of actual Israelite infants from Pharaoh's decree. It is the infants' *deliverance* that is the central topic of this tradition. The fact that they also sang at the sea is suggested by the demonstrative זֶה in Exod 15:2 and the recognition factor discussed above. Wis 10:21b, then, seems to be evidence of a "delivered infants" tradition that existed already in Ps-Solomon's day.

There is one final factor to introduce into the discussion that suggests not only the antiquity of some form of this tradition in Ps-Solomon's day, but also that the connection between Ezekiel 16 and Exodus is quite old as well. The relevant passage is Exod 1:7: וַתִּמָּלֵא הָאָרֶץ אֹתָם. From the point of view of Hebrew grammar, the nifal of מלא followed by the accusative is not at all unusual.[127] Nevertheless, this fact should not exert undue influence in our understanding of the interpretive possibilities that early exegetes might have seen in this grammatical construction. An early interpreter could easily (and purposefully) have read the verb as a piel, וַתְּמַלֵּא, thus yielding "the earth filled them," or something similar. In fact, the LXX seems to document just such a reading of Exod 1:7: ἐπλήθυνεν δὲ ἡ γῆ αὐτούς. Although the nifal of מלא plus the accusative is properly translated "the earth was full of them" or "was filled with them," such a translation of the corresponding LXX text is difficult to justify. Πληθύνω is a causal of πληθύω, and means "to make multiple" or "plurify."[128] Furthermore, this is the only place in the LXX where πληθύνω is used to translate the nifal of מלא (normally πίμπλημι, ἐμπίμπλημι, or πληθύω is used). Perhaps more significant is how πληθύνω is used elsewhere in LXX Exodus 1. The clear use of the passive earlier in v. 7 (ἐπληθύνθησαν, "the Israelites 'multiplied'") militates against reading ἐπλήθυνεν later in the same verse as anything other than active. In v. 20, ἐπλήθυνεν is used intransitively: "The people increased."

---

[127]Verbs that in the active voice take a double accusative retain an accusative in the passive voice. See G. F. Davies, *Israel in Egypt: Reading Exodus 1-2* (JSOT 135; Sheffield, 1992) 38, esp. n.1. B. K. Waltke and M. O'Connor refer to such a construction as a "complement accusative," and cite Exod 1:7 as an example (*An Introduction to Biblical Hebrew Syntax* [Winona Lake, IN: Eisenbrauns, 1990] 168). GKC §117z also adduces Exod 1:7 as an example of this construction meaning "to fill oneself with something" (see also §121d). Gen 6:11 is also cited, although this is without the direct object marker. Gen 21:8 is similar, but there the verb is גמל. See also Num 14:21. The same phenomenon occurs in biblical Greek (e.g., Zerwick, *Biblical Greek*, 26).

[128]LS, 2.1418.

We have, then, in the last few words of LXX Exod 1:7 an active
(ἐπλήθυνεν) transitive (αὐτούς) verb, which yields the translation "the
earth *increased them*," or something similar.[129] The point here is that LXX
Exod 1:7 may reflect an early attempt (whether original to the LXX or not
is beside the point) to link the allegory of Ezek 16:1-7 exegetically to
Exodus 1. I suggest that the specific passage that would have linked
Ezekiel 16 to Exod 1:7 is Ezek 16:7: "I made you grow like a plant in the
field" (השדה נתתיך רבבה כצמח).[130] If we understand ותמלא in Exod 1:7
as an active verb, precisely what we see in the LXX, a connection between
Ezek 16:7 and Exod 1:7 seems to present itself: the earth "multiplies" the
Israelites (Exod 1:7) like plants growing in the field (Ezek 16:7). Hence,
LXX Exod 1:7 may provide early evidence of a tradition that connected the
actual infants of Exodus 1 and those of Ezekiel 16.[131]

In any event, Ps-Solomon's terse statement, "made the tongues of
babes clear," certainly reflects a tradition of infants singing at the sea. In
this respect, this motif is distinct from the previous two (#s7 and 8), since a
clearly documented tradition seems to form the proper backdrop for Ps-
Solomon's statement. It is not clear, however, to what extent this tradition
had developed in Ps-Solomon's day, i.e., whether we can rightly say that

---

[129]See also the translations of the LXX by L. C. L. Brenton and C. Thomson. The former
has "the land multiplied them" (*The Septuagint Version, Greek and English* [reprint of 1844
edition; Grand Rapids: Zondervan, 1970) and the latter "The land caused them to abound"
(*The Old Covenant Commonly Called the Old Testament: Translated from the Septuagint*
[2 vols.; London: Skeffington & Son, 1904]). J. W. Wevers comments on LXX Exod 1:7
as follows: "The final clause uses the transitive verb ἐπλήθυνεν with an accusative αὐτούς
as though the verb were Hiphil [I am suggesting piel - P.E.], probably because of the
Hebrew's אתם. Note the attempt of mss. 53' to improve the sense by their επληθυνθη
αυτοις (*Notes on the Greek Text of Exodus* [SBLSCS 30; Atlanta: Scholars Press,
1990] 3). In the footnote to this statement, Wevers says, "The clause is more exactly
rendered by Aq and Sym with καὶ ἐπληρώθη ἡ γῆ ἀπ᾽ αὐτῶν." There is clearly an
awkwardness to the LXX.

[130]LXX Ezek 16:7 has πληθύνου (middle/passive imperative) for רבבה, which may
provide a further lexical connection between Exod 1:7 and Ezek 16:7.

[131]A second exegetical element, not related to the LXX, that serves to tie Ezekiel 16 to
Exodus 1 is the use of ילד and שלך. The second half of Ezek 16:5 reads: "You were
thrown (ותשלכי) into the field; you were neglected on the day of your birth (ביום הלדת)." A
similar fate befell the male children in Exod 1:22: "Every son who is born (הילוד) you will
cast (תשליכהו) into the Nile." It is beside the point that Ezek 16:5 refers to a field whereas
Exod 1:22 refers to the Nile. The fact remains that exegetical traditions exist that connect
the infants of Ezekiel 16 and those of Exodus 1, and שלך/ילד, along with the syntax of
Exod 1:7 discussed above, may have served, or even been exploited, to strengthen
that connection.

the later full-blown version of the tradition in all its detail, as reflected in
Exod. Rab. 23.8 and *T. Ps.-J.*, can be assumed to underlie Wis 10:21b.
Nevertheless, it seems certain that the tradition in some form must have
existed in Ps-Solomon's exegetical world in order for Ps-Solomon to have
said "made the tongues of babes speak clearly." We can hardly expect Ps-
Solomon's terse statement of babes singing at the sea to have been an
independent piece of interpretation aimed at connecting Ezek 16:1-7
and Exod 15:2.

If Wis 10:21b is indeed evidence of Ps-Solomon's participation in
some form of a tradition of "infants singing at the sea," we would seem to
have another example in the Book of Wisdom of differing comments on the
same biblical text or event. In Part I we saw that Wis 10:4 and 14:6
present two different explanations for the cause of the flood, Cain in the
former and the "arrogant giants" in the latter (pp. 32-34). Likewise, if the
babes who sing at the sea in Wis 10:21b are the very same babes who were
delivered from Pharaoh's edict in Exodus 1, then Wis 18:5 would say the
exact opposite.

> When they [=the Egyptians] determined to kill the children of the holy
> ones—though *one child* [=Moses] *had been exposed and rescued* (ἑνὸς
> ἐκτεθέντος τέκνου καὶ σωθέντος)—as punishment you took away a
> multitude of their children and destroyed them all together in raging water.

Although all the male children were subject to Pharaoh's decree, Moses
alone is said to have escaped. Hence, the νηπία who are said to sing in
10:21b have perished according to 18:5. The presence of conflicting
statements, then, would provide another example of the ease with which Ps-
Solomon can incorporate these traditions in his retelling of Scripture. The
"babes at the sea" tradition is clearly not the product of Ps-Solomon's own
interpretive energy. It is, rather, a pre-existing tradition either that he
consciously incorporated into his retelling or that came to be closely
associated with the biblical text itself so as to become actually part of the
retelling. (I prefer the latter option for reasons that will be presented
more fully in Part III.). Can the same be said for Wis 18:5? Although a
definitive conclusion does not present itself, 18:5 is more open than 10:21b
to a different solution. An important theme that is found throughout chaps.
11-19 is the principle of "measure for measure."[132] Wis 18:5 highlights

---

[132]The principle of "measure for measure" is stated clearly, for example, in Wis 11:4-9 in
connection with the plague of blood. See Y. Amir, "Measure for Measure in Talmudic
Literature and in the Wisdom of Solomon," *Justice and Righteousness: Biblical Themes*

the fact that only Moses escaped Pharaoh's decree, which may be a direct attempt on Ps-Solomon's part to show that the horrible punishment the Egyptians underwent (in both the tenth plague and the Red Sea incident) was fully justified in light of their own successful attempt to decimate the Israelite population through drowning. In any event, however we attempt to answer the question of the relationship between Wis 10:21b and 18:5, Ps-Solomon's participation in the "delivered infants" theme in 10:21b should not be obscured.

10. God Knew that the Egyptians Would Pursue the Israelites (19:1b)

In 19:1b, Ps-Solomon says that God *knew beforehand even their* [=Egyptians'] *future actions* (προῄδει γὰρ αὐτῶν καὶ τὰ μέλλοντα). Many commentators restrict their observations to the alleged moral difficulty of God punishing actions (v. 1a) that he foresaw would happen (v. 1b), i.e., what was in his power to prevent.[133] What is of exegetical interest, however, is Ps-Solomon's statement that God "knew beforehand" (προῄδει) the decision of the ungodly to pursue the Israelites after they had left Egypt. Winston produces an example from Philo's *Quod Deus sit Immutabilis* 29 expressing a similar idea, thus suggesting the presence of this notion of divine foreknowledge in Greek and Hellenistic writings, and, therefore, the influence of Greek thought on Ps-Solomon.[134] But adducing Hellenistic parallels will not go very far in explaining Ps-Solomon's

---

and Their Influence (eds. H. G. Reventlow and Y. Hoffman; JSOTSup 137; Sheffield: JSOT, 1992) 29-46.

[133] See, for example, Goodrick, 365; Deane, 214-15; Larcher, 3.1046-47.

[134] Winston, 323-24. The passage from Philo as cited by Winston is as follows: "God employs the forethought and foreknowledge (προμήθεια καὶ προνοία) which are virtues peculiarly of his own, and suffers nothing to escape his control or pass outside his comprehension. For not even about the future (τῶν μελλόντων) can uncertainty be found with him, since nothing is uncertain or future to God." God's foreknowledge (including the foreknowledge of prophets inspired by God) is also expressed by προγινώσκω (Rom 8:29; 11:2; 1 Pet 1:20; Wis 8:8; 18:6) and its noun cognate πρόγνωσις (Jdt 9:6; 11:19; Acts 2:23; 1 Pet 1:2). See also προοράω (Acts 2:31; Gal 3:8; Jos., *J. W.* 2.619). S. Sowers discusses the Stoic notion of providence (πρόνοια) and Ps-Solomon's reinterpretation of biblical history in Wisdom 10-11 ("On the Reinterpretation of Biblical History in Hellenistic Judaism," *Oikonomia: Heilsgeschichte als Thema der Theologie* [O. Cullmann Festschrift; ed. F. Christ; Hamberg-Bergstedt: Reich, 1967] 18-25).

comment. For one thing, God's foreknowledge is a common theme in the Hebrew Bible, not only in general (e.g., Gen 15:13-16; 45:1-8), but in the Exodus narrative. Specifically, Ps-Solomon's comment simply reflects Exod 14:1-5. There, YHWH tells Moses to take an unexpected route through the desert in an effort to confuse Pharaoh: "Pharaoh will think [אמר], 'The Israelites are wandering around in confusion, hemmed in by the desert.' And I will harden Pharaoh's heart and *he will pursue them*" (vv. 3-4a). In other words, YHWH anticipates, even causes, Pharaoh's next move, which is a change of heart and the decision to pursue the Israelites (v. 5). This is what Ps-Solomon has in mind when he says God "*knew beforehand even their future actions.*" Furthermore, the fact that God twice before in the biblical text of Exodus predicted Pharaoh's eventual unwillingness to let the Israelites go (3:19 and 7:4) argues that the theme of God's foreknowledge is integral to the Exodus narrative as a whole. There is simply no need to ascribe Ps-Solomon's comment to the influence of Greek thinking, especially since doing so would still leave unanswered why Ps-Solomon specifically connects this notion of foreknowledge to the *Pharaoh's decision to pursue the Israelites.*[135]

11. The Egyptians "Accompanied" the Israelites out of Egypt (19:2)

Ps-Solomon says that the Egyptians *hastily escorted* (μετὰ σπουδῆς προπέμψαντες) the Israelites out of Egypt. Saying that the Israelites were sent out "hastily" is directly tied to Exod 12:33 (למהר, LXX σπουδῇ; see also 12:39), and the commentaries routinely mention the point.[136] Philo's comment, μετὰ πάσης σπουδῆς (*V. Mos.* 1.139), is similar to Ps-Solomon's and suggests a common exegetical tradition based on the biblical text. But, again, although the biblical motive for Ps-Solomon's and Philo's comment is obvious, its significance should not be overlooked. This kind of comment suggests that Ps-Solomon's retelling of the Bible involves at some level a process that engages the biblical text specifically and

---

[135]See also the comment by W. P. Berwick: "Some Greek ideas in Wisdom are contained in all religious thought, e.g. the idea of Divine Providence is in the Old Testament as well as the Stoics and Plato" ("The Way of Salvation in the Book of Wisdom." [Ph.D. diss., Boston University, 1957] 150 and n. 1).

[136]Winston, 324; Goodrick, 365; Deane, 215; Reider, 216; Gregg, 181.

concretely, either on his own initiative or by interacting with exegetical traditions that do so.

Perhaps more important is Ps-Solomon's comment that the Israelites were "sent forth" (προπέμπω). As Winston observes,[137] Ps-Solomon is clearly operating within an exegetical tradition represented in *Mek. Besh.* 1.1-12. In commenting on Exod 13:17, (ויהי בשלח פרעה, "When Pharaoh had let the people go"), *Mek. Besh.* 1.1-3 reads,

> *Shiluaḥ* means nothing other than "escorting" [ליווי],[138] as it is said: "Abraham went with them to bring them on their way [לשלחם]" (Gen 18:16); "And Isaac sent them away [וישלחם]" (Gen 26:30). [139]

This tradition understands שלח in Exod 13:17 to mean "to escort,"[140] which is precisely what we find in Wis 19:2 with Ps-Solomon's use of προπέμπω, and seems to be clear evidence of his knowledge of the particular exegetical tradition cited above. The piel of שלח, which is what we see in Exod 13:17, typically means simply "to release, set free" or "send on one's way" (e.g., Gen 3:23; 30:25; 31:42; 32:27; Exod 22:4), which is reflected in the LXX rendering of Exod 13:17 ἐξαποστέλλω. The particular tradition of which Wis 19:2 is a part, however, evidently read this verb in light of other passages where it meant (or at least was understood to mean) "to escort" (Gen 12:20; 18:16; 37:14; 45:24), something that is not self-evident from the context of Exod 13:17 itself.[141]

---

[137]Winston, 324.

[138]The root לוה means "to escort" in the piel or hifil (M. Jastrow, *A Dictionary of the Targumim, the Talmud Babli and Yerushalmi, and the Midrashic Literature* [New York: Judaica, 1992] 697).

[139]The same notion is found in *Exod. Rab.* 20.3: "This [בשלח in Exod 13:17], however, is to teach that Pharaoh escorted (מלוה) them and said to them: 'Pray for me and ask for mercy for me,' as it says: *Take both your flocks and your herds, as you have said, and be gone; and bless me also* (Ex. 12:32). *Shiluah* here means nothing other than 'escorting' [לוה], as it says: *And Abraham went with them on the way* (Gen 18:16)." J. L. Kugel cites the comment on Gen 37:14 ("and he [=Jacob] sent [שלח] him [=Joseph] off from the valley of Hebron") in *Midrash Tanḥuma* (*In Potiphar's House*, 105, n. 20). The point of this midrash is explicit: to show that Jacob did not merely send Joseph on his way, but actually accompanied him, i.e., escorted him to the valley of Hebron.

[140]For προπέμπω meaning "to escort," see Acts 20:38; 21:5; Herodotus 1.111; Sophocles, *Oedipus Colonus*, 1667; Xenophon, *Hellenica*, 4.1.9-10; Aeschylus, *Persians*, 530. See also the use of συμπροπέμπω in LXX Gen 18:16 and 12:20.

[141]*Exod. Rab.* 20.3 makes clear that שלח must mean "escort" rather than "release," since the command to release the Israelites is God's alone (according to Num 23:22) and not Pharaoh's. The Israelites' triumphant departure was God's doing and not the command of a mere man. That Pharaoh "escorted" the Israelites was thus thought to

It is clear that Wis 19:2 is an early witness to this exegetical tradition. This is a particularly striking example of Ps-Solomon's exegetical activity in general and his acquaintance with early interpretive traditions founded on the Hebrew in particular, since the LXX has ἐξαποστέλλω rather than προπέμπω.

Ps-Solomon's comment also highlights the perversity of the Egyptians' "change of mind" (μεταμεληθέντης) in 19:2c. They did not merely *allow* the Israelites to leave, as if begrudgingly; they actually escorted them on their way. The remainder of *Mek. Besh.* 1.1-12 cited above makes special mention of the Egyptians' kindness for helping the Israelites on their way and their subsequent reward for doing so. Pharaoh's decision to pursue the Israelites might have been somewhat understandable if his initial decision to release them had been half-hearted.[142] But this is not the case according to the exegetical tradition represented here. That Israel was escorted implies a more sustained positive regard (although not necessarily lengthy) on Pharaoh's part toward the Israelites, rather than an impulsive decision.[143] This makes Pharaoh's subsequent decision to pursue all the more "foolish" (19:3c) and remarkable. It is worth noting again that a similar extreme shift from beneficence to malice is elaborated in 19:13-17, in which the actions of the Egyptians are compared to those of Sodom to Abraham, as recounted in Genesis 19 (see Part I, pp. 24ff.). There, too, the Egyptians' transgression is said to be inhospitality, i.e., first welcoming the Israelites as guests only to enslave them later (v. 14).

The "change of mind" we have been discussing is also clearly tied by Ps-Solomon to the biblical text, namely Exod 14:5, which says that Pharaoh and his officials ויהפך לבב. What is of particular interest here is Ps-Solomon's choice of words. Μεταμέλομαι has connotations of regret, i.e., "to feel sorry."[144] For Ps-Solomon, thus, Pharaoh did not merely change

---

highlight his importunity.

[142]This seems to be the sense of the comment in *Mek. Besh.* 2.63-64 on Exod 14:4 ("I will harden Pharaoh's heart"): "For Pharaoh was undecided [לב חלוק] whether or not to pursue [אם לרדוף אם לא לרדוף]."

[143]See also Ginzberg's comment: "The hatred of the Egyptians toward the Israelites changed now into its opposite. They conceived affection and friendship for them..." (*Legends*, 2.371).

[144]Although not every instance of μεταμέλομαι means "to regret" (see, for example, Sir 30:28 [33:19]; LXX Pss 105:45 and 109:4), this is the most common meaning. See LXX 1 Sam 15:35 (36); 1 Chr 21:15; Prov 5:11; 25:8; Jer 20:16; 1 Macc 11:10; Matt 21:32; 2 Cor 7:8. See also the many Hellenistic works cited in LS.

his mind (לבב ויהפך of Exod 14:5); he *regretted* his decision. Ps-Solomon is not alone in this comment.   Although a different word is used (μετανοέω), both Josephus and Philo express the same idea. In Jos., *Ant.* 2.320 we read: "But the Egyptians repented [μετενόουν] of having let the Hebrews go...." Philo says in *V. Mos.* 1.167: "And repenting [μετανοῶν] that he had let them go...."   This exegetical tradition represented by Josephus, Philo, and Ps-Solomon sharpens and clarifies the sense of Exod 14:5b, where the motive for Pharaoh's decision is given: "What is this that we have done? We have released the Israelites from our servitude." In this respect, Ps-Solomon's comment specifies, on the basis of Exod 14:5b, what precisely לבב ויהפך/μεταστρέφω in Exod 14:5a means.   By themselves, neither the Hebrew phrase nor the LXX equivalent carries any specific or necessary connotations of regret.[145]

12. The Egyptians' Decision to Pursue the Israelites Was Lacking in Intelligence (19:3c)

In 19:3c, Ps-Solomon comments further on the Egyptians' change of heart to pursue the Israelites: *they reached another foolish decision* (ἕτερον ἐπεσπάσαντο λογισμὸν ἀνοίας). On the one hand, the foolishness of Pharaoh's change of heart can be seen in his decision to ignore the previous warnings (plagues) given to him. After all, how much more opposition did he think Moses' God was going to tolerate? Yet it may also be significant that rabbinic sources speak of an actual, calculating decision made by the Egyptians. This tradition is found in the *Mek. Besh.* 2.41-43; 3.8-15; *Tg. Ps.-J.* to Exod 14:9; *Exod. Rab.* 15.15. These texts all refer to Pharaoh's foolish miscalculation in believing that the god Baal Zephon had trapped the Israelites in the desert, thus making them easy prey for his army.[146] The biblical motive for this tradition is certainly the mention of Baal

---

[145]Μεταστρέφω simply means "to turn, turn around," which in the context of Exod 14:5 may be understood as "to change one's mind." See Deut 23:5 (6); 1 Sam 10:9; 2 Chr 36:4; Pss 65 (66):6; 77 (78):44, 57; 104 (105): 25, 29; Jer 6:12; 21:4; Lam 5:2; Dan 10:8; Hos 7:8; 11:8; Amos 8:10; Joel 2:31 (3:4); Zeph 3:9; 1 Esdr 3:20; 7:15; Sir 11:31; 39:23; 1 Macc 9:41; 3 Macc 5:7; 6:22. See also the Hellenistic works cited in LS. Likewise, הפך לבב does not necessarily carry the nuance of regret. This clause occurs only four other times in the MT. Although Hos 11:8 and 1 Sam 10:9 have the same sense as Exod 14:5, Ps 105:25 and Lam 1:20 do not.

[146]Adducing this tradition to explain Ps-Solomon's comment finds support in some of the commentaries: Winston, 324; Reider, 216; Goodrick, 366.

Zephon (the geographical location) in Exod 14:2 and 9, which was understood to be a veiled reference to the name of the god.[147]   This tradition presents a motive for Pharaoh's pursuit: since Pharaoh believed a god was detaining the Israelites for capture, Pharaoh felt justified in going after them.[148]   But it is probably impossible to determine precisely whether this provides the background for Ps-Solomon's comment.   Other options should be explored to shed light on Pharaoh's "foolish decision" in Wis 19:3c.

There is a tradition, represented in *b. Soṭa* 11a (also *Exod. Rab.* 1.9), that speaks of the advice Pharaoh's counselors gave him regarding the manner of death they would inflict on the Israelites.   They conclude that death by water (throwing the Israelite male children into the Nile) would preclude God's taking vengeance on them, since they knew that he had promised he would never again bring a flood upon the earth (citing Isa 54:9; cf. Gen 9:11 and 15).   The midrash continues as follows:

> They were unaware [אינן יודעין], however, that while he would not bring a flood upon the whole world, he would bring it upon one people; or alternately, he would not bring [the flood] but they would go and fall [באין ונופלין] into it.   Thus it says, "And the Egyptians ran toward it" (Exod 14:27).   This is what R. Eleazar said: This is the meaning of what is written, "Indeed, in the very thing wherein they dealt proudly [זדו] against them."   In the pot in which they cooked were they cooked.[149]

This exegetical tradition clearly portrays the Egyptians' decision to pursue the Israelites as utter folly.   Their cleverness turned out to be foolishness: God's promise to Noah would not preclude their own death by water, as they had thought.   Their decision to pursue was foolish.

This passage from the Babylonian Talmud also hints at another reason why the Egyptian pursuit might be considered foolish.   This

---

[147]Perhaps לפי בעל צפן was read as "under the eye of Baal Zephon" (see the use of לפי in Deut 25:2 and 1 Sam 3:1), thus personifying Baal Zephon. Exod 14:2 would then read, "They are to encamp by the sea, under the eye of Baal Zephon." Also, "Zephon," from the root צפה (keep guard, watch) might also have prompted such a reading.

[148]Goodrick, for example, sees the Baal Zephon tradition as a justification for Pharaoh's actions rather than as evidence of his foolishness: "The folly of the Egyptians was, perhaps, not so great after all" (366).

[149]The last line of this midrash refers to Gen 25:29 and Jacob's cooking of stew (ויזד יעקב נזיד) for Esau. This is linked to Exod 18:11 on the basis of the root זיד/זוד, which is found in both. Hence, in drowning in the sea, the Egyptians are cooked in their own stew, so to speak. Although not connected to the Exodus, the root is used in a similar sense in Ps 124:5: "then the raging waters (המים הזידונים) would have swept us away."

midrash apparently understands Exod 14:27 to mean that the Egyptians "fell into" the water, as if to say they went in of their own accord. Exod 14:27 says,

> Moses stretched out his hand over the sea, and the sea returned at the break of dawn to its normal state [לְאֵיתָנוֹ] *and the Egyptians fled toward it* [וּמִצְרַיִם נָסִים לִקְרָאתוֹ]. Thus YHWH swept away the Egyptians in the midst of the sea.

The precise relationship between the clause וּמִצְרַיִם נָסִים לִקְרָאתוֹ and what precedes is ambiguous. The intention of the verse is certainly to be read "*while* the Egyptians fled toward it," i.e., the sea closed about them as they were making their way through water. Yet, if one reads the clause "*and* the Egyptians fled toward it," indicating sequence, one comes away with a different picture. Now the impression is that the Egyptians fled toward the sea [לִקְרָאתוֹ] *after* Moses returned the waters to their normal state. This implies that the Egyptians had not yet reached the water when Moses closed up the sea. Exod 14:27 does not say that Moses closed up the sea while the Egyptians were making their way through the sea, but rather while they were making their way *toward* the sea. And they could not have met their demise in the watery depths unless, even after the sea returned to its normal state, they had kept on marching into it! The Egyptians made a beeline for the sea, apparently after the parted waters had already returned to their former state.[150] Moreover, even if we read "*while* the Egyptians fled toward it," a similar situation could be envisioned. For if God closed up the sea while (at least some of) the Egyptians were not yet in it, but

---

[150]The Samaritan Pentateuch, perhaps in an attempt to alleviate this difficulty, has "retreated" (נסע) rather than "fled" (נס) which is in the MT. The reference to Exod 18:11 at the end of *b. Soṭa* 11a cited above puts this tradition into even sharper focus. In Mishnaic Hebrew, the hifil of זיד implies intentional wrongdoing (Jastrow, *A Dictionary of the Targumim*, 391). In this biblical passage, Jethro is praising YHWH for delivering Israel and punishing Egypt. Having seen God's deliverance, he is now convinced of YHWH's superiority over other gods (18:9-11a). Verse 11 in its entirety reads, "Now I know that YHWH is greater than all other gods, because in the manner in which they plotted evil against them." The seemingly incomplete sentence in v. 11b, כִּי בַדָּבָר אֲשֶׁר זָדוּ עֲלֵיהֶם, implies an unstated conclusion, such as, "because in the manner in which they plotted evil against them, *they themselves were punished*," or the like. (See *Exod. Rab.* 22.1, which reads עֲלֵיהֶם as the conclusion: "For the very manner in which they were presumptuous, *he was above them*.") This is certainly how the Talmud understands Exod 18:11: the drowning of the Egyptians in the sea, a death to which they rushed headlong, is fit punishment for their own plot against the Israelites in Exodus 1, the drowning of the Israelite male children.

outside running toward it, how could the Egyptians have been drowned, unless, foolishly, the Egyptians kept running, regardless, and ran right into the water? Thus, Wis 19:3c may be an effort to portray the Egyptian decision to follow the Israelites into the sea as completely lacking in judgment, and even intelligence, the basis of which is the syntax of Exod 14:27 and the prepositional phrase לקראתו.

This notion is further supported by the use of ἄνοια in Wis 19:3c. The term denotes a lack of understanding, i.e., with respect to one's mental capacity.[151] This also seems to be true of the clause חזק לב, used in Exod 14:4 (and throughout Exodus)[152] to describe Pharaoh's decision. חזק לב should not be understood entirely as an indication of Pharaoh's moral inclination, i.e., simply that he was stubborn. It may also be an indication of his incapacity to understand.[153] "Heart" in Hebrew is not normally the seat of one's moral faculties but of one's mental faculties. A particularly relevant passage is Exod 9:14, where Moses, speaking to Pharaoh on YHWH's behalf, says he will send "all my plagues to your heart" (כל־מגפתי אל־לבך). The result of such persuasion would be that Pharaoh would "know" (ידע) YHWH's incomparability, which could imply that Pharaoh's failure to recognize YHWH's might reflects his inability to *comprehend* the situation, rather than his unwillingness to comply. Such an understanding of the hardening of Pharaoh's heart can be seen in Ps-Philo's *Bib. Ant.* 10:6: "And God hardened their perception and *they did not know* that they were entering the sea" (*Et Deus obduravit sensum eorum, et non scierunt quoniam in mare ingrederentur*).[154] Similarly, Sir 16:15 reads: "The Lord hardened [ἐσκλήρυνε] Pharaoh so that he did not know [εἰδέναι]

---

[151] See Aeschylus, *Prometheus Bound*, 1079; Plato, *Timaeus*, 86b and *Republic*, 382c, e. Ps-Solomon uses the adjective in 15:18 regarding an animal's lack of intelligence. See also Larcher, 3.1050. Also, throughout the Wisdom of Solomon, Ps-Solomon's concern is the "foolish decisions" made by the ungodly (1:3, 5; 11:15; 12:10; 19:3). Deane defines ἄνοια as that "which signifies all wilful ignorance, sinfulness and carelessness, every act and habit opposed to the love of God and the practice of holiness" (25).

[152] Exod 4:21; 7:13, 22; 8:15; 9:12, 35; 10:20, 27; 11:10; 14:8, 17. See also קשה לב in 7:3 and כבד לב in 8:11 and 10:1.

[153] See also Sarna's comment on Exod 4:21: "The 'hardening of the heart' thus expresses a state of arrogant moral degeneracy unresponsive to reason and incapable of compassion" (*Exodus*, 23).

[154] H. Jacobson, too, makes the point that *Bib. Ant.* 10:6 refers to a dulling of their perception rather than stubborn behavior (*Commentary*, 1.442). He also cites several rabbinic passages in support of this notion, most notably *Mek. Besh.* 6.123-24: "He confounded them [דבמן] and mixed them up [ערבבן]; he took away their banners so that they did not know what they were doing."

him."[155] The result of this hardening is Pharaoh's failure to "know." More immediately relevant is Wis 16:15-16. With respect to the plagues, Ps-Solomon describes the Egyptians' behavior in terms of their mental processes: the ungodly "refused to know you" (ἀρνούμενοι γάρ σε εἰδέναι ἀσεβεῖς).[156] Furthermore, understanding the foolish decision of 19:3c to reflect לב חזק in Exod 14:4 helps us understand Ps-Solomon's seemingly inconsequential use of ἕτερον. The hardening of Pharaoh's heart to pursue the Israelites in Exodus 14:4 is not an isolated event, but yet "another" instance of what has been happening throughout the Exodus narrative—the hardening of Pharaoh's heart. When seen in this light, Ps-Solomon's statement in 19:3c comes into sharper focus.

In the final analysis, however, it is difficult to attribute Ps-Solomon's comment with any certainty to either of the options outlined above: Baal Zephon, a misunderstanding of God's promise in Gen 9:11 and 15, or a headlong rush into the sea. Still, Wis 19:3c clearly represents an understanding of the Egyptians' pursuit of the Israelites as an egregiously dimwitted, cognitive act—a "foolish decision"—and this comment likely reflects some exegetical tradition to which Ps-Solomon had access. [157]

---

[155]The verb σκληρύνω is used in the LXX throughout Exodus for the Hebrew factitive verb חזק. Sir 16:15-16 is attested only in Codex Alexandrinus, Codex Sinaiticus, and a second translation of the Greek (i.e., after that of Ben Sira's grandson). This, however, should not keep us from appreciating the relevance of the exegetical tradition contained therein.

[156]This is similar to Isa 6:9-10, where the prophet's message is said to have a dulling effect on the people's perception: השמן לב־העם הזה (v. 10a). The point is that Isaiah's message will not be understood.

[157]Although the word ἄνοια is not used, Wis 12:23-27 and the whole of 15:14-19 also attribute "foolishness" (ἄφρων) to the Egyptians, in this case specifically for their idolatry. Wis 12:26 also mentions that, after the plagues, the Egyptians came to know God whom they had "previously refused to know" (πάλαι ἠροῦντο εἰδέναι). Once again, the Egyptians' antagonism toward YHWH is expressed by Ps-Solomon as a conscious decision. See also Amir's observation that Ps-Solomon throughout the Wisdom of Solomon is primarily concerned not with wicked *deeds* but "with the wicked thoughts which underlie them" ("Measure for Measure," 38). One final possible biblical motive for Pharaoh's "foolish decision" pertains to another portion of Exod 14:5 not yet considered. This is the curious statement that Pharaoh *was told* that the Israelites had left. It was upon receiving this information that Pharaoh and his officials decided to pursue them. The question of course is why Pharaoh would have to be told in the first place. He is the one who gave the order, yet the news seems totally unexpected to him. Had he forgotten already?

13. The Israelites Were "Begged" to Leave Egypt (19:3d)

The fact that the Egyptians were now pursuing (διώκω) as fugitives (φυγάς) those whom they had previously gone to such lengths to drive out of their presence highlights the foolishness of their decision in v. 3c-d: they were the ones who had permitted the Israelites to leave; indeed, they had insisted upon it. Now they chase them as fugitives from justice.[158] After continually resisting Moses' call to release the Israelites, Pharaoh finally succumbs to the effects of the plagues, particularly the tenth plague, and does what one would expect of anyone with any appreciation for the gravity of the situation: he insists that the Israelites leave at once. The urgency of their expulsion is expressed well by the use of ἐκβάλλω. In saying that the Israelites were "cast out," Ps-Solomon is simply following the Exodus narrative. The same verb is used in LXX Exod 11:1 and 12:39 (MT גרש) and 12:33 (MT שלח). The Exodus narrative leaves the clear impression that the departure of the Israelites was nothing short of forced expulsion. Moses and Aaron were, after all, summoned at night (12:31), thus suggesting the urgency of the matter; the Israelites were urged to leave quickly (12:33), so quickly in fact that they did not have adequate time to prepare for their departure (12:39).

What is of greater interest for this study, however, is Ps-Solomon's description of the Israelites being *beseechingly* (ἱκετεύοντες) cast out.[159] This is more subtly associated with the Exodus narrative. For one thing, the verb ἱκετεύω does not appear in the LXX of Exodus. Neither is the notion of petitioning overtly present. If anything, the presence of ἐκβάλλω/גרש in Exod 11:1; 12:33 and 39 suggests a less polite motivation for Israel's hasty departure. What, then, would prompt Ps-Solomon to say such a thing? The same tradition is found in *Tg. Ps.-J.* to Exod 12:31-33. The key passage is the Targum's addition to 12:31 ("And he [=Pharaoh] called to Moses and Aaron at night"). The Targum adds the following: "His voice could be heard as far as the land of Goshen. Pharaoh *entreated* them with a sorrowful voice." The key word is "entreat," מתחנן, the hitpᵉel of חנן. *Tg. Ps.-J.* to Exod 12:31-33 as a whole is relevant.

---

[158]The use of φυγάς also provides thematic links between the Israelites' crossing of the sea, Jacob's flight from Esau, and Lot's flight from Sodom (see appendix to 19:3c and φυγάς).

[159]See the similar use of ἱκετεύω in 2 Macc 11:6 (Lysias' siege of Beth-zur), 1 Clem. 7:7 (Jonah) and 48:1 (beseeching God with tears).

(31) Now the territory of the land of Egypt was a distance of 400 miles.[160] The land of Goshen, where Moses and the Israelites were, was in the middle [במציעתה] of the land of Egypt, whereas Pharaoh's royal palace [ופלטרין דבית מלכותא דפרעה] was at the beginning of the land of Egypt. So he called to Moses and Aaron on the night of the Passover. His voice could be heard as far as the land of Goshen. Pharaoh entreated [מחזנן] [them] with a sorrowful voice [בקל עציב]. He said, "Get up. Leave my people's presence, you and the Israelites, too. Go worship YHWH as you have said. (32) Take also your sheep and your cattle and from my belongings [ומן דילי], as we have spoken, and go. I ask only that you pray for me that I not die." (33) When Moses and Pharaoh and the Israelites heard Pharaoh's weeping voice [קל בכותא], they did not pay attention [לא אשגחו] until he and all his officials and all the Egyptians came. They urged the people of the house of Israel to hurry and leave the land, for they said, "If they remain here one more hour, we will all die."[161]

But what of the origin of the tradition? If "petitioning" is not part of the Exodus narrative, why would the tradition have arisen in the first place? As indicated in the Targum, the biblical motive seems to be Exod 12:31. There, the urgency and panic of Pharaoh's actions are evident. It is the Passover. Moses and the Israelites have been instructed by YHWH to remain indoors, in Goshen, to escape death. Pharaoh is in his palace surrounded by the shrieks of terrified countrymen. What does he do? He "calls to Moses and Aaron" (ויקרא למשה ולאהרן, v. 12:31a). The Targum understands the *lamed* not in the sense of summoning them by means of a messenger, but actually calling to them, perhaps a loud cry of frustration and grief, or even yelling out the window! They hear him, of course (or else the ensuing commands of Pharaoh would not be heard), even halfway across the country, 200 miles away. But according to the Targum, the Israelites do not react until their enemies suffer further humiliation and present themselves. Also, Pharaoh calls to them at night (לילה), which further emphasizes the urgency of the matter; this simply could not keep until morning. The words of Pharaoh that follow in vv. 31b-32 sound like complete capitulation: "Take everything, whatever you want, sheep, cattle, anything. Just get out. The only thing we want from you is your blessing: make the plague stop."[162] Although Pharaoh's actions are not explicitly

---

[160]The Aramaic is פרס, representing Persian miles.

[161]Ginzberg retells a similar midrash, but, unfortunately, without notes as to its origin (*Legends*, 2.368-70).

[162]Ginzberg also comments on the urgency of the expulsion, but, again without notes: "So the Egyptians were happier to be rid of the Hebrews than these were to be free" (*Legends*, 2.374). See also Ps 105:38: "The Egyptians rejoiced when they left."

labeled "begging," this is precisely what he is doing. These are not the words of a powerful ruler bent on keeping his slaves under his thumb. Rather, he is now himself playing the role of the slave, begging his master for mercy. The Egyptians, too, join in the begging (Exod 12:33 וַתֶּחֱזַק מִצְרַיִם עַל־הָעָם לְמַהֵר] and *Tg. Ps.-J.* to Exod 12:33).[163]   Hence, the biblical motive for this tradition may be seen both in the clear implication of the Exodus passage as well as, more specifically, in the curious statement in Exod 12:31a, "He called to Moses and Aaron at night."

At this juncture, two observations can be made. First, it is apparent that both Ps-Solomon and the Targum have a similar understanding of the biblical text, though the Targum's version is much more elaborate. Indeed, all five of the Targum's expansions to the Exodus account serve to underscore Pharaoh's and the Egyptians' importunity.   Thus, (1) the Targum provides the geographical information in v. 31 in order to emphasize the strength of Pharaoh's lament: the latter could be heard 200 miles away in the land of Goshen. (2) Pharaoh does not wait to find Moses and Aaron; rather he does so immediately, on the very night of Passover. (3) Pharaoh is specifically said to have "entreated" Moses and Aaron "with a sorrowful voice;" here is a beaten ruler groveling for mercy.   (4) Pharaoh not only allows the Israelites to leave with the sheep and cattle (what he had previously disallowed in Exod 10:24), but, in a desperate move, he now offers Moses his own possessions as well (v. 32). And, (5) in v. 33, the Israelites are said to ignore their plea until Pharaoh, his officials, and all the Egyptians come personally. They come and, as with relatives who overstay their welcome, they "urge" them to leave, having not even one hour to spare.

A second observation concerns the direction of influence, if any, between Ps-Solomon and the Targum. It is immediately clear that the Targum's presentation is not in any sense dependent on Wis 19:3d; Ps-Solomon's comment is too incidental to have spawned the elaborate retelling we find in the Targum. Rather, Ps-Solomon's terse statement seems to be an abridgment of an existing tradition rather than his own creation. But neither can we say that Ps-Solomon derives his comment from the Targum. Although this is possible in the abstract, there is no evidence for the existence of *Tg. Ps-Jonathan* in Ps-Solomon's day. It is far

---

[163]The fact that not only Pharaoh but the Egyptians as well urge the Israelites on their way may be significant, since Ps-Solomon also speaks in the plural: "they beseechingly cast them out."   Although not in the MT, LXX Exod 12:39 also expresses the same idea: ἐξέβαλον γὰρ αὐτοὺς <u>οἱ Αἰγύπτιοι</u>.

more likely that neither is dependent on the other, but both Ps-Solomon and the Targum are witnesses to an exegetical tradition that is older than either of them. This is further evidence of Ps-Solomon's familiarity with exegetical traditions current in his day, and the subtle, almost unconscious manner in which he incorporates these traditions into his retelling of the biblical narrative.

14. The Egyptians Were Drowned in the Sea as Fitting Punishment for the Drowned Israelite Children (19:4-5)

Ps-Solomon's comment in 19:4-5 reflects not only the principle of *talion*, which is so prevalent throughout the Wisdom of Solomon, but a well known exegetical tradition. By drowning in the sea, the Egyptians got exactly what they deserved: *For a deserved fate drew them to this end and made them forget what had happened, so that they might fill up the punishment that was lacking in their torments* (εἷλκεν γὰρ αὐτοὺς ἡ ἀξία ἐπὶ τοῦτο τὸ πέρας ἀνάγκη καὶ τῶν συμβεβηκότων ἀμνηστίαν ἐνέβαλεν, ἵνα τὴν λείπουσαν ταῖς βασάνοις προσαναπληρώσωσιν κόλασιν; 19:4). It is only the death in the sea, what Ps-Solomon calls "deserved fate" (ἡ ἀξία...ἀνάγκη), that will satisfy God's justice.[164] What torments (βάσανος) they had heretofore experienced in the plagues were not yet the full punishment they deserved. The fact that Ps-Solomon portrays their death in the sea as their "deserved fate" and the fullness of their punishment indicates that he is another witness to a fairly widespread exegetical tradition: the death of the Egyptians at the sea was the fitting punishment for Pharaoh's decree in Exod 1:22 to throw every male infant into the Nile. This tradition is found in the Wisdom of Solomon, as we saw earlier, not only in 19:4-5, but in 18:5 as well:

> When they [=the Egyptians] determined to kill the children of the holy ones—though one child [=Moses] had been exposed and rescued—as punishment you took away a multitude of their children and destroyed them all together in raging water.

---

[164]In 17:17, Ps-Solomon also speaks of the Egyptians' punishment in the ninth plague as ἀνάγκη. The word appears nowhere else in the Wisdom of Solomon. On divine retribution, see also S. Sowers, "On the Reinterpretation of Biblical History in Hellenistic Judaism," 18-25.

This principle is clearly articulated in *Mek. Besh.* 7.3-22 (to Exod 14:28).
Note particularly lines 4-7:

> Let the wheel turn against them and bring back upon them their own
> violence. For with the same devices with which Egypt planned to destroy
> Israel, I am going to pass sentence on them. They planned to destroy my
> children by water, so I will likewise punish them by water.

Other sources for this tradition include *Exod. Rab.* 22.1, 1.9; *b. Soṭa* 11a
(commenting on Exod 18:11); *Jub.* 48:14.[165]   The clear exegetical
justification for this tradition is the obvious fact that water was the medium
for both Pharaoh's decree and YHWH's punishment. After all, why, of all
the means by which YHWH could have brought an end to the Egyptians,
did he have them drown in the sea? Early interpreters seized upon the
opportunity to explain the manner of the Egyptian death as retribution for
their treatment of the Israelites. Although the principle of *talion* by water
is not made explicit in the Exodus narrative, the connection between
chap. 1 and chap. 14 is certainly the biblical basis for this tradition.
In fact, the Exodus narrative itself seems to encourage the reader to make
this connection.

Furthermore, Ps-Solomon's word choice in v. 4a supports the notion
that the Egyptian death in the sea was a just punishment for their previous
actions against the Israelites. First, ἕλκω has connotations of compulsion
or forced compliance, i.e., that their fate was inexorable.[166]   Second,
ἄξιος connotes something that is of equal worth or value. Third, ἀνάγκη
in Hellenistic writings means "necessity."[167]   If we understand ἀνάγκη in
this way, the discussion found in some of the commentaries regarding
the apparent contradiction in the term "deserved fate" recedes to the
background. "Fate" need carry no necessary connotations of divine
predestination.[168]   The punishment of the Egyptians is not *fated*, i.e., by

---

[165]*Jub.* 48:14 reads: "And all the people whom he [=Prince Mastema] brought out to
pursue after Israel the LORD our God threw into the middle of the sea into the depths of the
abyss beneath the children of Israel. Just as the men of Egypt cast their sons into the river
he avenged one million. And one thousand strong and ardent men perished on account of
one infant whom they threw into the midst of the river from the sons of your people"
(Charlesworth, *Pseudepigrapha*, 2.140).

[166]See *Iliad*, 3.383; 24.52 and *Odyssey*, 16.276. See also Larcher, 3.1051.

[167]On the meaning of the word see Reese, *Hellenistic Influence*, 4 and 101, n. 67.

[168]Here I am in agreement with Reider (216), Grimm (292-93) Winston (324) and
Goodrick (366). Goodrick, however, contradicts himself earlier by remarking: "the
student must be warned that he will find in Pseudo-Solomon no exact philosophical

divine fiat, but *necessary*, i.e., commensurate with their actions against the Israelites.[169] In other words, according to Ps-Solomon, the Egyptians were *compelled* (ἕλκω) to accept a punishment that was *necessary* (ἀνάγκη) and *of equal value* (ἄξιος) to their own treatment of the Israelites. Wis 19:4 is another witness to the *talion* tradition cited above.

Ps-Solomon further states in 19:4 that the impetus for their decision to follow the Israelites was that they were "made to forget what had happened" (τῶν συμβεβηκότων ἀμνηστίαν ἐνέβαλεν). This appears to be a direct comment on Exod 14:17: "I will harden the heart [מחזק הנני ואני את־לב] of the Egyptians so that they will go after them." Ps-Solomon understands the hardening of the heart as "forgetting." Once again, this reinforces the notion that, at least for Ps-Solomon, the hardening of the heart refers to a mental process (see comments on #12 above, pp. 99ff.). This then ties "forgetting" to the "foolish decision" in v. 3c, which is also brought on by their hardened hearts. After all, how else could one explain the Egyptians so soon forgetting their recent misery and pursuing the Israelites without fear of further retribution?[170]   Ps-Solomon describes the Egyptians' cognitive processes in clear terms: they were foolish. And once again, in doing so he is also providing some rationale for the events described in the Exodus narrative itself, i.e., Pharaoh's impulsive change of heart, first to implore the Israelites to leave, and no sooner having done so, to attempt to bring them back.

Saying that the Egyptians were made to "forget" (ἀμνηστία), besides being motivated by Exod 14:17, also helps Ps-Solomon justify the death of

---

reasoner, but rather a loose rhetorical thinker, who uses the first word that comes to hand, and that will round off a period" (40). The following footnote reads: "An example of confusion of ideas is to be found in 19:4—ἡ ἀξία ἀναγκή, a plain contradiction in terms." Not only does Goodrick contradict himself here, but his pessimism, here and throughout his commentary, regarding Ps-Solomon's ability to express his thoughts accurately detracts greatly from an otherwise excellent scholarly work.

[169]See also Larcher: "...la Nécéssité qui poussait les Égyptiens jusqu'à ce point extrême était une nécessité méritée..." (3.1051).

[170]Relevant here is 19:3a-b, where the Egyptians are said to make their decision to pursue during their period of grief, *while they were still mourning and lamenting at the graves of their dead.* Juxtaposing the Egyptians' grief with their decision to pursue seems to add some emphasis to the foolishness of their decision in v. 3c. Is it not precisely at this time of overwhelming grief that the Egyptians should have been least likely to forget that it was their persistent failure to obey the God of Israel that led to their grieving in the first place? Yet, contrary to all reason and common sense, the Egyptians *in their grief* mobilize themselves for one last futile act of hostility against the Israelites, what Ps-Solomon calls a "foolish decision."

the Egyptian soldiers. In 19:4, it is the soldiers themselves who are the particular objects of God's wrath, not those who made the decision to pursue. The contexts of both Wis 19:4-5 and Exod 14:17 clearly imply that the topic of discussion is the pursuit of the soldiers, those actually entering the sea. By saying that God made the *soldiers* forget what had happened, Ps-Solomon may be trying to justify their death and apply more consistently his principle of *talion*. This also seems to be happening in the Exodus narrative itself. Once God had hardened the heart of Pharaoh and his *officials* to make the decision to pursue (14:4, 8), Pharaoh and his *army* cornered the Israelites against the sea. At this point, apparently the soldiers themselves needed a dose of hardening to continue their pursuit (14:17). Why? Perhaps without this divine initiative they would not have been so foolish as to embark on such an obviously doomed chase. They clearly pursued the Israelites *because* God hardened their heart (hence Wis 19:4, they pursued because God made them forget). The effect is not only to give some rationale for why the soldiers would behave in a manner contrary to all military sense,[171] but also to justify God's punishment of an "innocent" party. The basis for the soldiers' punishment is identical to that of Pharaoh's: both had their hearts hardened. As Pharaoh got what he deserved, so did the soldiers—God's punishment is just. The death of Pharaoh's army in the sea "filled up the punishment that was lacking in their torments" (19:4).

Similarly, 19:5, with reference to the verses preceding it, also expresses a type of measure-for measure punishment: the means by which God punished the Egyptians are said to be the very means by which he aided the Israelites: *and that your people might experience an incredible journey but those others might find a strange death* (καὶ ὁ μὲν λαός σου παράδοξον ὁδοιπορίαν πειράσῃ ἐκεῖνοι δὲ ξένον εὕρωσιν θάνατον). Reider suggests that this "incredible journey" refers to the Israelites' desert wandering, i.e., after the crossing of the sea.[172] I am not in favor of this view, since this would disrupt the chronology of the passage. In recounting the departure from Egypt, I see no convincing reason to suggest that Ps-Solomon would begin with the Egyptians' decision to pursue (19:1-4) and then make a passing comment on the forty-year wilderness period (v. 5a), only to return to the crossing of the sea (vv. 5b-8) and the Song at the Sea (vv. 9-10). It is not until v. 11 that he mentions the desert experience

---

[171]It is these very same soldiers who are later said to flee "toward" (לקראתו) the sea in Exod 14:27, as we have seen above under #12.
[172]Reider, 216. See also Clarke, 126.

(quail). Verse 11 begins "afterwards" (ἐφ᾽ ὑστέρῳ), i.e., after the events of the departure recounted in the previous verses. A comment on the desert in v. 5a would be out of place.

Another weakness in Reider's comment is that he does not account for the parallelism in v. 5. The death of the Egyptians in v. 5b is sharply contrasted to the "incredible journey" of the Israelites in v. 5a. The force of this contrast would be altogether lost if the cataclysmic and sudden death of the Egyptians were played off against the forty-year desert wanderings. Rather, their journey must refer to some event associated with the crossing of the sea.   Nor should παράδοξος be translated "unexpected," as does Larcher, i.e., with reference to Israel's unexpected route to the sea in Exod 13:17-14:4.[173] Although this is possible, another reading is more consistent with Ps-Solomon's use of the word elsewhere in the Book of Wisdom. The word occurs in 5:2 and 16:17, and both times has connotations of something supernatural or miraculous (See Jdt 13:3 and 3 Macc 6:33). In 5:2 the topic is the righteous man's salvation as he stands before the fearful ungodly at the last judgment. In 16:17, Ps-Solomon refers to the fire's effect (i.e., the fire that came with the hail in Exod 9:23) even in water as "most unusual of all" (παραδοξότατον). The point is not that these vehicles of divine judgment were merely "contrary to expectation," but that they were of divine origin: they were miraculous. This suggests that παράδοξος in 19:5a also refers to some divine intervention of a more dramatic nature than merely the unexpected itinerary of the Israelites. It is probably the "miracle" at the sea that Ps-Solomon has in mind.[174] Ps-Solomon's point in v. 5 is succinctly expressed in 11:5: "For through the things by which their enemies were punished, they themselves received benefit while in need" (δι᾽ ὧν γὰρ ἐκολάσθησαν οἱ ἐχθροὶ αὐτῶν, διὰ τούτων αὐτοὶ ἀποροῦντες εὐεργετήθησαν). Such a view is also found in *V. Mos.* 1.143: "And the strangest thing of all was that the same elements in the same place and at the same time brought destruction to one people and safety to the other." So here, not only is God's drowning of the Egyptians deserved, but God also uses the same Red Sea by which he punished the Egyptians in order to save the Israelites. This is precisely the point of Ps-Solomon's choice of words in 19:5: it was God's own intervention that made possible the "incredible journey" though the sea, just as this same intervention brought a "strange death" (the

---

[173]Cf. Larcher, 3.1054.

[174]Reese, 197; Grimm, 292. Reider, too, thinks of miraculous signs, but in conjunction with the desert wanderings, as remarked above (216).

miraculous closing of the sea) to the Egyptians. It follows, then, that the "strange death" of v. 5b refers to the manner in which the Egyptians met their fate.[175]

Like παράδοχος in 19:5a to describe the "incredible journey," ξένος in 19:5b also implies divine intervention. This is supported by Wis 16:16b: "for the ungodly, refusing to know you, were scourged by the strength of your arm, pursued by strange rains (ξένοις ὑετοῖς) and hail and relentless storms, and utterly consumed by fire." The strength of God's arm is seen in these "strange" rains and hail. In other words, what makes ξένος a fitting description of these phenomena is the fact that they are of divine origin. This is also the case in 16:3. Ps-Solomon here refers to the provision of quail in the desert as ξένην γεῦσιν, a "strange delicacy." Once again, what is strange about this delicacy is not the bird itself, but how the Israelites got it. This is further established by the context of the passage. God punished the Egyptians by the very creatures they worshipped (16:1). This *punishment* by God through *animals* is immediately contrasted to 16:2: "Instead of this punishment, you (=God) showed *kindness* to your people: you prepared *quails* to eat, a strange delicacy for satisfying the desire of appetite." In other words, not only is the Egyptians' punishment just (they worshipped animals and are therefore plagued by them), but God used the same means of intervention, in this case animals, to aid the Israelites. In sum, then, Ps-Solomon is concerned in 19:4-5 to justify the nature of God's punishment: the Egyptians got what they deserved, and in doing so participate in a broader *talion* tradition such as we find in *Mek. Besh.* 7.3-22.

15. The Redemption of the Israelites at the Sea Was a "New Creation" (19:6-7b)

In describing the deliverance of the Israelites at the sea in 19:6, Ps-Solomon says that *the whole creation was fashioned all over again in its own nature* (ὅλη γὰρ ἡ κτίσις ἐν ἰδίῳ γένει πάλιν ἄνωθεν διετυποῦτο); Israel's deliverance was a "new creation." The presence of this theme here is further suggested in v. 7, where Ps-Solomon describes the crossing of the sea in ways reminiscent of the creation in Genesis 1: the cloud overshadowing the camp in v. 7a calls to mind the spirit of God hovering over the waters in Gen 1:2, and, more clearly, the emergence of

---

[175]Gregg, 182; Deane, 216; Reider, 216; Clarke, 126; Larcher, 3.1054.

dry land in v. 7b calls to mind the appearance of dry land in Gen 1:9. [176]
We have already seen Ps-Solomon's use of this theme in his reference to the
Red Sea as ἄβυσσος (#5 above).

What apparently motivated Ps-Solomon to describe the crossing of
the sea as he does is an attempt to express biblical truth in a way that would
not violate the philosophical sensibilities of his audience, something we
have seen above concerning the "flame of stars" (#3, Wis 10:17d).[177] The
universe behaves as it was designed to behave, and any deviation from that
design—for example, a body of water parting—requires an explanation
that accounts for the phenomenon without violating the physical laws
of that design. Ps-Solomon's answer is that the sea was temporarily infused
with new physical properties that allowed it to behave as it did—it was
created anew and obeyed a new design. Ps-Solomon speaks of this
suspension of the natural order elsewhere, namely in 19:18-21 and 16:16-
19. Both of these passages refer to the effects on nature of God's
deliverance of the Israelites. The natural elements behave contrary to their
natural properties: fire burning even in water (16:17-19; 19:20-21), land
and sea creatures exchanging their habitats (19:19).[178] These are the types
of "unnatural" (or to use the vocabulary of v. 5, "strange") occurrences
that Ps-Solomon would have been hard pressed to explain on the basis of
natural law.[179]

---

[176]W. Vogels is particularly helpful in establishing the creation imagery in Wis 19:6 ("God
who Creates," 330). He mentions, for example, that the "kinds" spoken of by Ps-
Solomon (ἐν ἰδίῳ γένει) recall the use of למין/κατὰ γένος of Genesis 1.

[177]Several commentaries offer this as an explanation (Winston, 324-25; Reider, 217;
Goodrick, 367; Reese, 197; Larcher, 3.1056). Gregg (182) seems to be the first of several
commentators to cite Epictetus in support of this view (3.24; cf. *V. Mos.* 2.267; see also
1.154). See also the discussion in Larcher (*Études*, 166-68) and the comment by E.
Beaucamp regarding 7:17-20: "[Ps-Solomon is] seeking to show himself well informed as
to the views of his contemporary scientists and philosophers" (*The Bible and the Universe:
Israel and the Theology of History* [trans. D. Balhatchet; London: Burns & Oates, 1963]
44). Winston convincingly argues that Ps-Solomon's view of creation as *ex amorphou
hyles* rather than *ex nihilo* is clearly at work here: "[H]ad the author of Wisdom held the
doctrine of *creatio ex nihilo*, he could hardly have been troubled by lesser miracles and
sought a philosophical principle to explain them, for *creatio ex nihilo* is the miracle of
miracles" ("The Book of Wisdom's Theory of Cosmogony," *HR* 11 [1971] 194).

[178]According to Gregg, the latter refer to the Israelites ("land creatures") passing through
the sea, and the frogs coming on land (188). See also J. P. M. Sweet, "The Theory of
Miracles in the Wisdom of Solomon," *Miracles* (ed. C. F. D. Moule; London: A. R.
Mowbray, 1965) 115-16.

[179]Such an understanding of Ps-Solomon's motives can also put 19:5 into proper
perspective: another way of expressing "incredible" and "strange" is to say that God's aid

Noah's deliverance, by contrast, although likewise by God's hand,[180] is in perfect harmony with the created order and Ps-Solomon explains it as such (14:1-7). God may be the primary cause for Noah's salvation, but the immediate cause is the physical property that God has given to wood: it floats. This property, being part of the created order, is immutable and obeys whomever is driving the ship, whether idolaters (v. 1), the unskilled (v. 4), or the righteous Noah (vv. 6-7). In bringing Noah through the water, therefore, God did not violate the created order. Such a philosophically pleasing explanation, however, will not do for the Exodus. There the elements behave in ways inexplicable by natural law. And as God cannot transgress his own laws, another explanation is in order: there is a "new creation." This is anticipated earlier in the book. In 7:22, wisdom is called "the fashioner of all things" (ἡ...πάντων τεχνῖτις), the same wisdom who is also responsible for saving God's people (9:18), from Adam to Joseph (10:1-14) and the Israelites from Egypt (10:15-21; 19:1-9). It would be difficult for Ps-Solomon to posit wisdom as the fashioner of the marvelous created order around us only for her to break these very laws, which she herself enacted, in delivering the Israelites. Ps-Solomon's "new creation" is a solution that obviates this difficulty.

This helps us to understand what Ps-Solomon means in v. 6b, "complying with your commands" (ὑπηρετοῦσα ταῖς σαῖς ἐπισαγαῖς). As a new creation, it follows that the parting of the sea must, like the first creation, result from a divine command—a spoken word. Ps-Solomon's comment appears to be a reference to Exod 14:16 and 21, where Moses is

---

to his people and his corresponding punishment of the Egyptians are outside the normal parameters of physical laws. The events at the sea are not to be explained on the basis of laws immanent in the natural order. The sea opening up to allow the Israelites to pass through and then crashing together to kill the Egyptians are difficult to explain as anything other than acts of divine intervention. The point is that it is apparently not enough for Ps-Solomon simply to say that the Israelites walked through the water and the Egyptians drowned; he makes a point of adding that this is a divine act, and therefore "incredible" and "strange." Also, it is worth mentioning the presence of the "new creation" theme in the NT, since it is roughly contemporaneous with the Book of Wisdom. Some clear examples are the prologue to John (1:1-5), Paul's teaching of Christ as the second or new Adam (Rom 5:12-21; 1 Cor 15:22), and Paul's description of the Christian life as a "new creation" (καινὴ κτίσις, 2 Cor 5:17). The presence of this theme not only in the NT but in the Hebrew Bible and other works of antiquity should caution us against attributing Ps-Solomon's comment entirely to philosophical concerns. Our author does not employ a novel theme to handle his philosophical dilemma.

[180] 14:3 speaks of God as "Father." Throughout chaps. 11-19, God, not wisdom, is the active agent.

told by God to raise his staff and part the sea. It is through Moses' raising of his staff that the water divides and the dry land (יבשה) appears in Exodus 14, just as the waters divided and the dry land (יבשה) appeared in Gen 1:9. Where the parallel between the two events breaks down is in the fact that Ps-Solomon assigns the parting of the sea unequivocally to divine activity, whereas Exod 14:16 and 21 credit Moses (at least to a certain extent; see following paragraphs) with the event. This should be no surprise, however, since, as we have already seen, Ps-Solomon elsewhere attributes almost everything to divine activity, even events that in the Hebrew Bible are the domain of human activity.[181]

The creation theme is certainly evident in v. 6, but there is another point that also bears mentioning. The fact is that there is ambiguity in the Exodus narrative itself over whose command is ultimately responsible for the events at the sea. Although it is Moses who raised the staff/stretched out his hand (Exod 14:16 and 21) to part the sea, and afterwards again stretched out his hand to bring the waters crashing down on the Egyptians (14:27), it is God who is said to command Moses to do so (14:15-16). More importantly, in 14:21 and 27, *both* Moses and YHWH are said to command the sea. Exod 14:21 reads: "*Moses* stretched out his hand over the sea and *YHWH* drove back the sea all night with a strong east wind." Likewise, v. 27 reads: "*Moses* stretched out his hand over the sea, and the sea returned to its normal state (לאיתנו)....So *YHWH* swept away [נער] the Egyptians in the midst of the sea." This raises the obvious question of who is ultimately responsible for the parting of the sea and the subsequent death of the Egyptians, a question dealt with, not surprisingly, in rabbinic sources, specifically *Mek. Besh.* 5.58-79.[182] This midrash recounts an

---

[181]See again 10:16b: "She [=wisdom as a hypostasis of God] withstood dread kings with wonders and signs." Moses' role in performing the signs recedes completely to the background.

[182]This tradition is also fully retold in Ginzberg, *Legends*, 3.18-20. Commenting on the *Mekilta*, D. Boyarin writes that Exod 14:21 is, "problematic from the point of view of the narrative logic. If Moses has been empowered to split the sea with his hand, as implied by God's command to him in the previous verse, 'stretch out your hand over the sea and split it,' then why does God intervene directly and perform the splitting himself?" (*Intertextuality and the Reading of Midrash* [Bloomington: Indiana University Press, 1990] 96). Along with the *Mekilta*, Ps-Philo, *Bib. Ant.* 10:5-6 seems to have the same concern: "And God said, 'Why have you cried out to me? Lift up your rod and strike the sea, and it will be dried up.' And when *Moses* did this, *God* rebuked the sea and the sea was dried up....And while the Egyptians were in the sea, *God* again commanded the sea and said to *Moses*, 'Strike the sea yet once more.' And he did so. And the LORD commanded the sea, and it started flowing again and covered the Egyptians and their chariots and horsemen"

argument between the sea and Moses. When Moses commands it to part, as God had told him to do, the sea refuses: it will only listen to God's command, not man's. The sea relented only when it saw God himself.[183] The difficulty this tradition is dealing with is the ambiguity in Exod 14:16, 21, and 27 mentioned above.

The problem is solved by acknowledging that, although Moses raised the staff, it is at God's command that the water finally parted, and this explanation could be seen as being behind Ps-Solomon's particular observation, that by parting, the water "complied with your [i.e., God's] command." This is a fairly well documented exegetical tradition and would be consistent with Ps-Solomon's comment. Admittedly, however, there is very little to go on here in making the concrete connection between Wis 19:6 and this exegetical tradition. Despite the fact that Ps-Solomon's allusions to exegetical traditions are typically terse, one would need more substantive information than simply a reference to *God's* commands (in contrast to *Moses'* commands) to justify positing a tradition that speaks of a protracted argument between the sea and Moses. It appears that the more likely motive for Ps-Solomon's comment is his tendency to ascribe Israel's deliverance to divine activity.

We see the "new creation" theme continued in v. 7a-b as well: *The cloud was seen overshadowing the camp; where water had previously been, dry land rose up,* (ἡ τὴν παρεμβολὴν σκιάζουσα[184] νεφέλη, ἐκ δὲ προϋφεστῶτος ὕδατος ξηρᾶς ἀνάδυσις γῆς ἐθεωρήθη).[185] This mention of the cloud overshadowing the camp is similar to Ps-Solomon's statement in 10:17c, although in 10:17c there is the apparent identification of wisdom and the cloud, something that is not found in 19:7a.

(Charlesworth, *Pseudepigrapha*, 2.317; my emphasis). See also the discussion by S. Loewenstamm of the same problem (*Evolution*, 280-91), and a similar problem pertaining to the instigation of the plagues (130-54).

[183] *Mek. Besh.* 5.72-74. The *Mekilta* cites Ps 114:3: "The sea saw and fled" (ראה הים וינס). See also Ps 77:17: "The sea saw you, O God, the sea saw you and writhed; even the depths trembled."

[184] The use of σκιάζω here resembles LXX Num 9:18 and Isa 4:5 (σκιάσει νεφέλη ἡμέρας); cf. Winston, 325; Deane, 216.

[185] I read the finite verb ἐθεωρήθη, the only finite verb in v. 7, as referring to all four phenomena described in v. 7: the cloud (v. 7a), dry land (v. 7b), the path through the sea (v, 7c), and the grassy plain (v. 7d). One should also note the parallel prepositional phrases in v. 7 all beginning with ἐκ and which are governed by the singular verb ἐθεωρήθη. This suggests that along with "the cloud overshadowing the camp," the following phenomena "were seen": dry land rising from the water; an unhindered way from the Red Sea; a grassy/herb-bearing plain from the raging wave.

Nevertheless, 19:7a and 10:17c seem to be talking about the same event. [186] With respect to the new creation, some commentators have made the connection between 19:7a and the spirit of God hovering over the waters in Gen 1:2.[187] When taken together with what follows in vv. 7b, and especially when read in light of the introduction of new creation imagery in v. 6, the connection to Genesis in Wis 19:7a seems clear. In v. 7b, the appearance of dry land where water once was is an almost unmistakable allusion, as we have seen, to Gen 1:9.[188] As God at creation gathered the waters together to one place and dry land appeared (תֵּרָאֶה הַיַּבָּשָׁה/ὤφθη ἡ ξηρά), so did God in Exodus drive back the sea (Exod 14:21) and make dry land appear (בַּיַּבָּשָׁה/κατὰ τὸ ξηρόν, 14:22). A comment in *Pirqe R. El.* 42 is evidence of this tradition. Speaking of the Exodus, this midrash remarks, "On the day when He said 'Let the waters be gathered together' (Gen 1:9), on that very day were the waters congealed (נִקְפְּאוּ)."[189] This

---

[186] As for biblical connections, there appears to be at least a superficial similarity between 19:7a and Exod 14:24, since both locate the cloud above somewhere. In Exod 14:24, YHWH is said to "look down" (וַיַּשְׁקֵף). Likewise, in 19:7a, "overshadowing" assumes that the cloud's location is above. Wis 10:17c, however, bears a stronger similarity to Exod 13:21-22, where the cloud guides the Israelites *in front*, or 14:19-20, where it serves to separate them from the Egyptians. Exod 14:24 further specifies that YHWH is looking down upon the *camp* (אֶל־מַחֲנֵה/ἐπὶ τὴν παρεμβολὴν), which is exactly what we find in Wis 19:17a: "the cloud overshadowed the camp." Unlike the Wisdom of Solomon, however, Exod 14:24 specifies whose camp: ἐπὶ τὴν παρεμβολὴν τῶν Αἰγυπτίων. Might we then take the additional step and conclude that Wis 19:7a is also referring to the Egyptian camp? (In this case, Ps-Solomon would be juxtaposing YHWH's confusing the Egyptian army [Exod 14:24-25] in v. 7a with the deliverance of the Israelites through the sea in vv. 7b-9.) This is very unlikely, however, since Exod 14:19-20 twice specifies the Israelite camp. Moreover, the remainder of Wis 19:7 as well as vv. 8 and 9 are focused on God's deliverance of the Israelites. It is easiest to read v. 7a as doing likewise. The camp mentioned in Wis 19:7a, therefore, most certainly refers to the Israelites. The issue is not discussed in the commentaries. All seem to be working with the assumption that the Israelite camp is in view. See for example Larcher, "L'auteur mentionne donc d'abord la nuée qui couvrait le camp des Hébreux....Le référence à *Ex.*XIV, 19-20 est certaine..." (3.1058).

[187] Winston, 325; Reese, 197; Gilbert, "La Relecture de Gn 1-3," 339-41. W. Vogels also makes this point, but on the faulty premise that the cloud in Wis 19:7a is *above* while the cloud in Exodus 14 is merely *between* the two armies ("God who Creates," 330-31). But, as we have seen above, the location of the cloud in the Exodus narrative is in front (13:21), behind (14:19), and above (14:25). The creation connection in Wis 19:7a holds, but not for the reason given by Vogels.

[188] Gilbert, "La Relecture de Gn 1-3," 339-41.

[189] On the relationship between Creation and Exodus in the Hebrew Bible, see also R. Le Déaut, *La Nuit Pascale: Essai sur la signification de la Pâque juive à partir du Targum d'Exode XII 42* (Rome: Biblical Institute, 1963) 88-93.

midrash not only points out the similarity between Genesis and Exodus, but is also an overt attempt to bring the two together. Interestingly, although Ps-Solomon's comment is on the Exodus, it resembles more Gen 1:9 than anything in the Exodus narrative. In saying that the "dry land appeared/was seen" (aorist passive of θεωρέω), Ps-Solomon is very close to Gen 1:9, "dry land appeared/was seen:"

Wis 19:7b   ξηρᾶς...γῆς ἐθεωρήθη
Gen 1:9 LXX ὤφθη ἡ ξηρά
Gen 1:9 MT   ותראה היבשה (nifal).[190]

Besides the use of ξηρά in both the Wisdom of Solomon and the LXX, the verbs in all three cases are passive verbs of seeing. Also, Ps-Solomon's choice of the rare προϋφίστομαι, "previously existing," may carry some creation overtones, and hence further suggests the connection between the Exodus and Creation.[191] In any event, Ps-Solomon's use of creation imagery to describe the Exodus is clear.

16. The Bottom of the Sea Was an "Herb-Bearing Plain" (19:7d)

Ps-Solomon's description of the bottom of the sea in 19:7d as χλοηφόρον πεδίον, typically translated "grassy plain," must first be considered in light of the "unhindered way" (ὁδὸς ἀνεμπόδιστος) mentioned in v. 7c. In one sense, saying that the Israelites' way through the sea was "unhindered" may be understood as an attempt by Ps-Solomon to contrast the ease of their journey to the difficulty the Egyptians had in making the same journey in 14:25 (וינהגהו בכבדת/καὶ ἤγαγεν αὐτοὺς μετὰ βίας). In this respect, Wis 19:7c would be an implied contrast between God's treatment of the Israelites and the Egyptians.[192] This is consistent with 17:20, the only other use of ἀνεμπόδιστος in the Book of Wisdom, where there is a clear

---

[190]W. Vogels makes precisely the same observation ("God who Creates," 331), as does Schwenk-Bressler (*Sapientia Salomonis*, 308).

[191]This is, according to Winston, the first attestation of this compound (325). Creation overtones for this word are suggested by the verb cognate ὑφίστημι, which can mean "to give substance to, cause to subsist" (see Plotinus, *Philosophus*, 6.7.40) or "to conceive" (see Diodorus Siculus, 1.11). The noun cognate ὑπόστασις can also carry similar connotations (e.g., LXX Ps 138:15).

[192]Schwenk-Bressler also mentions this as a possibility (*Sapientia Salomonis*, 307).

contrast between "the whole world," which "engaged in unhindered work" (ὅλος...ὁ κόσμος ἀνεμποδίστοις συνείχετο ἔργοις) and the Egyptians who alone suffered under the pale of darkness (ninth plague).

Deane, however, tersely cites Isa 63:13 in his comment on ἀνεμπόδιστος, which is in the long run more valuable for understanding not only v. 7c, but v. 7d as well.[193] What is immediately attractive about this suggestion is the fact that 19:9 (#19 below) is routinely, and I think correctly, said to reflect Isa 63:13-14.[194] Isa 63:11-12 asks a series of rhetorical questions concerning YHWH's deliverance of his people out of Egypt. The prophet's last question is in v. 13:

> [Where is he] who led them through the depths? Like a horse in the open country [במדבר/δἰ ἐρήμου] they did not stumble [לא יכשלו/οὐκ ἐκοπίασαν].

I agree with Deane that Ps-Solomon's reflection on this passage begins already with ἀνεμπόδιστος in v. 7c.[195]

Understanding the "unhindered way" in v. 7c as reflecting Isa 63:11-14 brings the "grassy plain" of v. 7d into sharper focus. This most likely reflects Isa 63:14, "like cattle going down into the valley" (בקעה/πεδίον).[196] Connecting Ps-Solomon's comment to Isa 63:14 helps make sense of what had been a difficult problem in the scholarly literature, and many past attempts have not adequately addressed the issue. Most commentators consider the "grassy plain" to be a legendary elaboration of some sort, which simply assumes that Ps-Solomon's comment is without exegetical value. Goodrick, for example, calls Ps-Solomon's comment a "gross exaggeration."[197] He then suggest that the grassy plain is "possibly

---

[193]216. Larcher, citing Deane, is the only other commentator to mention Isa 63:13 (3.1060). Gregg, on the other hand, treats "grassy plain" as one of the several "legendary embellishments of the Scriptural narrative" in v. 7, and is typical of the opinion of many commentators (183).

[194]Both the MT and LXX of Isa 63:13-14 are presented below under #19 (pp. 131ff.), where the passage is discussed in more detail.

[195]It is worth observing that connecting ἀνεμπόδιστος in Wis 19:7c to Isa 63:13 is not in the least inconsistent with connecting it to the Egyptians' "hindered" way in Exod 14:25 mentioned above. In fact, Isa 63:13 may itself be seen, at least in part, as an exegetical tradition motivated by Exod 14:25: the Egyptians' way was difficult, but the Israelites, like horse in an open country, did not stumble.

[196]This translation of Isa 63:14 is based on the MT, which differs somewhat from the LXX (see #19 below).

[197]368.

a fantastic description of the actual bottom of the Red Sea," citing Pliny, *Natural History*, 13.25 as a parallel.[198]   It is somewhat surprising that Deane calls it a "poetical amplification," particularly in view of the fact that he himself cites Isa 63:13 with respect to the preceding line.

The difficulty with the above mentioned observations is that they do not take into account *T. Ps.-J.* to Exod 15:19, which is clearly relevant to the discussion.[199]   The Targum repeats Exod 15:19 and adds the following:

ותמן סלקון עינוון בסימן ואילני מיכלא וירקי ומיגדי בארעיה ימא

Sweet springs rose up there, along with edible trees, herbs, and fruit, at the bottom of the sea.

The Targum is another witness to the description of the bottom of the sea like that seen in Pliny, but, as distinct from Pliny, the Targum clearly represents a Jewish tradition of relative antiquity.   This is of no small importance for our understanding Ps-Solomon's reference to the "grassy plain" in Wis 19:7d.   Ps-Solomon is operating within a Jewish exegetical tradition that, for some reason, described the bottom of the sea using vegetal imagery.   Although this is not to dismiss the broader relevance of Pliny's remark to the discussion (he was, after all, a rough contemporary of Ps-Solomon), it should at least be said that citing Pliny does not really bring us any closer to understanding Ps-Solomon's "grassy plain."   What must be brought into the discussion, indeed given prominence, is viewing Ps-Solomon's comment in the context of the early history of biblical interpretation rather than as a scientific catalog of submarine vegetation. Furthermore, what might offer a concrete lexical connection between the Wisdom of Solomon and the Targum is χλοηφόρον, literally "bearing

---

[198]In the Loeb series, this relevant passage is found in 13.48-50 (vol. 4, pp. 179, 181). For example, Pliny states "Shrubs and trees also grow at the bottom of the sea—those in the Mediterranean being smaller size, for the Red Sea and the whole of the Eastern Ocean are filled with forests....[I]n the Red Sea there are flourishing forests, mostly of bay and olive, both bearing berries and in the rainy season funguses, which when the sun strikes them change to pumice. The bushes themselves grow to a yard and a half." Reider also cites Pliny, calling the entire tradition a "legendary embellishment" (218). See also Gregg (183, cited above, n. 259), Reese ("imaginative details," 197) and Winston (325). For R. T. Siebeneck, it is a legendary addition to "make the biblical story appear more grand" ("The Midrash of Wisdom 10-19," *CBQ* 22 [1960] 180). F. Feldmann, like Goodrick, considers this to be an abbreviated description of the bottom of the sea: "Der Verfasser stellt die nüchterne Wirklichkeit in poetischem Gewande dar" ("Die literarische Art von Weisheit Kap. 10-19," *TGl* 1 [1909] 183).

[199]Clarke seems to be the only commentator to mention this source, but he does not develop its significance (126).

greens/herbs,"[200] and יָרָק "herbs." In this respect, a better translation for χλοηφόρον πεδίον might be "herb-bearing plain" rather than "grassy plain." I propose that Wis 19:7d is an abbreviated version of the tradition that the Targum describes more fully.

Another important piece of evidence, although found in a medieval compilation,[201] is *Midr. Teh.* 114.38. According to this midrash, there were ten miracles at the sea, the tenth of which is as follows: "God made it [the sea] into a kind of valley (כמין בקעה) that sprouted grass (והעלתה עשבים), and Israel grazed in it, as it is said *As the cattle that go down to the valley* (Isa 63:14)." This midrash is significant not only in that it parallels both the Targum and Wis 19:7d in its description of the way through the sea, but in that it draws upon the language of Isa 63:14 as the basis for that description. This adds some weight to the argument that Ps-Solomon's description of the sea represents a tradition that incorporates this Isaianic imagery, and that Wis 19:7d is an early documented witness to that tradition. Moreover, we see once again the shorthand manner in which Ps-Solomon brings a particular tradition into his comment, a fact that argues for the popularity and antiquity of that tradition.

The exegetical impetus for describing the bottom of the sea in this way is at least in part the connection to Isa 63:13-14. Apparently understanding "cattle going down into the valley" as a comment on the crossing of the sea, early interpreters filled in the gap by providing a description of the plain itself. The elaborate description of this valley is suggested not only by the Isaianic imagery, but by Ps 106:9, a text overlooked by many modern commentators,[202] although it did not escape the rabbis: "He led them through the depths (בתהמות) as through the desert (במדבר)." The reference to המדבר in both Isa 63:13 and Ps 106:9, which describe the crossing of the sea, clearly suggests the connection to the forty-year period במדבר subsequent to Israel's crossing of the sea. And so we read in *Exod. Rab.* 21.10:

---

[200]For χλόη, LS gives "vegetables, herbs, greens" for one of it's meanings, citing Antiphones, 1.5 and Sotades, 1.9 as examples.

[201]It is worth reiterating Vermes's observation, that although the compilation is late, one cannot assume that the traditions represented therein are necessarily late as well (*Scripture and Tradition*, 95). See also Part I, p. 13, n. 16.

[202]But see M. J. Suggs et al., eds., *The Oxford Study Bible* (New York: Oxford University Press, 1992) 773 and K. Barker et al., eds., *The NIV Study Bible* (Grand Rapids: Zondervan, 1985) 1109.

> An Israelite woman would pass through the sea holding her child by the hand; and when he would cry, she would stretch out her hand and pick an apple or a pomegranate from the sea and give it to him, for it says, *And He led them through the depths, as through the wilderness* (Ps 106:9). Just as they lacked nothing in the wilderness [במדבר], so also in the depths [במצולה] they lacked nothing. This is what Moses said to them: *These forty years the Lord your God has been with you; and you lacked nothing* (Deut 2:7).[203]

Calling the path through the sea "the wilderness," as do Isa 63:13 and Ps 106:9, invites the comparison to the forty-year wilderness period. After all (our ancient interpreters might think), what other reason would Isaiah and the Psalmist have for describing the path through the sea as "the wilderness" rather than something else? Moreover, the use of the definite article might have suggested not just any patch of desert, but precisely what it says: *the* wilderness, i.e., the wilderness of the wandering Israelites. The comparison between the two is clear in *Exod. Rab.* 21.10 just cited. There are, therefore, extant witnesses to a tradition that describes the passage through the sea in vegetal imagery, and of which Ps-Solomon's comment on the "herb-bearing plain" is one succinct example. Wis 19:7d, indeed, appears to be the earliest documented witness to this tradition.

In light of this, I am led to disagree not only with those who would attribute this account of the sea to Ps-Solomon's imagination, but also with the suggestion that the "grassy plain" carries through the creation imagery of vv. 6a-7b (new creation, God's command, cloud overshadowing the camp, emergence of dry land).[204] This suggestion, to be sure, is a genuine attempt to explain Wis 19:7d, and is more helpful than the approach taken in some of the older commentaries. Nevertheless, although the creation motif is certainly evident in general in this passage, this is not to say that the imagery of Genesis 1 specifically extends to every line, particularly since there is no such imagery in vv. 8 and 9. I propose simply that Ps-Solomon depicts only the cloud of v. 7a and the emergence of dry land in v. 7b in the specific creation imagery of Genesis 1. In v. 7c, he continues his comment on God's deliverance but now employs the imagery of Isa 63:13-14, imagery that is explicit in v. 9. Furthermore, the fact that the

---

[203] *Exod. Rab.* 21.10 is clearly also another source that speaks of the bottom of the sea in vegetal imagery.

[204] This view is held, for example, by Winston ("If we see in the leafy plain a continuation of the creation motif [cf. Gen 1:11-13: 'Let the earth sprout vegetation...'], then the sequence becomes perfectly clear" [325]), Gilbert ("La Relecture," 340-41), Vogels ("God who Creates," 331), and Schwenk-Bressler (*Sapientia Salomonis*, 307-8).

"unhindered way" in v. 7c cannot be readily connected to the creation imagery in Genesis also militates against reading v. 7d in terms of creation imagery. The "herb-bearing plain" of Wis 19:7d is much more easily associated with the exegetical tradition described above than anything in Genesis 1.

17. The Israelites at the Sea Were "One Nation" (19:8a)

In 19:8a, Ps-Solomon describes the Israelites passing through the sea "as one nation" (πανεθνεὶ), or perhaps more precisely, "as a whole nation."[205] Like other of Ps-Solomon's comments, this seems quite incidental and is easy to pass over. Yet, it is striking. Why, after all, would Ps-Solomon bother to make this superfluous comment? Why would anyone think that the Israelites would have passed through the sea as anything other than "one nation?" What can "as one nation" possibly add to one's understanding of the crossing of the sea? It is precisely because this is such a curiously incidental remark that it deserves our attention. There are several options that need to be considered in discerning the motive for this comment.

Deane tersely offers a solution that is attractive for its simplicity: emphasizing that Israel crossed the sea as one nation brings to light the frustration of what had been Pharaoh's intention throughout, i.e., to allow only some of the Israelites to leave.[206] Exod 10:8-10 speaks of the disagreement between Moses and Pharaoh over just who would be leaving. Moses insists, "We will go with our young and with our old, with our sons and with our daughters; we will go with our sheep and our cattle, for we are to celebrate a festival to YHWH" (v. 9). Pharaoh replies that only the men are to go, leaving the women and children behind (v. 10). But of course, Pharaoh capitulates completely and sends all the Israelites, along with their livestock, on their way (12:30-31). Hence, πανεθνεὶ could be seen as a comment on Exod 12:30-31. Although this is an attractive solution in some respects, Exod 10:9 and 12:30-31 are somewhat removed from Ps-Solomon's topic in 19:8a, the crossing of the sea. Moreover, if the point was that women and children accompanied the men, πανεθνεὶ would not strike one as a particularly adequate way of describing this phenomenon. What follows are three other possible explanations more closely associated with the Song at the Sea.

---

[205]The rare adverb is attested only in Strabo 5.1.6. (see Winston, 325; Goodrick, 369).
[206]Deane's entire comment consists of "Comp. Ex. x. 9" (217).

One solution is to see this comment as analogous to 10:20c discussed above, where Ps-Solomon's "they sang with one accord" reflects the unexpected singulars of Exod 15:1, יָשִׁיר and אָשִׁירה. There is a similar grammatical situation in Exod 14:30-31 that may have some bearing on Ps-Solomon's comment in 19:8a.

> YHWH delivered *Israel* on that day from the hand of the Egyptians and *Israel saw* [וַיַּרְא/εἶδεν] the Egyptians dead on the shore. *Israel saw* [וַיַּרְא/εἶδεν] the mighty display of power that YHWH had performed against the Egyptians. So the people [הָעָם/ὁ λαός] feared YHWH and trusted YHWH and his servant Moses.

It strikes the eye somewhat that the Israelites would be referred to here as "Israel" (יִשְׂרָאֵל) rather than בְּנֵי־יִשְׂרָאֵל. It is in this passage, Exod 14:30-31, that "Israel" is used for the first and only time in Exodus 1-15 as the subject of a verb, whereas up to this point, בְּנֵי־יִשְׂרָאֵל has been used throughout.[207] This somewhat abrupt use of "Israel" plus the corresponding singular verb may have been something that early interpreters found worthy of comment. Why, an early interpreter might have asked, is this expression used for the first time in Exod 14:30 and 31 rather than the expected וַיִּרְאוּ בְּנֵי־יִשְׂרָאֵל? Perhaps "Israel" (plus the corresponding singular verb) indicates a certain "togetherness" at the sea that had not been evident before. This grammatical phenomenon might have been explained by Ps-Solomon's πανεθνεί.

A second solution is similar in that it also concerns Israel's national identity at the sea. Its biblical motive is Exod 15:16:

> Terror and dread fell upon them;
> by the might of your arm they became as silent as stone,
> *until your people* (עַמְּךָ) *passed by*, O YHWH,
> *until the people* <u>you</u> <u>created</u> (עַם־זוּ קָנִיתָ) *passed by.*

---

[207]Of the eighteen occurrences of "Israel" in Exodus 1-15, thirteen are with a construct noun and never as the subject (זִקְנֵי-3:16, 18; 12:21; אֱלֹהֵי-5:1; מִקְנֵה-9:4, 7; עֲדַת-12:3, 6, 19, 47; מַחֲנֵה-14:19, 20; מִפְּנֵי-14:25). Besides 14:30 and 31, "Israel" appears in the absolute state only three other times, but never as the subject. It appears as a predicate nominative in 4:22, referring to Jacob in 6:14, and as the direct object of the verb in 14:30. "Israel" does appear as the subject in 12:3 and 47, but only with the construct כָּל־עֲדַת. Of the 59 occurrences of בְּנֵי־יִשְׂרָאֵל in Exodus 1-15, it is the subject sixteen times (1:7; 2:23; 6:12; 12:28, 35, 37, 46, 50; 13:18; 14:8, 10(2), 16, 22, 29; 15:19).

In v. 16d, the Israelites are referred to as God's עַם whom he "created" at the crossing of the sea, i.e., it was at the Exodus that the Israelites received their national identity.[208]   But what is the significance of essentially repeating v. 16c in v. 16d but adding something about the "creation" of an עַם at the sea? The answer may be found in Exod 12:38. There we read of a "mixed multitude" (עֵרֶב רַב) that came out of Egypt with the Israelites, most likely indicating that these were non-Israelites (so later interpreters understood it),[209] perhaps including some "God-fearing" Egyptians (cf. Exod 9:20). It is worth noting that we never hear about this diverse group again. One might think from reading Exod 15:16 that only the Israelites, i.e., "your people," crossed the Red Sea. Perhaps Ps-Solomon's words are specifically designed to counter such an understanding of Exod 15:16. He says that they "crossed over" (διέρχομαι = עָבַר) "as one nation," and in so saying, he successfully defuses the implication of Exod 15:16, that the mixed multitude had somehow been left behind. Ps-Solomon's "as one nation" would indicate that the mixed multitude had not been forgotten: *all* the people were "created," i.e., made into one עַם.[210]

---

[208]The immediate question is how to translate קָנָה (see Part II, n. 75). In Biblical and Mishnaic Hebrew, the root has a fairly broad semantic range: "to buy, redeem, beget, acquire, create." With "God" as the subject, however, the meaning "to create," although not necessary, becomes likely. Some examples include Gen 14:19, 22 (קֹנֵה שָׁמַיִם וָאָרֶץ), Ps 139:13 (כִּי־אַתָּה קָנִיתָ כִלְיֹתָי), and Prov 8:22 (יהוה קָנָנִי i.e., wisdom). See also Deut 32:6, where קָנָה is used in conjunction with other "creation" vocabulary: "Is he not your father, your creator [קָנֶךָ], who made you [עָשְׂךָ] and formed you [יְכֹנְנֶךָ]?" R. Le Déaut remarks that the use of קָנָה in Exod 15:16 reflects the notion of the Exodus as a new creation [*La Nuit Pascale*, 96-100]. He also cites Prov 8:22 [97-98].) And although *Targum Onqelos* reads "redeemed" or "delivered" (פְּרַק; *Targum Ps-Jonathan* has קְנָה, and therefore tells us nothing about how the word was understood), the LXX has κτίζω, "to create." The point, therefore, is that whatever עַמּוּ קָנִיתָ might have meant to the writer of the song, it meant, at least to some early interpreters, "a people you have created." Furthermore, it is certainly a debatable point whether this creation actually took place *at the sea*. Exod 15:16 does not actually say this. Still it seems to me quite likely that the reference in 15:16d is to the Exodus event in some sense, especially since the song as a whole is concerned to relay YHWH's deliverance of the Israelites from Egypt.

[209]See, for example, Rashi; *Exod. Rab.* 18.10; *Qoh. Rab.* 2.8; *b. Beṣa* 32b.

[210]Ps-Solomon's comment has a particular nuance that would have struck a cord with any Hellenized Jew. If πανεθνεί is to be understood as "*as* one nation," Ps-Solomon would not be saying that the mixed multitude actually *became* Israelites, but the exact opposite! They were not really one people, as if Israelites and non-Israelites suddenly merged, but they passed through the sea "*as* one nation," simply meaning that they all came out together. It might have been a problem for Ps-Solomon to accept the notion that non-Jews would have been so effortlessly incorporated into Israel without some official acknowledgment of their conversion. At this juncture, however, a text-critical issue

There is a third solution, however, that in the long run is perhaps more valuable in accounting for Ps-Solomon's "as one nation." Several ancient sources attest to a notion that the trek through the sea was not an altogether harmonious undertaking by the twelve tribes. Such an idea is found in several forms. We see, for example, Benjamin going down into the sea first and Judah retaliating by pelting them with stones (*Mek. Besh.* 6.1-28).[211] Similarly, Ps-Philo, *Bib. Ant.* 10:3 and *Mek. Besh.* 3.128-36 portray the Israelites at the sea as an indecisive assembly of tribes who each have a different opinion about what to do: some tribes want to perish in the sea, some want to return to Egypt, some want to wait on YHWH's deliverance, and some want to fight. There is also the popular (and intricate) exegetical tradition of a "premature Exodus" by the tribe of Ephraim (*Mek. Besh.* 1.45-53; *b. Sanh.* 92b; *Tg. Ps-J.* to Exod 13:17; Targums to Ezekiel 37, Ps 78:9 and 1 Chr 7:20ff.).[212] This tradition apparently arose in an attempt to explain the circumstance of the death of Ezer and Elead, sons of Ephraim, at the hands of "the native-born men of Gath" (אנשי־גת הנולדים) in 1 Chr 7:21, otherwise unattested. The confrontation between the Ephraimites and the men of Gath is thought to have taken place subsequent to the Ephraimites' lone crossing of the sea at the time of the Exodus. The connection to the Exodus is made on the basis of two related biblical texts. The first is Ps 78:9-16, which speaks of the Ephraimites' covenant unfaithfulness and obstinacy on the day of battle (ביום קרב, v. 9). What battle, and when did it take place? Since the context of Ps 78:9-16 is the Exodus (v. 13), it is thought that Ephraim crossed the sea prematurely and engaged the Philistines in battle. This premature Exodus of the Ephraimites is considered an act of disobedience to God (Ps. 78:10-11) and as a result some/many are slain (1 Chronicles 7). This then is connected more explicitly to the Exodus by virtue of the

---

concerning πανεθνεί becomes relevant. Some commentators prefer the variant πᾶν ἔθνος, which would be the subject of διῆλθον (Goodrick, 369; Deane, 217). If this is the preferred reading, a very debatable point either way, then this particular nuance disappears. Ps-Solomon would then be asserting that "one nation" passed through the sea. See also Ziener's observation that the Book of Wisdom puts Jews and Gentiles in the same covenant category, they are both "righteous" insofar as they are both participants in the covenant. Ziener seems to deny any "fanatischen Nationalismus" in Wisdom 10-19 (*Begriffssprache*, 96-97).

[211] See also Weingreen, *From Bible to Mishna*, 18.

[212] J. Heinemann has done a thorough study of this tradition as it affects the tradition of the Messiah of Ephraim ("The Messiah of Ephraim and the Premature Exodus of the Tribe of Ephraim," *HTR* 68 [1975] 1-15, esp. 10-12).

curious syntax of a second passage, Exod 13:17: "Now when Pharaoh released the people, God did not lead them by the way of the land of the Philistines, כִּי קָרוֹב הוּא...." This Hebrew phrase is usually translated, "*even though* it [the way through Philistine country] was nearer," i.e., it highlights the Israelites' circuitous route to the sea. Heinemann, however, translates כִּי not concessively, but causally, as early interpreters might: "*because* that was near."[213] Because *what* was near? Exod 13:17 continues: "...lest the people change their mind when they see war and return to Egypt." The "it" that was near was the war referred to in the subsequent sentence. And to which war does Exodus refer? To the war between the Ephraimites (who had left Egypt prematurely) and the Philistines, more specifically, the carnage (1 Chr 7:21) that followed this encounter. In other words, God did not lead the people through Philistine country so as to keep the people from seeing the dead Ephraimites, a sight that would have been sure to discourage them.[214]

What all of these traditions have in common is that they attribute to the Israelites a lack of tribal unity at the sea. There is a certain attractiveness in reading Wis 19:8a in light of this tradition, since Ps-Solomon is apparently concerned to show that the crossing of the sea was a unified national event; πανεθνεὶ serves to counter any notion of an Exodus other than one that involved all twelve tribes together, which is certainly the sense of the Exodus narrative itself. The problem with this proposed solution, however, is that there does not seem to be another extant example of a similar counter-tradition. Nevertheless, the national overtones of

---

[213]Ibid., 11. N. Liebowitz discusses the translation of this difficult clause by Rashi, Ibn Ezra, and Ramban (*Studies in Shemot* [Jerusalem: The World Zionist Organization, 1976] 234-37).

[214]Other than merely to explain the difficult syntax of Exod 13:17 (although I agree with Heinemann's observation), another motive for connecting this midrash to the Exodus may be the ambiguity of Ps 78:9-16 itself. Ephraim is specifically mentioned in v. 9 as, (1) one armed for battle who turned back (הָפַך) on the day of battle (v. 9); (2) who did not keep God's covenant and refused to walk in his laws (v. 10); (3) who had forgotten God's deeds and the wonders he had shown them (v. 11, הֶרְאָם). The plural suffix in v. 11 clearly refers to the Ephraimites. The psalm continues: (4) "He performed wonders in the sight of their fathers" (v. 12, אֲבוֹתָם). Whose fathers? Again, the suffix would seem to refer to the Ephraimites. Then v. 13 begins: (5) "He divided the sea and led *them* through" (וַיַּעֲבִירֵם). Whom did God lead through? To whom does the plural suffix refer? To the Ephraimites, of course, but understood to refer not to the nation of Israel as a whole, but to the tribe of Ephraim alone. Apparently, this verse was thought to mean that God led *them* through the sea without the other eleven tribes. I suggest that the ambiguity of Ps 78:9-16 is a significant factor that brought about the exegetical tradition of the premature Exodus of the tribe of Ephraim.

πανεθνεὶ fit well in the context of this tradition, and, hence, I prefer this solution to the first two I proposed.[215]

18. There Were Miracles (Plural) Performed at the Sea (19:8b)

In 19:8b, Ps-Solomon makes another passing comment that deserves close attention. He says that the Israelites passed through the sea *after gazing on marvelous wonders* (θεωρήσαντες θαυμαστὰ τέρατα). The question is to which "marvelous wonders" does Ps-Solomon refer? Since τέρατα is plural, one initial reflex might be to think of the plagues, especially since τέρας is used in this way in Wis 10:16 and 17:15. This is unlikely, however, since the sense of 19:8 as a whole, in fact all of 19:6-9, is that

---

[215]One final aspect of Wis 19:8a that deserves at least a passing comment concerns the protection of the Israelites by God's "hand" during their trek through the sea. In one sense, this may be nothing more than Ps-Solomon's use of a common biblical idiom. In another sense, attributing God's deliverance of the Israelites to God's "hand" is also quite common throughout the Exodus narrative specifically (3:19, 20; 6:1; 7:4, 5; 9:3, 15; 13:3, 9, 14, 16; 14:31). Furthermore, an immediate exegetical motive also presents itself, i.e., "your right hand" (ימינך) in Exod 15:6 and 12. Ps-Solomon's comment here is quite at home in the Exodus narrative in general and in the Song at the Sea in particular, which is the subject of Wis 19:9. At the very least, therefore, there is no need to attribute Ps-Solomon's comment to Isa 51:16 (ὑπὸ τὴν σκιὰν τῆς χειρός μου σκεπάσω σε), as do Goodrick (369), Gregg (183), and Larcher (3.1061), or other similarly remote passages. If Isa 51:16 shares anything concrete with Wis 19:8a, it is the fact that both recontextualize the Exodus: Isaiah does so by applying Exodus imagery to the return from Babylon and Ps-Solomon by applying it to immortality (see appendix). Both Reese (*Hellenistic Influence*, 139) and Ziener (*Begriffssprache*, 125) read 19:8a as a "flashback" (to use Reese's term) to 5:15-23, where the focus is the victory of the righteous over the ungodly, a victory that culminates in immortality (vv. 15-16). 5:16 is the only other use of σκεπάζω in the Wisdom of Solomon, where it refers to God's protection of the righteous with respect to their immortality. Furthermore, 5:17 and 20 make explicit that the entire passage is to be understood as God employing creation to redeem his people, the same theme found in 19:6-7b (see also M. Marböck, "'Denn in allem, Herr, hast du dein Volk großgemacht!' Weish 18,5-19,22 und die Botschaft der Sapientia Salomonis," *Lehrerin der Gerechtigkeit: Studien zum Buch der Weisheit* [ETS 19; Leipzig: St. Benno-Verlag, 1991] 160-61). Hence, 5:15-23 is a clear and striking example of Ps-Solomon's recontextualization of the Exodus to refer to the "departure" (cf. ἔξοδος in 3:2 and 7:6) of the godly from this life to the next. This may provide a valuable background for the prevalence of this theme in the NT (e.g., Heb 3:1-4:13 and Jesus as the new Moses). In any event, what is important here is that Ps-Solomon's comment is easily explained on the basis of the immediate context of the Exodus narrative.

these "wonders" occur at the sea. In addition, a passing remark on the plagues would be out of place in v. 8b because Ps-Solomon has been only remotely interested at best in the plagues throughout vv. 1-9.[216] These "wonders," whatever they are, are to be associated with the crossing of the sea.

What, then, are these wonders and why are there are more than one? Is the parting of the sea not simply one event? LXX Exod 15:11 provides a starting point for investigating Ps-Solomon's "wonders" in 19:8b:

> Who is like you among the gods, O YHWH? Who is like you, majestic in holiness, awesome (נוֹרָא/θαυμαστός), renowned, working wonder[s] (עֹשֵׂה פֶלֶא/ποιῶν τέρατα)?[217]

The use of θαυμαστός as well as the mention of "wonders" (τέρατα) bears more than a coincidental resemblance to Wis 19:8b. The Hebrew פֶלֶא, however, is singular. Although it is possible to construe the singular form as a collective (as seems to be the case, for example, in Ps 77:12, 18), there would be no real reason to do so here, since the topic of the Song at the Sea is clearly the parting of the sea; this is what פֶלֶא refers to.[218] Yet, the LXX has the plural τέρατα, as does the Wis 19:8b. Did Ps-Solomon read the LXX in this one instance, see the plural, and write it down? This is unlikely. Rather, it appears that Wis 19:8b and perhaps LXX Exod 15:11 are early witnesses to a very popular exegetical tradition that spoke of a multiple number of miracles at the sea. Several sources mention ten miracles at the sea, specifically: *Mek. Besh.* 5.1-14;[219] *Midr.*

---

[216]The reference to the tenth plague in v. 3a-b is brought in to highlight the foolishness of the Egyptians' decision to pursue the Israelites.

[217]Schwenk-Bressler mentions in a footnote the similarity between Wis 19:8b and Exod 15:11, but does not develop the significance of this connection (*Sapientia Salomonis*, 309, n. 534).

[218]The entire Song at the Sea is a song about what YHWH did at the sea. Verses 1-12 specifically are concerned entirely with the death of the Egyptians in the sea and God's deliverance of the Israelites. The immediate context of v. 11 is clearly the death of the Egyptians. Verse 10 ends: "They sank like lead in the mighty water." Verse 12 reads: "You stretched out your right hand; the earth swallowed them." It is precisely between these two statements that YHWH works his פֶלֶא. Hence, פֶלֶא does not refer to the plagues or any of the other miracles in conjunction with the departure from Egypt, but to the parting of the sea. Compare this to the use of נִפְלָאוֹת in Pss 78:11 and 106:7, where the plagues are most likely in view, in contrast to פֶלֶא in Ps 78:12, which seems to refer specifically to the crossing of the sea in v. 13.

[219]The *Mekilta* actually lists eleven. See W. S. Towner, *The Rabbinic "Enumeration of Example,"* 147, n. 1.

Teh. 114.38; 136.7; *b. Soṭa* 37a; *Pirqe R. El.* 42; *m. 'Abot* 5.4; *'Abot R. Nat.* A 33 (B=36).[220] The motive behind the number "ten" is apparently to correspond to the number of plagues upon the Egyptians (see especially the last three sources just listed).[221] There can be little question that Ps-Solomon is a succinct witness to such a general tradition of "wonders" at the sea.[222] "Gazing at marvelous wonders" is not a surprising comment.

Finally, it is worth mentioning more specifically *Midr. Teh.* 114.38 cited above. According to this source, the last of the ten miracles at the sea is "a kind of valley that sprouted grass," citing Isa 63:14 ("As cattle that go down into the valley"). This continues the allusion to Isaiah 63 that, as I have argued, began in 19:7d (#16 above) and that is explicitly referred to in the final comment to be considered in this study.

---

[220]Larcher (alone) mentions this tradition, citing Ginzberg 2.22 and 6.6 (n. 36), but he does not explicitly connect it to Ps-Solomon's comment (3.1061).

[221]A similar type of exegesis can also be seen with respect to the number of plagues the Egyptians suffered at the sea. The Passover Haggadah and *Exod. Rab.* 23.9, for example, number these plagues at fifty, the reason for the number being that, since God's "finger" smote the Egyptians (Exod 8:15), resulting in ten plagues, the "hand" of God that delivered the Israelites (14:31) must yield five times as many plagues upon the Egyptians! Both texts also number the plagues at 200 (up to 250 in the Passover Haggadah). There are no traditions to my knowledge, however (with the exception of *Mek. Besh.* 5.1-14 mentioned above), that have more than ten miracles at the sea.

[222]Acts 7:36 may also reflect multiple miracles at the sea: "He [=Moses] led them out, performing wonders and signs in the land of Egypt, at the Red Sea, and in the desert for forty years" (οὗτος ἐξήγαγεν αὐτοὺς ποιήσας τέρατα καὶ σημεῖα ἐν γῇ Αἰγύπτῳ καὶ ἐν Ἐρυθρᾷ Θαλάσσῃ καὶ ἐν τῇ ἐρήμῳ ἔτη τεσσεράκοντα). Without pushing the limits of Greek grammar beyond reasonable bounds, the performance of "wonders and signs" in this passage could be understood to describe Moses' activity at *each* of the three subsequent locations mentioned: miracles were performed (note the use of ποιέω as in LXX Exod 15:11) in Egypt (the plagues) *and* at the Red Sea (the "wonders") *and* in the desert (manna, quail, water). This is not by any means the only reading. Still, ἐν γῇ Αἰγύπτῳ must certainly be understood adverbially as modifying ποιήσας, i.e. signs and wonders were performed in Egypt. This at least introduces the possiblity, perhaps even likelihood, that the following two parallel prepositional phrases also modify ποιήσας. On a marginally related topic, see S. Loewenstamm's comment on whether Acts 7:36 can be considered another example of the exegetical tradition (represented, for example, in *Exagoge* 132) that Moses was the sole producer of the plagues (*Evolution*, 135-36 and n. 90).

19. The Israelites Were "Horses" and "Lambs" at the Sea (19:9)

The commentaries are in overwhelming agreement that Isa 63:13-14 lies behind Wis 19:9: *For they grazed as horses and skipped as lambs, praising you, O Lord, who delivered them* (ὡς γάρ ἵπποι ἐνεμήθησαν καὶ ὡς ἀμνοὶ διεσκίρτησαν αἰνοῦντες σε, κύριε, τὸν ῥυόμενον αὐτούς). Both passages recount the Exodus and employ similar imagery. I lay out the texts below as a basis for comparison.

Wis 19:9a   ὡς γάρ ἵπποι <u>ἐνεμήθησαν</u>
               For <u>they grazed</u> as horses.

LXX Isa 63:13   ἤγαγεν αὐτοὺς διὰ τῆς ἀβύσσου ὡς ἵππον δι' ἐρήμου <u>καὶ οὐκ ἐκοπίασαν</u>
               [He] led them through the depth like a horse through a desert, <u>and they did not stumble.</u>

MT Isa 63:13   מוליכם בתהמות כסוס במדבר <u>לא יכשלו</u>
               [He] was leading them into the depths like a horse in the desert; <u>they did not stumble.</u>

Wis 19:9b-c   καὶ ὡς <u>ἀμνοὶ διεσκίρτησαν</u>
               αἰνοῦντές σε, κύριε, τὸν ῥυόμενον αὐτούς
               and <u>skipped</u> as <u>lambs</u>
               praising you, O Lord, who delivered them.

LXX Isa 63:14   καὶ ὡς <u>κτήνη διὰ πεδίου,</u> κατέβη πνεῦμα παρὰ κυρίου καὶ ὡδήγησεν αὐτούς.
               οὕτως ἤγαγες τὸν λαόν σου ποιῆσαι σεαυτῷ ὄνομα δόξης.
               And like <u>cattle through a field</u>, the spirit of the Lord came down and led them.
               Thus you led your people to make a glorious name for yourself.

MT Isa 63:14   <u>כבהמה בבקעה תרד</u>   רוח יהוה תניחנו
               כן נהגת עמך לעשות לך שם תפארת
               Like <u>cattle going down into the valley</u>, the spirit of YHWH gave them rest.
               Thus you led your people to make a glorious name for yourself.

The similarity between Wis 19:9 and Isa 63:13-14 is clear, and one may safely conclude that Ps-Solomon is employing the Isaianic imagery in his comment on the Exodus.[223]   There are some differences between the passages, however, that are equally significant.   For one thing, in Wis 19:9, horses *graze* and *lambs skip*; in Isa 63:13-14, horses *don't stumble* and *cattle* are *in a field*.   Also, Isaiah explicitly speaks of the crossing of the sea: "[He] led them into the depths" (63:13); "The spirit of YHWH gave them rest...you led your people" (63:14; LXX: "The spirit of the Lord came down and led them. Thus you led your people").   If Isaiah is explicit in juxtaposing the zoological imagery to the *crossing* of the sea, Ps-Solomon is just as explicit in juxtaposing it to the *Song at the Sea*.   The syntax of v. 9, particularly the present participle αἰνοῦντες in v. 9c, indicates that the act of praising the Lord (the Song at the Sea) is concurrent with the grazing and skipping of v. 9a-b.[224]   The actual crossing of the sea, as we have seen, is the topic of v. 8, not v. 9.   It should also be kept in mind that Isaiah does not mention the song at all.   His purpose in recounting the crossing of the sea was to show how YHWH guided his people, thereby bringing glory to himself (63:14).   Although Ps-Solomon would probably concur with such a statement, this is not what he says in 19:9.   Ps-Solomon says that, while the Israelites were in the state equivalent to horses grazing and lambs skipping, they praised God.

In view of these differences between Isaiah and the Wisdom of Solomon, one may wonder, if Ps-Solomon is following Isa 63:13-14 (as he certainly is), why does he not do a better job?   What can account for the differences between the Wisdom of Solomon and Isaiah, particularly Ps-Solomon's application of the Isaianic imagery to the Song at the Sea?   It seems clear that Isa 63:11-12 and 13-14 are parallel.   Verses 11-12 speak of

---

[223]Schwenk-Bressler maintains that Wis 19:9 continues the new creation theme that was begun in v. 6 (*Sapientia Salomonis*, 310-12). For the reasons stated above, I do not think the application of the creation imagery of Genesis 1 extends beyond 19:7b. To be sure, Schwenk-Bressler mentions (albeit in passing) Isa 63:13-14 (as well as Pss 76:21; 77:52; 113:4-6; Mal 3:19-20) with respect to Wis 19:9, yet he seems to dismiss its relevance, since he understands Wis 19:9 to employ new creation imagery, and this imagery is lacking in Isa 63:13-14. Unfortunately this assertion obscures the obvious relavance that Isa 63:13-14 has to the discussion.   On another matter, it is worth pointing out that both Isa 63:13-14 and Wis 19:9 are examples of the recontextualization of the Exodus; the Exodus is recounted for the purpose of encouraging their respective communities. For Isaiah, it is the "Exodus" from Babylon, for Ps-Solomon the "Exodus" from this life to the next (see appendix).

[224]For this use of the present participle see Moulton, 3.79-81, and E. Mayser, *Grammatik der griechischen Papyri aus der Ptolemäerzeit* (2 vols.; Berlin: de Gruyter 1926) 1.175ff.

Moses shepherding his flock across the sea. God sent his spirit to Moses to
enable him to divide the waters "to make for himself an everlasting name"
(ποιῆσαι αὐτῷ ὄνομα αἰώνιον/לעשות לו שם עולם, v. 12). Verses 13-14
seem to recount the same event, but this time using zoological imagery
(perhaps thus picking up on the notion of shepherding in v. 11). Verse 14
ends virtually the same way as v. 12: "to make for yourself a glorious
name" (ὄνομα δόξης/שם תפארת). These two passages are parallel and
exhibit basically an AB:AB structure.

What I suggest here, however, is that Ps-Solomon read these verses
not as parallel, but consecutively. What might have bothered Ps-Solomon
(or some other early interpreter) is the repetition in vv. 12 and 14. Ps-
Solomon might have concluded that this is no mere repetition, but only
apparently so. Rather, Isa 63:12-14 are in fact talking about two different
things. For him, the description of the crossing apparently ends at Isa
63:12; v. 13 picks up with the next event, which is the Song at the Sea
itself. This explanation may also account for why, if Ps-Solomon is in fact
following Isa 63:13-14, he does not reproduce anything, at least in v. 9,
that might suggest the crossing of the sea. Any such reference, which is
most of the passage, is missing. All he says is that the Israelites were like
grazing horses and skipping lambs; he does not tell us where. He is not
concerned to tell us that the Israelites were kept from stumbling. This
would clearly evoke the trek through the sea. Rather, he speaks of
"grazing horses" and "skipping lambs," imagery which seems more
appropriate after the crossing when the Israelites are safely on the other
side.[225] In this respect, the imagery is more reminiscent of Mal 3:20b
("You came out [ויצאתם] and pawed the ground [ופשתם] like calves
released from their stalls [כעגלי מרבק]"), rather than Ps 114:4, which is
often cited.[226] The topic of Psalm 114 is creation's spasmodic response to
God's redemptive activity at the Exodus and crossing of the Jordan. The
sea looked and fled (וינס), the Jordan turned back (יסב, v. 3); the *mountains*
skipped (רקדו) *like rams*, the *hills like lambs* (כבני־צאן, v. 4); the earth
trembled (חולי) at YHWH's power (v. 7). It is difficult to see Ps-Solomon
employing this imagery of terror in his comment on the Israelites' safe and

---

[225]See also U. Offerhaus: "Das Bild von den springenden Lämmern, das die Freude und
den Jubel der Geretteten ausdrückt, leitet unmittelbar zur Erwähnung des Lobes Gottes
über, den die Israeliten im Mirjam-Lied (Ex 15) angestimmt haben (v. 9c)" (*Komposition
und Intention*, 172).

[226]See, for example, Winston, 325; Goodrick, 369; Deane, 217 (who also cites Mal 3:20b
[EV. 4:2]).

joyful passage through the sea. Like Mal 3:20b, Wis 19:9c describes the
activity of God's people after a period of confinement. The Israelites are
safe and sound, praising YHWH, and, employing the imagery of Isa 63:13-
14, are described appropriately: like grazing horses and skipping lambs.

Part III

The Wisdom of Solomon and the State of Biblical Interpretation during Ps-Solomon's Time

Summary and Conclusions

We have seen that Ps-Solomon's comments on the departure from Egypt have many parallels in other ancient sources, including the Apocrypha, the Pseudepigrapha, Targums, Josephus, Philo, and rabbinic works. We have also seen that many of these traditions are truly *exegetical*, i.e., they are motivated by factors in the biblical texts themselves. The following list is a synopsis of the nineteen comments by Ps-Solomon discussed in this study including parallels, both direct and indirect, in other sources (where relevant), and the biblical passage(s) that may have motivated these motifs.

1. *Egypt Had "Kings" during the Plagues* (10:16b)
   parallel sources. Sir 45:3
   biblical motive. Ps 105 (104):30; Ps 135 (134):9; Exod 7:11, 20-22, etc.

2. *Israelites Received "Payment" for Their Period of Slavery* (10:17a)
   parallel sources. Jub 48:18; V. Mos. 1.141; Exagoge 162-66
   biblical motive. Exod 12:35-36 (3:21-22; 11:2-3)

3. *The Pillar of Cloud Was for the Purpose of "Protecting/Sheltering" the Israelites* (10:17c):
   a) a "protection" from the Egyptian army
   parallel sources. V. Mos. 1.178; Tg. Ps.-J. to Exod 14:19 and 20; Mek.
         Besh. 5.43-50, 15-36; Tg. Neof. to Exod 14:20;
   biblical motive. Exod 14:19-20
   b) a "covering" overhead signifying God's presence with the Israelites
   parallel sources. Midr. Teh. 105.34-35; Cant. Rab 1.44; Num. Rab 21.22;
         Mek. Besh. 1.178-92; 1 Cor 10:1
   biblical motive. Ps 105:39; Exod 40:34, 38; Isa 4:5-6; Exod 14:19-20, 24

135

4. *The Sea "Cast Up" the Egyptians so as to Allow the Israelites to "Plunder" Them*
   (10:19b-20a)
       parallel sources. V. *Mos.* 2.255; *Mek. Besh.* 7.94-108; *b. Pesaḥ.* 118b; *b.*
          'Arak. 15a; *Mek. Shir.* 9.7-15; *Midr. Teh.* 22.39-42; *Pirqe R. El.*
          42; Jos., *Ant.* 2.349; *Memar Marqah* 2.7
       biblical motive. Exod 14:28, 30; 15:1, 4, 5, 10, 12

5. *The Red Sea Was a "Bottomless Depth"* (10:19b)
       biblical motive. Exod 15:5, 8; many other passages

6. *Israelites Sang "To Your Holy Name"* (10:20b)
       biblical motive. Exod 15:1

7. *The Israelites Sang "With One Accord" at the Sea* (10:20c)
       parallel sources. Mek. Shir. 1.11-12; *Cant. Rab.* 4.2; *Mek. Besh.* 3.22-25;
          Gen. Rab. 99.7
       biblical motive. Exod 15:1

8. *The "Dumb" Sang at the Sea* (10:21a)
       parallel sources. Cant. Rab. 1.49; *Mek. Besh.* 3.140-49
       biblical motive. Exod 14:14

9. *"Babes" also Sang at the Sea* (10:21b)
       parallel sources. Exod. Rab. 23.8; *Tg. Ps.-J.* to Exod 15:2; *t. Soṭa* 11b; *b.*
          Soṭa 30b; *Pirqe Rab. El.* 42; *Pesiq. Rab. Kah.* 47
       biblical motive. Exod 15:2; Ezek 16:1-7

10. *God Knew that the Egyptians Would Pursue the Israelites* (19:1b):
        biblical motive. Exod 14:1-5

11. *The Egyptians "Accompanied" the Israelites out of Egypt* (19:2)
        parallel sources. V. *Mos.* 1.139; *Mek. Besh.* 1.1-12; *Exod. Rab.* 20.3
        biblical motive. Exod 13:17

12. *The Egyptians' Decision to Pursue the Israelites was Lacking in Intelligence*
    (19:3c)
        parallel sources. b. Soṭa 11a; *Exod. Rab.* 1.9; *Bib. Ant.* 10:6 (Sir 16:15)
        biblical motive. Exod 14:27; 14:4, etc.

13. *The Israelites Were "Begged" to Leave Egypt* (19:3d)
        parallel sources. Tg. Ps.-J. to Exod 12:31-33
        biblical motive. Exod 11:1; 12:31-33, 39

14. *The Egyptians Were Drowned in the Sea as Fitting Punishment for the
    Drowned Israelite Children* (19:4-5)
        parallel sources. Mek. Besh. 7.3-22; *Exod. Rab.* 22.1, 1.9; *Jub.* 48:14 (*b.*
           Soṭa 11a)
        biblical motive. Exod 1:22/14:27-28

15. *The Redemption of the Israelites at the Sea Was a "New Creation"* (19:6-7b)
    common biblical and extra-biblical theme

16. *The Bottom of the Sea Was an "Herb-Bearing Plain"* (19:7d)
    parallel sources. Tg. Ps.-J. to Exod 15:19; *Exod Rab.* 21.10; *Midr. Teh.*
        114.38
    biblical motive. Isa 63:14; Ps 106:9

17. *The Israelites at the Sea Were "One Nation"* (19:8a)
    biblical motive. Exod 10:8-10; 12:28; 14:30-31; 15:16

18. *There Were Miracles (Plural) Performed at the Sea* (19:8b)
    parallel sources. Mek. Besh. 5.1-14; *b. Soṭa* 37a; *Pirqe R. El.* 42; *Midr.*
        Teh. 114.38; *m. 'Abot* 5.4; *'Abot R. Nat.* (A) 33 (B=36)
    biblical motive. Exod 8:15/14:31

19. *The Israelites Were "Horses" and "Lambs" at the Sea* (19:9):
    biblical motive. Isa 63:13-14 (Mal 3:20b)

The general picture presented by these data leads to a number of
conclusions concerning the nature of Ps-Solomon's comments on the
Exodus. What he says about the Bible is often evidence of exegetical
traditions arising out of something specific in the biblical text. This is very
apparent in several clear-cut examples: "cast up" from the sea (#4; 10:19b-
20a); "hymned your holy name" (#6; 10:20b); God's foreknowledge of the
Egyptian pursuit (#10; 19:1b); the Egyptians "escorted" the Israelites (#11;
19:2). Such "triggers" in the biblical text are also discernible in other
instances: sang "with one accord" (#7; 10:20c); the "dumb" and "babes"
sang at the sea (#s 8 and 9; 10:21a-b); the Egyptians "beseechingly" cast out
the Israelites (#13; 19:3d); the Israelites passed through the sea "as one
nation" (#17; 19:8a), and others.[1] Many of the exegetical traditions
represented in the Wisdom of Solomon were, thus, ultimately motivated by
something in the biblical text itself, especially by some grammatical
irregularity or gap in the narrative. As such, these traditions are products
of truly "close readings" of the Bible. Furthermore, it has been argued

---

[1] Others of Ps-Solomon's comments that seem to be connected to the Exodus narrative (and
are therefore mentioned at best only briefly in Part II) are the following: (1) wisdom
"entered" Moses (10:16a) [Exod 3-4 (4:16/7:1)]; (2) Moses as a "servant" (10:16a) [Exod
4:10]; (3) "Red Sea...water" (10:18) [reflects parallelism in Exod 14:16, 21, 22, 29];
(4) YHWH's "champion might" delivers the Israelites (10:20c) [Exod 14:31; 14:14, 25;
15:3]; (5) Israelites' way through the sea was "unhindered" (19:7c) [Isa 63:13; Exod
14:25]; (6) Israelites "protected by God's hand" (19:8a) [Exod 3:19, 20; 6:1; 7:4, 5; 9:3,
15; 13:3, 9, 14, 16; 14:31; 15:6, 12].

that at least two of these examples, "with one accord" (#7) and "beseechingly cast out" (#13) likely stem from factors found only in a Hebrew text rather than a Greek translation. Even in the unlikely event that Ps-Solomon read the Bible in Hebrew, are we to assume that his readers would have been able to do likewise? If not, why is it that Ps-Solomon would allude to features of the biblical text not found in the LXX, the Bible of his audience? The simple answer seems to be that these interpretations did not originate with him. He did not have a Hebrew text before him, or for that matter a Greek one. He was not engaging the text in any immediate sense. Rather, he was, in a manner of speaking, simply a conduit for pre-existing exegetical traditions. The presence of these traditions in the Wisdom of Solomon shows that Ps-Solomon's retelling of Scripture is firmly at home in the milieu of Second Temple biblical interpretation. Comments such as these are not his own creation.

This last observation is strengthened by looking at how other interpreters, both before and after Ps-Solomon, understood the same passages in the Exodus narrative. We have seen that Ps-Solomon's understanding of the Bible cannot be fully appreciated in isolation. Throughout 10:15-21 and 19:1-9, many of Ps-Solomon's comments have been shown to be but one witness to a broader exegetical family that incorporated similar or identical explanations of the Bible. Of the nineteen comments discussed in this study, thirteen are found in other sources (#s 1, 2, 3, 4, 7, 9, 11, 12, 13, 14, 15, 16, 18). It goes without saying that the Wisdom of Solomon cannot be considered the point of origin for these traditions. For one thing, several of these traditions are extant in some form in writings that are either earlier or roughly contemporaneous with the Wisdom of Solomon: "kings" during the plagues in 10:16b (#1; Ben Sira); "payment for services rendered" in 10:17a (#2; *Jubilees, Exagoge*, and *Vita Mosis*); sea "cast up" the Egyptians in 10:19b (#4; *Vita Mosis*); Israelites "escorted" out of Egypt in 19:2 (#11; *Vita Mosis*); Egyptians' decision is "foolish" in 19:3 (#12; *Biblical Antiquities*).[2]

More important is the fact that Ps-Solomon does not reproduce these traditions in their entirety. His allusions to these exegetical traditions are just that, allusions; he refers to them in little more than a phrase, or, in some instances, merely a word. This exegetical "shorthand" in particular speaks to the antiquity and widely dispersed nature of these traditions by the first century AD. How else are we to understand, for example, his almost offhand mention of "babes" singing at the sea (#9), the payment the

---

[2]See also wisdom "entered" Moses in 10:16a (*V. Mos.* 1.158; Sir 45:2).

Israelites received for their period of slavery (#2), or the grassy path through the sea (#16) if not within a well established context of Second Temple interpretive activity? Unless we assume some level of pre-understanding on the part of the author and his audience, comments such as these would be inexplicable. Moreover, we see in the Wisdom of Solomon not only later, brief versions of some exegetical traditions found in earlier sources, but also *early* hints of exegetical traditions that are otherwise only documented in *later* and *fuller* versions. Examples include: pillar of cloud as "shelter" in 10:17c (#3; *Mekilta, Targum Neofiti, Canticles Rabbah*, and *Numbers Rabbah*); "babes" sing at the sea in 10:21b (#9; *Mekilta, Targum Ps-Jonathan*, Talmuds, *Pirqe de-Rabbi Eliezer*, and *Pesiqta de-Rab Kahana*); Israelites "beseeched" to leave in 19:3 (#13; *Targum Ps-Jonathan*); bottom of sea as a "grassy plain" in 19:7d (#16; *Targum Ps-Jonathan*); "wonders" at the sea in 19:8b (#18; *Mekilta*, Babylonian Talmud, *Pirqe de-Rabbi Eliezer*, and *Midrash Tehillim*).

The rabbinic material is vital for our understanding of the Wisdom of Solomon. How is it that Ps-Solomon and later rabbinic texts can say very similar things about the same biblical phenomenon? What is the link between them? We can, first of all, dismiss as most unlikely the notion that the authors of these later works read the Wisdom of Solomon and developed full-blown midrashim on the basis of Ps-Solomon's terse comments. It is, rather, Ps-Solomon's terse comments that presume the existence of a more developed tradition. But (quite obviously) we can not say that Ps-Solomon had access to specifically these later rabbinic versions of these traditions! There is, it seems, no direct path of influence between Ps-Solomon and the later texts. How, then, are the similarities to be explained? It seems that, well before the Wisdom of Solomon was written, these exegetical traditions existed, and both Ps-Solomon's terse allusions and the later, fuller versions attest to their existence. It is precisely the brevity of Ps-Solomon's allusions to these interpretive traditions, when seen in the context of the fuller versions, both earlier and later, that shows how firmly at home this ancient interpreter was in the world of Second Temple biblical interpretation.

We may take this last observation a step further by suggesting that there was a pre-existing "corpus" of comments (by which I certainly do not mean written or officially recognized in some sense) on the Bible that, by Ps-Solomon's time, had became closely associated with the "retelling" of the Bible, so closely, in fact, that the biblical texts and their explanations went hand in hand: the explanations actually became part of the retelling.

We must keep in mind that Ps-Solomon was not a Tannaitic rabbi, or even a Palestinian Jew, but an Alexandrian Jew, writing in Greek for his immediate countrymen. Moreover, his agenda was not biblical exposition simply for its own sake, nor was he interested in exploiting the "playfulness" of the text. Rather, the book itself gives strong indication that it had a more practical focus: it was written, at least in part, to offer encouragement in troubled times. Although there are differences of opinon regarding the date of composition, scholars routinely agree that some type of persecution forms the historical backdrop for the Wisdom of Solomon.[3] The book is addressed to the rulers of the earth (1:1),[4] who are chided for reasoning unsoundly (2:1) by not following the path of wisdom. They say that the here-and-now is all that matters. There is no afterlife (2:2-5); their time is best spent enjoying what they have now (2:6-9). And, inspired, perhaps, by their conviction that no judgment awaits them after death, they take it upon themselves to oppress the righteous poor, those who foolishly reproach the rulers for their ungodly conduct (2:10-20). The oppression of the righteous likely included those taken before their time, perhaps in the prime of their youth (3:10-4:19). Ps-Solomon even

---

[3] See, for example, Winston's observation: "[Ps-Solomon] attempts to justify their present suffering though the promise of immortality as a reward for their steadfast perseverance in the pursuit of righteousness....By presenting Judaism in intellectually respectable terms, he sought to shore up the faith against hostile anti-Semitic attacks from without and gnawing doubts from within, and through a determined counterattack against the immoral world which he threatened with divine retribution, he attempted to revive the flagging spirits of his hard-pressed people" (63-64). Reider has a helpful overview of the various theories concerning Ps-Solomon's purpose (9-12; see also Lillie, *History of Scholarship*, 36-45), and concludes not only that "the purpose of the Book of Wisdom is primarily to strengthen the faith of the pious Jews," but also "to convert the apostate or renegade Jews to such a faith, and to convince the heathen of the folly of their idolatry" (10-11). Ps-Solomon's ultimate reasons for writing this book are certainly manifold, but it is also certain that offering comfort to his people is one of them, especially in light of the repeated references to the oppression of the righteous and their ultimate immortality in chaps. 1-5. See also Larcher, 1.114-19 and most recently J. M. G. Barclay, *Jews in the Mediterranean Diaspora: From Alexander to Trajan (323 BCE - 117 CE)* (Edinburgh: T & T Clark, 1996) 181-91.

[4] Although the book is addressed to the pagan rulers, I do not think that these rulers were the actual, intended audience, but merely provided the literary context in which Ps-Solomon could address his beleaguered countrymen. Could we really expect the rulers of Ps-Solomon's day to have been moved by his warnings to follows the way of wisdom? It seems more likely that even these opening chapters are addressed to Jews. Ps-Solomon is telling his audience, "See, these pagan rulers are doomed to certain judgment and destruction. They mean you no good and their end is certain. Do not be like them or the people they rule. They do not follow wisdom's path, but you should."

envisages a heavenly scene in which the persecuted righteous face their oppressors in the heavenly court (4:20-5:14). The end of the ungodly are like chaff in the wind (5:14), but the righteous live forever (5:15). Surely, the Book of Wisdom is written with these oppressed righteous ones in mind. Chapters 6-9 reiterate the warning to the ruler of the earth to heed wisdom's warning. Their dominion is from God's hand (6:3), and they ought to follow in step with God's ways (6:21). The remainder of chaps. 6-9 is largely a praise of wisdom, meant to inspire these rulers to follow her with all their might.

It is clear from even a glance at the opening chapters of the Book of Wisdom that oppression of some sort is very much on the author's mind, but his consolatory agenda does not end with chap. 9. Beginning in chap. 10, Ps-Solomon continues to offer comfort to God's people to endure their hardship, and he does so by relating to them the stories of God's care for his people throughout biblical history (10:1-14), and especially during the Exodus (10:15-19:21).[5] The righteous Israelites have a long history of divine aid in times of trouble, and Ps-Solomon takes great care to spell that out clearly. If, then, persecution forms the proper historical backdrop from which to view the Wisdom of Solomon, the smattering of interpretive traditions that color Ps-Solomon's comments on Scripture needs to be explained. Ps-Solomon was an Alexandrian Jew, whose mind was particularly concerned to address the oppression of his countrymen. Biblical exposition was for him no mere academic exercise. Yet, in his comments on Scripture, he relates not simply Scripture to his readers, but "Scripture plus." In light of such dire circumstances, it seems somewhat far-fetched to think that Ps-Solomon incorporated these interpretive traditions merely to add some flourish or spice to his otherwise drab comments. Rather, the Wisdom of Solomon was a literary product of some urgency, the purpose of which was to help his people, not to set them on an exegetical adventure. He was concerned with nothing less than providing scriptural *proof* that God does indeed deliver his people: he has done it in the past and he is sure to do it now. It is hard to escape the conclusion that for Ps-Solomon, the interpretative traditions that find their way into his

---

[5] I disagree with Berwick, that the purpose of chaps. 10-19 is "to convert the Greek by showing Jehovah's dealings in the history of Judaism" (*Way of Salvation*, 103). I understand these chapters, as can be seen especially in the transition from chap. 9 to 10 and the contents of chap. 10 as a whole, as concrete examples of how wisdom has provided for the righteous (see below). As such, chaps. 10-19 offer further encouragement to a beleaguered people.

exposition of Scripture actually represent his *understanding* of what the passages in question actually said.   He is, therefore, not so much an interpreter of Scripture in the narrow sense; it is not *he* who is grappling directly with the exegetical particulars of the biblical text. This has already been done for him. He is, rather, an inheriter of an interpreted Bible, and, therefore, an interpreter in a broader sense: his role is to bring the message of this interpreted Bible to bear on his people's situation. Already by his time these exegetical traditions had become so intimately associated with the Bible that an Alexandrian Jew under dire circumstances was able to retell them succinctly and with conviction as nothing less than the Bible itself, and, moreover, expect to be understood by readers who certainly had other things on their minds than gaps and grammatical irritants in the biblical narratives.

We should also pause here to consider the density of these allusions. In the sixteen verses in which Ps-Solomon discusses the Exodus, he incorporates no less than thirteen interpretive traditions that are also found in other sources. It is almost as if he cannot say *anything* about the Bible without referring to these interpretive traditions. And these traditions are found not only in chap. 10, where one might expect to see them; the density of these allusions is no less in chap. 19. Furthermore, Part II of this study has focused only on one relatively small theme in the Wisdom of Solomon, the departure from Egypt. But more briefly, we have discussed the presence of these traditions elsewhere, i.e., in Ps-Solomon's retelling of Adam to Joseph in 10:1-14. We have seen how Abraham was delivered from "nations in wicked agreement" (10:5), a statement which, along with other Second Temple sources, seems to place Abraham in Babel during the Tower episode. The sin of Sodom was, for Ps-Solomon, not specifically their sexual behavior, but their inhospitality to foreigners (10:6-8; 19:13-17), an interpretive tradition found not only in extra-biblical sources, but in Ezek 16:49-50 as well. Jacob is said to have been guarded from enemies who were lying in ambush for him (10:12), an event that does not appear in the Genesis narrative but is found in *Jubilees* 37-39. Joseph seems to have been wrongly accused of sexual misconduct not only by Potiphar's wife, but by other members of her household (10:14), a tradition found also in Philo's *De Iosepho* 51 (and perhaps *Gen. Rab.* 87.8 and 88.1). Ps-Solomon's account of the Flood is particularly interesting in that he offers two explanations for the cause of the deluge, Cain (10:4) and the "giants" of Gen 6:1-4 (14:6), the latter interpretation being common in Second

Temple literature.[6] All of these factors—the density of this interpretive material in the Wisdom of Solomon, his "shorthand" manner of expressing these traditions, and the setting in which he and his audience lived—attest not so much to Ps-Solomon's own notions of biblical interpretation, but to the general, popular notions of biblical interpretation current in his day.

As such, the Wisdom of Solomon is a valuable witness to the nature of biblical interpretation in the century before the close of the Second Temple period, and, by implication, long before. We gain insight not so much into the nature of Ps-Solomon the *interpreter*, i.e., his exegetical method, but what constituted proper biblical *understanding* for Ps-Solomon and his readers. Ps-Solomon was heir to an interpreted Bible, and much of what he said about Scripture was not his own creation but the fruit of previous exegetical activity. What remains to be seen is to what extent, if at all, Ps-Solomon was cognizant of this previous exegetical activity. In other words, was he actually aware that his comments on Scripture went "beyond the text," so to speak? Was he conscious that he was in fact *incorporating* these "traditions" into the sacred text? The degree to which the inclusion of these exegetical traditions was a conscious activity on Ps-Solomon's part is a matter that goes well beyond any demonstrable proof. Still, I would venture to say that these traditions had simply come to be a part of what constituted a proper biblical understanding for Ps-Solomon and the people for whom he wrote. Ps-Solomon was not in any sense *interacting* with past exegetical activity when he wrote his book, nor was he necessarily even aware of such activity. All he knew is what the Bible "says," and his goal was to bring that message to the people as best he could. In this sense, Vermes's observation on the manner in which exegetical traditions are incorporated into the *Genesis Apocryphon*, the expansive retelling of portions of Genesis found among the Dead Sea Scrolls, is apt.

> The author never attempts to introduce unrelated or extraneous matter. His technique is simple and he exercises no scholarly learning, no exegetical virtuosity, no play on words. His intention is to explain the biblical text, and this he does either by bringing together various passages of Genesis, or by illustrating a verse with the help of an appropriate story. The resulting work is certainly one of the jewels of midrashic exegesis, and the best

---

[6]Some of Ps-Solomon's comments on the plagues may also betray some knowledge of interpretive traditions, e.g., Israel's being attacked by *wild beasts* in the desert (16:5); *bites* of locusts and flies (16:9); simultaneity of the plagues (16:18).

illustration yet available of the primitive haggadah and of the unbaised
rewriting of the Bible.[7]

Vermes's insight is largely applicable to the Wisdom of Solomon.

The Wisdom of Solomon in the Broader Context of Second Temple Wisdom

In addition to the foregoing remarks about the exegetical traditions that
pervade Ps-Solomon's comments on the Exodus, a number of observations
may be made concerning Ps-Solomon's use of Scripture and its place in the
broader context of the Second Temple period. First, although the focus of
this study has been to highlight the traditions to which Ps-Solomon
certainly had access and the exegetical processes that underlie these
traditions, there are instances where Ps-Solomon seems to engage the
biblical texts on a more direct level. This, of course, is fully to be
expected, and this study is in no way intended to suggest that Ps-Solomon's
understanding of the Bible is merely a by-product of the work of others.
Although Ps-Solomon's understanding of Scripture was heavily influenced
by the exegetical world of which he was a part, this does not mean that he
himself was incapable of engaging Scripture in a more immediate sense.
One aspect of his exegesis that we have seen is that it seeks to harmonize
the biblical material with the prevailing philosophical notions of his day:
recall "flame of stars" (discussed under #3; 10:17d) and his description of
the crossing of the sea (#15; 19:6-7b). These instances are more amenable
to the theory that Ps-Solomon was an interpreter dealing directly with the
scriptural material in an effort to explain it in such a way that does not
violate the philosophical sensibilities of his audience (although even here,
this philisophical agenda has ample precedent in Philo's writings). What
might also be considered an example of Ps-Solomon's direct interaction
with Scripture is his use of Isa 63:12-14 (#s16 and 19). The point here is
not so much that he brings this passage into the discussion (not a
particularly daring exegesis, since Isa 63:12-14 is obviously concerned with
the Red Sea), but that he seems to have introduced an innovative
understanding of the passage: v. 12 refers to the crossing of the sea while
vv. 13-14 refer to the Song at the Sea. Since there is no other extant
example of such an interpretation of Isa 63:12-14, the possibility that this

---

[7]Vermes, *Scripture and Tradition*, 126.

exegesis is the fruit of Ps-Solomon's own exegetical labor should at least be given consideration, although, admittedly, the matter is ultimately impossible to determine, nor is it vital for this study. The point remains that in the context of his brief exposition of the Exodus, Ps-Solomon's understanding of the Exodus is at some level influenced by passages outside of the bounds of the Exodus narrative. We see something similar in chaps. 13-15 where he calls upon the biblical idol-polemic motif in the broader context of the Exodus/Wilderness theme of chaps. 10-19. It seems that for Ps-Solomon, the parts of Scripture are not separated by such incidentals as authorship or date, but that the parts "speak" to each other. By Ps-Solomon's day, "commenting on the Pentateuch" did not mean that one was restricted to examining the particular passage in isolation.[8] There was enough of a notion of the simultaneity of Scripture to allow for some communication between texts. And, as in the case of the "flame of stars" or the crossing of the sea, Ps-Solomon's exegesis can go outside of the bounds of the Bible entirely.

A second characteristic is Ps-Solomon's appeal to Scripture to show the workings of divine justice. What is the Exodus story about? It is certainly more than an account of God's deliverance of the ancient Israelites in the past. Rather, it is a paradigm for how God has ordered all of creation. God is just and will deliver the faithful throughout history and punish all those who wrong them. Has he not already shown this to be the case? Were not Adam, Noah, Abraham, Lot, Jacob, Joseph, and, most important of all, the Israelites under Moses, delivered by wisdom from their oppressors (10:1-21)? Despite the appearance of things, there is an underlying plan of God that will right all wrongs; the plan is firmly in place, but it calls for patience on the part of the faithful:

> For what man can know the counsel of God, or who can reflect on what the Lord wills? For the reasoning of mortals is worthless, and our designs are likely to fail, for a perishable body weighs down the soul, and this earthly tent burdens a mind full of cares. We can scarcely guess at what is on earth, and what is at hand we find with difficulty. Who, then, has traced out what is in the heavens? Who has learned your counsel, unless you have given wisdom and sent your holy spirit from on high? This is how the

---

[8]In this respect, see also Ps-Solomon's comments on kings during the plagues (Pss 105 [104]:30 and 135 [134]:9), Sodom's inhospitality (Ezek 16:49-50), the military conflict between Esau and Jacob (Obad 14), and infants singing at the sea (Ezek 16:1-7). Although these are likely not examples of Ps-Solomon's own notion of intertextuality but of his awareness of an existing exegetical tradition, they demonstrate a nascent intertextuality before Ps-Solomon's time and in which he likely participated.

> paths of those on earth were set right, and people were taught what pleases
> you, and were saved by wisdom (9:13-18).

These verses introduce Ps-Solomon's review of Israel's history in chaps.
10-19, which is no mere "review" of history but a lesson in God's justice.
History itself, like the physical universe (7:22-24), has become wisdom's
stage. Since *eternal* wisdom has been active throughout history to save
God's people, the faithful can, even now, far after the passing of these
historical events, rest assured that they have not been forgotten, despite
their present afflictions. And, as the opening chapters of the book make
clear, the certainty of deliverance extends beyond this life into the life to
come (see 1:13-14; 2:21-3:9; 4:7-17; 5:15-23). Even if deliverance does
not come now, the passing from this life into the next does not thwart the
plan of God. Rather, it is part of God's "secret purposes" (μυστήρια,
2:22) that the righteous will receive immortality (3:1-9; 5:15). What is in
store for the righteous at death is not the cessation of participation in the
divine plan, but a better realization of that plan.

In light of this, the unifying theme of the Wisdom of Solomon
presents itself: "wisdom delivers"—whether now or later, past or
present, this life or the next. This is, in fact, how the Book of Wisdom
ends (19:22):

> For in every way (κατὰ πάντα), O Lord, you have exalted and glorified
> your people. At every time and in every place (ἐν παντὶ καιρῷ καὶ τόπῳ)
> you have not neglected to help them.

Wis 19:22 is a summary statement for the book as a whole: God never
neglects his people. It matters little what the circumstances are; he is with
them κατὰ πάντα.[9] Nor is God's saving power relegated to a bygone era;
he is with his people ἐν παντὶ καιρῷ. And God's saving power knows no
boundary; he is with his people ἐν παντὶ τόπῳ—even death. God has
always been with his people, for absolutely nothing, neither time, place,
nor circumstance, is outside of the reach of God's overarching plan and

---

[9]In fact, according to Wis 15:1-3, God's presence with his people extends even to their sin:
"For even if we sin, we are yours, knowing your power." God is with his people not only
when they are hard-pressed by some outside forces, but even when they themselves are
turning from him. God is kind, patient, and merciful (15:1) toward his people. Knowing
his power is the "root of immortality" (ῥίζα ἀθανασίας; 15:3). For a discussion of 15:3
specifically, see R. E. Murphy, "'To Know your Might is the Root of Immortality' (Wis
15,3)," *CBQ* 25 (1963) 88-93.

purpose, which will not be frustrated and will come to pass: "She reaches mightily from one end of the earth to the other and she orders all things well" (8:1).

Here, also, the background of persecution mentioned above helps us see more clearly this unifying theme of the book by providing some sense to the book's structure. In the early chapters, Ps-Solomon's emphasis is clearly on the afterlife (chaps. 1-5, see also 8:13-17). Furthermore, Ps-Solomon refers to this movement from the present life to the next as an "exodus" (ἔξοδός; 3:2 and 7:6), in which the faithful are delivered not only from persecution, but from the confines of a material existence (9:14-15). When we turn to chaps. 10-19, Ps-Solomon begins to recount wisdom's acts of deliverance throughout Israel's history, focusing in particular on the Exodus and subsequent wilderness wandering. In light of Ps-Solomon's clear purpose of giving encouragement to a people facing the very real possibility of death, one begins to see the motive behind not only his emphasis on the "Exodus" in the opening chapters, but his choice of Israel's *Exodus* experience as the primary topic of conversation in chaps. 10-19. Israel's Exodus, her passage from "death to life," as it were, is the prime biblical portrait of what wisdom is doing now in the lives of these persecuted Alexandrian Jews, their own passage from death to life, their own Exodus. Hence, Ps-Solomon's treatment of death and the afterlife in the early chapters of the book is a recontextualization of the Exodus of the Bible; he has brought the biblical event of the past into the people's present. This thematic overlap between the early chapters of the Book of Wisdom and the "historical" section in chaps. 10-19 is not only one argument for a two-fold division of the book (with the second part beginning at 10:1; see Part I, n. 15), but a demonstration of the book's unity. 9:13-18, cited above, serves to link the section on immortality and the praise of wisdom in chaps. 1-9 to the rehearsal of wisdom's activity in Israel's history in chaps. 10-19: it is wisdom who saves, and the retelling of Israel's history supports that fact.[10] The appendix to this study is a preliminary attempt to support this notion by demonstrating the lexical overlap between the two parts of the book, i.e., Ps-Solomon's use of similar vocabulary throughout the book to speak of wisdom's deliverance of the faithful.

A third characteristic of Ps-Solomon's use of Scripture, which follows closely upon the second, concerns the manner in which he presents the figures of Israel's past. Simply put, biblical characters are

---

[10]A. Schmitt is particularly convincing in establishing the links between 9:18 and 10:1-21 ("Struktur, Herkunft und Bedeutung der Beispielreihe in Weish 10," *BZ* 21 [1977] 1-22).

models of virtue. There is no ambiguity about their moral character. Rather, the heroes of the Bible are presented by Ps-Solomon as exempla for the faithful of his own day, and as such, it will not do to present these figures from the past in anyway other than the ideal. Abraham in Wis 10:5 does not doubt YHWH as he does, for example, in Gen 17:17-18; rather he is simply "righteous" (cf. Paul's similar presentation of Abraham in Rom 4:20-21). The same holds for Ps-Solomon's presentation of Lot and Jacob: they are models of absolute virtue, whereas the biblical narratives paint a more subtle and varied moral portrait.[11]   And, of course, there is no mention of Moses' (near fatal) slip-up on the way from Midian (Exod 4:18-26), or his disobedience at Meribah (Num 20:7-12) and his subsequent punishment of being denied entrance into Canaan. Rather, all these figures are painted with broad strokes of black and white, something typical not only of the Wisdom of Solomon as a whole, but of the genre of Wisdom literature (especially post-biblical literature) of which this book is a part.[12] That these figures from the past serve as paradigms for the present also helps to explain Ps-Solomon's avoidance of naming these figures. *Who they were then* is of little importance; *what they represent now*, patterns of wise conduct, is all that matters.   These biblical figures have become democratized: they represent models of conduct for the readers of the

---

[11]Lot's "righteousness" may be called into question in view of his choice of the "cities of the plain" for a homestead. Was he not aware of Sodom's reputation? Of all places to settle, why would he choose a site anywhere near Sodom? Likewise, Jacob's deceit ought to have raised an eyebrow. Even righteous Joseph is not without fault. Later rabbinic sources seem determined to put some blame on Joseph for putting himself in a compromising situation with Potiphar's wife in the first place (see Kugel, *In Potiphar's House*, 94-96).

[12]The appendix in part attempts to draw attention to this phenomenon in 10:15-21 and 19:1-9 specifically, and throughout the Wisdom of Solomon. Regarding the ideal portrayal in antiquity of biblical characters, see J. J. Collins and G. W. E. Nickelsburg, *Ideal Figures in Ancient Israel: Profiles and Paradigms* (SBLSCS 12; Chico, CA: Scholars Press, 1980), and M. E. Stone, "Ideal Figures and Social Context: Priest and Sage in the Early Second Temple Age," *Ancient Israelite Religion: Essays in Honor of Frank Moore Cross* (eds. P. D. Miller, P. D. Hanson, and S. D. McBride; Philadelphia: Fortress, 1987) 575-86. The ideal presentation of past figures is not, however, simply a post-biblical phenomenon. Within the Bible itself, the Chronicler, for example, paints an idealized portrait of Israel's past. In particular, David's reign and the transition of power from David to Solomon are presented in a way that removes David's foibles and the political machinations that characterize the Deuteronomist's account.

Wisdom of Solomon. In the midst of daily challenges to their faith, the word of God must speak clearly to their present situation.[13]

These developments during the Second Temple period are not limited to the Wisdom genre, and a brief look at contemporary analogies developments will help to put into sharper focus the preceding discussion. G. Anderson, for example, has pointed out the changing significance of sacrifice during this same period, which he calls the "scripturalization" of sacrifice, i.e., the "transfer of biblical sacrifice from temple-practice to exegetical artiface."[14] An example Anderson adduces to make his case concerns the differences in the ordinances for the purification offerings in Leviticus 4 as compared to Num 15:22-31.[15] There are a number of differences between these two passages, most notably, Anderson argues, the requirement of a bull for the purification offering in Leviticus 4, whereas Numbers 15 requires a calf for the purification offering and a bull for the burnt offering. Rather than explaining this difference, as is often done, by seeing these texts as reflecting *historical* developments concerning the cult, Anderson suggests that,

> Num 15:22-31 is a systematic *exegetical reworking* of Leviticus 4. No longer are we speaking of *development of cultic practice* but rather of *learned reflection on a developing canon of textual material.*[16]

Sacrifice has become more than "simply a matter of what takes place in the temple; it is also a matter of *recovering* what a *textual* law requires."[17] Sacrifice, in other words, has gone beyond the temple walls and has been

---

[13]Commenting on Ben Sira's "catalog of heroes" (Sir 44-50), J. L. Kugel writes: "for him [Ben Sira] Josiah and Zerubbabel dwell in the same mythic fog as Abraham or Enoch. These once-real people have become, essentially, *lessons*, whose importance can be captured in a line or two" (*Early Biblical Interpretation* [Philadelphia: Westminster, 1986] 49; his emphasis). See also A. Schmitt's comment: "Es geht bei unserer Beispielreihe [Wis 9:18-10:21] nicht um eine bloße Historisierung, sondern vor allem um eine Aktualisierung der Heilsgeschichte. Indem nämlich Personen verschiedener Epochen mit dem Nomen δίκαιος belegt werden, stellt man sie auf die glieche Ebene. Das zeitliche Intervall is damit relativiert; für sie all gilt: Als δίκαιοι haben sie die heilsame und rettende Macht der σοφία an sich erfahren, zu welcher Zeit sie auch lebten. Diese Typisierung läßt der Hoffnung Raum, daß für hier und heute das Gleiche gilt" ("Beilspielreihe," 21).

[14]G. Anderson, "Sacrifice and Sacrifical Offerings," *ABD* 5.885.

[15] Ibid., 883-84. See also G. Anderson, "The Interpretation of the Purification Offering (חטאת) in the *Temple Scroll* (11QTemple) and Rabbinic Literature," *JBL* 111 (1992) 17-35.

[16]"Sacrifice and Sacrificial Offerings," 883 (his emphasis). Anderson is building on the work of A. Toeg ("Numbers 15:22-31—Midrash Halakha," *Tarbiz* 43 [1974] 1-10).

[17]"Sacrifice and Sacrificial Offerings," 884 (his emphasis).

transformed into an exegetical endeavor. This development of the understanding of sacrifice in the Second Temple period demonstrates the increasingly important role Scripture played in Judaism.[18] With the cessation of prophecy and the Jerusalem cult during the exile, focus began to shift to a continuation of the divine-human discourse by means of exegesis of Scripture.[19] Exegesis became the vital link between God and his people; it was through a proper understanding of Scripture that God's will could be known. As M. Fishbane puts it,

> [S]cripture has become the vehicle of new revelations, and exegesis the means of new access to the divine will. Thus, complementing the divine revelation now embodied in a written Torah, the sage seeks from God the grace of an *ongoing revelation* through the words of scripture itself—as mediated *through exegesis*.[20]

Anderson's "scripturalization of sacrifice" is just one example of the increased importance placed on the written word during the Second Temple period, evidence of which is found in a number of places within the Hebrew Bible itself. Fishbane's work has also helped clarify the significance of this phenomenon. For example, he spends nearly 200 pages of his *Biblical Interpretation in Ancient Israel* discussing various examples of legal exegesis, not unlike that mentioned by Anderson, within

---

[18]This is what J. L. Kugel refers to as the "rise of Scripture" (*Early Biblical Interpretation*, 13-26). For a more recent study of the role of Scripture and the increasing importance of exegesis in the Second Temple period, see W. M. Schniedewind, *The Word of God In Transition: From Prophet to Exegete in the Second Temple Period* (JSOTSup 197; Sheffield: Sheffield Academic Press, 1995). Schniedewind's focus is on the Chronicler's work.

[19]See Kugel, *Early Biblical Interpretation*, 13-17. The matter of what is meant by the "cessation" of prophecy in the post-exilic period is far more complicated than I am suggesting here, but a fuller treatment is not necessary in this context. For a brief review of the discussion on this issue, see Schniedewind, *Word of God*, 11-29; J. Barton, *Oracles of God: Perceptions of Ancient Prophecy in Israel after the Exile* (London: Darton, Longman and Todd, 1986). The recent monograph by R. Gray treats this issue with specific reference to Josephus (*Prophetic Figures in Late Second Temple Jewish Palestine: The Evidence from Josephus* [New York/Oxford: Oxford University Press, 1993] 7-34). In any event, it is safe to say that so-called "classical" prophecy, the *spoken* word, ceased during this period, and that this historical phenomenon coincides with the increased importance of the *written* word.

[20]M. Fishbane. "From Scribalism to Rabbinism: Perspectives on the Emergence of Classical Judaism." *The Sage in Israel and the Ancient Near East* (eds. J. G. Gammie and L. G. Perdue; Winona Lake, IN: Eisenbrauns, 1990) 442-43 (his emphasis).

the Hebrew Bible.[21] Elsewhere, Fishbane discusses other examples of the biblical evidence for the increasing importance of Torah exegesis. [22] In Neh 8:1-8, Ezra receives inspiration (cf, 8:6, 9) in order to interpret the "Book of the Law of Moses." Likewise, the writer of Psalm 119 is apparently assuming a written law when he asks for divine enablement to understand it (see esp. vv. 18 and 135). The Chronicler, in retelling the history of monarchy for the returnees from Babylon, appeals to the importance of heeding prophetic words of the past (see 2 Chr 20:20). Also, Daniel's inspired interpretation of Jeremiah's prophecy concerning the "70 weeks" (see Dan 9:2, 20) is a clear example of the trend we have been discussing.

Even these brief examples are sufficient to illustrate the increasing importance of biblical interpretation during the Second Temple period and to sketch the broader context of that interpretation within which one might understand the specific of the Wisdom circles. The scripturalization of sacrifice in particular is similar to what we see in the development of the Wisdom tradition in the Second Temple period. As disparate cultic laws were read in such a way as to bring harmony between them, so, too, the Torah as a whole came to be read in such a way as to make clear, unambiguous declarations of God's dealings with his people. We can appreciate, then, the need to "tidy up" the biblical data in an effort to make all Scripture speak more clearly to the ever-changing situations of the readers. This is why Ps-Solomon portrays the heroes of Israel's past in black and white catagories: they have become models of virtue. This is also why these heroes have become nameless figures: the past is dehistoricized in an effort to bring that past more forcfully into the present. In calling upon this dehistoricized past, Ps-Solomon is telling his readers that the God of Israel is still with them, that who they are now amid the changing fortunes of history must be seen in light of the never-changing God who has never failed to deliver the faithful who have gone before. Idealizing the past does not obliterate history but makes it transportable. The idealized past, therefore, is the only proper backdrop for viewing one's present, historical situation. It is the solid rock that stands high above the ebb and flow of history. And, according to Ps-Solomon, it is wisdom herself who has been God's active agent throughout Israel's history in bringing the godly through trying times. His readers, therefore, are exhorted to seek (6:12-16), honor (6:21), pray for (7:7),

---

[21]Fishbane, *Biblical Interpretation in Ancient Israel,* 91-277.
[22]For the following, see "From Scribalism to Rabbinism," 439-56.

love (8:2), and befriend (8:18) her. Acquiring wisdom now is the key to the present, for it is wisdom who has been active throughout Israel's past.

That Ps-Solomon portrays wisdom as the primary player in Israel's history will naturally lead to placing such an understanding of wisdom in the context of the Second Temple period in general. We see already in Proverbs 8 the personification of wisdom who has some special status in creation, either as the first of God's creations (Prov 8:22)[23] or as actually having a hand in creation itself (Prov 8:30; cf. perhaps Prov 3:19). Proverbs 8 is one of the few expressions (and certainly the clearest) of the personification of wisdom in the Hebrew Bible (see also Job 28; Proverbs 1, 9), a fact which, it is fairly safe to say, encouraged early interpreters to find out more about the nature of wisdom's activities in the world. The reticence with which the Hebrew Bible speaks of personfied wisdom may be contrasted to the importance this theme takes on in post-biblical times. Specifically, there is a well documented post-biblical tendency to equate personified wisdom with Torah.[24] The most explicit text in drawing the connection between Torah and wisdom, and certainly among the earliest, is Sir 24:1-29. For Ben Sira, Torah is the source of wisdom, a point he makes unequivocally clear in 24:23. First, Ben Sira places personified wisdom at creation: she is the first of God's creations existing from eternity to eternity (24:9; see also 1:4, 9).[25] She then is said to make her

---

[23]The root קָנָה in Prov 8:22 is open to several meanings, including "beget" and "acquire" in addition to "create." See W. McKane, *Proverbs: A New Approach* (Philadelphia: Westminster, 1970) 352 and R. B. Y. Scott, *Proverbs, Ecclesiastes: Introduction, Translation and Notes* (AB; Garden City, N.Y.: Doubleday, 1965) 71-72. See also nn. 75 and 208 in Part II. Settling the matter is not of vital importance here; in any case, wisdom's place was "beside" God (אֶצְלוֹ, v. 30) at the "beginning" (רֵאשִׁית, v. 22)

[24]For a study of wisdom and law in Ben Sira, intertestamental literature, Dead Sea Scrolls, and the Apostle Paul, see E. J. Schnabel, *Law and Wisdom from Ben Sira to Paul* (WUNT 2, Reihe 16; Tübingen: J. C. B. Mohr [Paul Siebeck], 1985). See also R. Wilken, ed., *Aspects of Wisdom in Judaism and Early Christianity* (Notre Dame: University of Notre Dame Press, 1975); J. Blenkinsopp, *Wisdom and Law in the Old Testament: The Ordering of Life in Israel and Early Judaism* (Oxford: Oxford University Press, 1983); G. Boccaccini, *Middle Judaism: Jewish Thought, 300 B.C.E. to 200 C.E.* (Minnealpolis: Fortress, 1991) 81-99; Winston, 33-38. Many rabbinic passages assume the equation of Torah and wisdom, while referring specifically to Prov 8:22: e.g., *Mek. Shir.* 9.123, which cites Prov 8:22 as a proof text that *Torah* is a possession (קִנְיָן) of God. See also *Gen. Rab.* 1.4; *Lev. Rab.* 11.3; 19.1; *Cant. Rab.* 5.11.

[25]Ben Sira certainly models his disussion of wisdom after Proverbs 8 (P. W. Skehan, "Structures in Poems on Wisdom: Proverbs 8 and Sirach 24," *CBQ* 41 [1979] 365-79). In contrast to Ben Sira, however, Ps-Solomon presents wisdom as having a role in the act of creation itself (Wis 7:22; 8:4, 6).

dwelling in Israel (vv. 8-11). She "takes root" among God's people and grows tall and flourishes (vv. 12-17). Having thus described wisdom, Ben Sira bids the readers to come and eat their fill of wisdom's produce (v. 19), for this will bring ample reward: they will never hunger nor thirst again (v. 21), nor will they ever be put to shame or sin again (v. 22). The phrase ταῦτα πάντα, which begins v. 23, "introduces to his readers an encapsulated summation or clarification of the whole previous section."[26] "All this," i.e., the content of Sir 24:1-22, is to be equated with βίβλος διαθήκης θεοῦ ὑψίστου νόμον ὃν ἐνετείλατο ἡμῖν Μωυσῆς, "the Book of the Covenant of God Most High, the Law which Moses commanded us" (see also Sir 39:1). What follows is praise for the *law* of Moses, which "fills men with *wisdom*" (σοφία; v. 25) and "*understanding*" (σύνεσις; v. 26). Beginning at least in v. 23, the topic is "plainly a recital of the history of Wisdom who resides in Israel as the Torah."[27] What distinguishes Sir 24:1-29 from Wis 10:1-21 is the fact that Ps-Solomon deals with the specifics of wisdom's participation in Israel's history, whereas Sir 24:1-29 mentions only creation and a vague notion of wisdom's presence in Israel. But this distinction only pertains to Sir 24:1-29. Ben Sira turns to the topic of wisdom's participation in Israel's history in great detail in Sira 44-50, where, very similar to Wis 10:1-21, the author recounts the deeds of "famous men" (44:1) whose lives stand as permanant examples of righteous lives, righteous because they exemplify the wisdom ideal (see 44:2-6).[28]

Scripture, specifically Torah, has become the depository of wisdom. The role of wisdom, as G. T. Sheppard puts it, has moved from "mundane advice to Wisdom's recital of her participation in Israel's traditions."[29] In Wisdom books like Proverbs, Job, or Qohelet, we find scarcely a single, clear scriptural allusion. Starting with Ben Sira[30] and the Wisdom of Solomon, however, we see books of Wisdom that are steeped through and through with references to biblical figures and events. This fact does not make these two books any less a part of the Wisdom genre. Rather, it is the nature of "wisdom" that has shifted. Whereas the sages of the Hebrew

---

[26]G. T. Sheppard, *Hermeneutical Construct*, 61.

[27]Ibid.

[28]In this context, one thinks, too, of the catalog of heroes in Hebrews 11. A. Schmitt cites a number of examples of *historische Beispielreihe* in antiquity, including biblical, apocryphal, pseudepigraphal, Hellenistic and classical Greek literature ("Struktur," 1-22).

[29]*Hermeneutical Construct*, 6.

[30]J. G. Gammie offers a general overview of Ben Sira's conception of the sage ("The Sage in Sirach." *The Sage in Israel and the Ancient Near East* [eds. J. G. Gammie and L. G. Perdue; Winona Lake, IN: Eisenbrauns, 1990] 355-72).

Bible were concerned with observing patterns in the created order as the basis for godly conduct, "exegeting the world" so to speak, Ben Sira and Ps-Solomon were concerned with observing the nature of God's activity by exegeting the Book; the sage's repertory of knowledge now includes Scripture. The Wisdom of Solomon, therefore, is not a *commentary* on Scripture, but a *search for wisdom*, for God's overarching, eternal plan, on the basis of Scripture. God's eternal wisdom is to be learned from the Bible, for it is Scripture that is the depository of wisdom.

We can see, then, why a proper understanding of Scripture becomes all important. Scripture must be read aright. It is fraught with meaning, and therefore careful attention must be paid to its details: a grammatical or syntactical irregularity must mean something; disharmony between passages or narrative gaps are not hindrances, but opportunities to search for hidden meaning. Biblical interpretation gained such importance in the Second Temple period because Scripture is God's wisdom. It is rich in meaning and invites, even demands, the search for meaning that necessarily goes beyond the plain sense of the text. It is precisely because Torah, including the non-legal potions, *is* wisdom that it takes wisdom to discern its meaning. It is little wonder, then, that the exegetical traditions witnessed to in the Wisdom of Solomon came to be so closely associated with the biblical text. Scripture must be properly interpreted in order for it to be a guide for living. A biblical passage is of little use in revealing to the reader the eternal and immutable pattern of the universe if its meaning is unclear. But when "interpreted," its meaning becomes clear. The presence of these exegetical traditions in the Wisdom of Solomon are not mere legends or artistic embellishments. They are, rather, the fruit of sagely activity that treated the Bible as a gift from God for a standard of faith and conduct with, at least for Ps-Solomon, eternal consequences.

For these reasons, an investigation of biblical interpretation in the Wisdom of Solomon must treat Ps-Solomon's comments on Scripture as part of the broader interpretive movement of which he was a part. Such an investigation will give us a glimpse not only of the state of biblical interpretation in Alexandria during Ps-Solomon's lifetime, but of the nature of biblical interpretation during the Second Temple period as a whole.

Appendix

Ps-Solomon's Use of Vocabulary to Contrast Israel to Egypt in 10:15-21 and 19:1-9, and throughout the Book

Although the main purpose of this study is to draw out the interpretive traditions that underlie Ps-Solomon's comments on the departure from Egypt, this is not to say that every one of his comments, either in the passages we have discussed or in the book as a whole, bears witness to such antecedent exegetical activity. The opening comments in both 10:15-21 and 19:1-9 do not appear to reflect any interaction with any particular exegetical tradition. Nevertheless, these comments are valuable for other reasons, for it is here that Ps-Solomon displays a manner of expression that is typical of what he does throughout the book, as well as characteristic of Wisdom literature in general. Therefore, since these comments are so representative of both the contents and the genre of the Wisdom of Solomon, they merit some attention.

In 10:15, Ps-Solomon's description of Israel is one of many examples in the Wisdom of Solomon of the "black and white" categories that are a recognized characteristic of Wisdom literature:[1] *She* [=Wisdom] *delivered a*

---

[1] On this "black and white" (Georgi, 391) mode of expression (e.g., the contrasting destinies of the "righteous" and the "wicked") in Wisdom literature, see the following studies: G. von Rad, *Wisdom in Israel* (London: SCM, 1972) 124-37; J. K. Kuntz, "The Retribution Motif in Psalmic Wisdom," *ZAW* 89 (1977) 223-33, and "The Wisdom Psalms of Ancient Israel—Their Rhetorical, Thematic and Formal Dimensions," *Rhetorical Criticism: Essay in Honor of James Muilenburg* (eds. J. J. Jackson and M. Kessler; PTMS 1; Pittsburgh: Pickwick, 1974) 186-222; R. B. Y. Scott, *Proverbs-Ecclesiasties* (AB 18; Garden City, N.Y.: Doubleday, 1965), and *The Way of Wisdom in the Old Testament* (New York: Macmillan, 1971) 190-222; W. S. Towner, "Retributional Theology in the Apocalyptic Setting" *USQR* 26/3 (1971) 203-14; R. E. Murphy, "A Consideration of the Classification, 'Wisdom Psalm'," *Congress Volume: Bonn 1962* (VTSup 9; Leiden: E. J. Brill, 1963) 156-67, reprinted in *Studies in Ancient Israelite Wisdom* (ed. J. L. Crenshaw;

holy and blameless seed from a nation of oppressors (Αὕτη λαὸν ὅσιον καὶ
σπέρμα ἄμεμπτον ἐρρύσατο ἐξ ἔθνους θλιβόντων). This is a somewhat
stunning assertion in view of Israel's less than exemplary behavior
throughout the Exodus narrative. Yet our author presents such a view of
God's people not only here but throughout the book. We see, for
example, constant reference to the righteous (δίκαιος)[2] and the ungodly
(ἀσεβής).[3] These two are sharply contrasted in 3:10; 4:16; 5:14-15; 10:6,
20; 12:9; 16:16-17. This absolute contrast between the two types of
people has ample biblical precedent in the Psalms[4] and throughout
Proverbs 10-29.[5] Such a contrast also fuels the speeches of Eliphaz, Bildad
and Zophar in Job. Ps-Solomon's treatment of Lot is a particularly
noticeable example of the author's tendency to view things in terms of
strong contrasts. By calling Lot "righteous" (10:6 and 19:7), Ps-Solomon
is assigning to Lot's character an extreme positive evaluation that Genesis
19 leaves more ambiguous.[6]

New York: Ktav, 1976) 456-67; S. Mowinckel, "Psalms and Wisdom," *Wisdom in Israel
and in the Ancient Near East* (H. H. Rowley Festschrift; VTSup 3; Leiden: E. J. Brill,
1955) 205-24; H. Gunkel, *Einleitung in die Psalmen* (4th ed.; Göttingen: Vandenhoeck &
Ruprecht, 1985); H.-J. Kraus, *Psalmen* (2 vols.; BKAT 15; Neukirchener Verlag, 1960).
With respect to the Wisdom of Solomon itself, see Y. Amir, "Measure for Measure," 37.
M. Kolarcik argues that the effect of 1:1-15 as a whole is to set up this notion of absolute
contrasts (*The Ambiguity of Death*, 63-68). See also R. Lothar, "Gerechte und Frevler
(Gottlose) in Sap 1,1-6,21. Zum Neuverständnis und zur Aktualisierung alttestamentlicher
Traditionen in der Sapientia Salomonis," *Weisheit Salomos im Horizont biblischer
Theologie* (Biblische-Theologische Studien 22; ed. H. Hübner; Neukirchen-Vluyn:
Neukirchener Verlag, 1993) and F. Focke, *Die Entstehung der Weisheit Salomos*
(FRLANT 5.5; Göttingen: Vandenhoeck & Ruprecht, 1913) 19-24.

[2]2:10, 12, 16, 18; 3:1, 10; 4:7, 16; 5:1, 15; 10:4, 5, 6, 10, 13, 20; 11:14; 12:9, 15, 19;
14:30; 16:17, 23; 18:7, 20; 19:16, 17. See also δικαιοσύνη 1:1, 15; 2:11; 5:6, 18; 8:7 (2);
9:3; 12:16; 14:7; 15:3, and δικαίως 9:12; 12:15; 19:13.

[3]1:9, 16; 3:10; 4:3, 16; 5:14; 10:6, 20; 11:9; 12:9; 14:16; 16:16, 18; 19:1. See also
ἀσέβεια and ἀσέβω, both in 14:9.

[4]Examples include the "Wisdom Psalms" (1, 32, 34, 49, 112, 127, 128, and 133). The
list belongs to Kuntz ("Retribution Motif," 224-25). Other lists differ somewhat.

[5]Examples abound throughout Proverbs. Some passages include 10:1; 11:2-3; 12:5-7;
13:5-6; 14:11; 15:6-9; 16:8; 17:24; 18:13-15; 19:8-9; 20:4, 7; 21:12; 22:3; 24:7; 25:26;
26:12; 27:12; 28:1; 29:1-4.

[6]See also 2 Pet 2:7, where Lot is called δίκαιος, Luke 17:28, where a positive view of Lot
seems to be implied, and *Apos. Con.* 8.12.22 (12:61): "[You] snatched away pious
Lot from the burning" (Charlesworth, *Pseudepigrapha*, 2.693). *Jub.* 16:7-9, for example,
portrays Lot very negatively: because he "lay with his daughters...he committed sins upon
the earth which were not [committed] on the earth from the days of Adam until his time..."
(Charlesworth, *Pseudepigrapha*, 2.88). See also J. A. Loader, *A Tale of Two Cities:*

There are also terms in 10:15 that our author uses throughout the book to describe God's people and contrast them to Israel's enemies. One such term is ὅσιος (holy), which appears again in v. 17a.[7] Another word is λαός, regularly λαὸς σου. This is a favorite designation of Ps-Solomon throughout the second part of the book (chaps. 10-19) for the Israelites of the Exodus generation.[8] This may be contrasted, for example, to the "nations" (ἔθνος), a title that is consistently applied to the enemies of God's people.[9] Likewise, σπέρμα also describes the inhabitants of Noah's ark, another beneficiary of divine deliverance, in 14:6.[10] The use of σπέρμα in both 14:6 and 10:15 may then be contrasted to the description of Canaan in 12:11. Here, Canaan is not simply σπέρμα, but "a race *accursed* from the beginning" (σπέρμα γὰρ ἦν κατηραμένον ἀπ᾽ ἀρχῆς). Ps-Solomon's reference to Israel as "holy," "your [God's] people" and "seed" in 10:15, insofar as it serves to contrast Israel and other nations, is a function of the genre of Wisdom literature and is consistent with Ps-Solomon's outlook throughout the book.

We also find Ps-Solomon's bold contrasts in 19:1-9. Many commentators consider this passage to be the final "antithesis" in the book contrasting God's care for the Israelites and his punishment of the Egyptians.[11] In addition, this passage also forms a larger contrast to 18:20-

Sodom and Gomorrah in the Old Testament, Early Jewish and Early Christian Traditions (Kampen: J. H. Kok, 1990) 77-79; T. D. Alexander, "Lot's Hospitality: A Clue to His Righteousness," *JBL* 104 (1985) 289-91. *Pirqe R. El.* 25 and *Gen. Rab.* 49:13 seem to explain Lot's righteousness on the basis of the dialogue between Abraham and the angels in Gen 18:23-32. The "righteous" on whose behalf Abraham asks for mercy is understood to be Lot.

[7]Other instances in the Wisdom of Solomon are 3:9 (2); 4:15 (2); 6:10; 7:27; 18:1, 5, 9. In the last three verses just cited, God's holy people are explicitly contrasted to idolaters. See also ὁσιότης 2:22; 5:19; 9:3; 14:30 and ὁσίως 6:10.

[8]12:19; 15:14; 16:2, 20; 18:7, 13; 19:5, 22. Cf. G. Ziener, *Begriffssprache*, 80.

[9]See 12:12 (Canaanites); 14:11 and 15:15 (nations that practice idolatry). The relevant passages in the first part of the book are 3:8; 6:2; 8:14. "As one nation" (πανεθνεί), however, does describe the Exodus community in Wis 19:8, but see the discussion in Part II under #17, pp. 123ff.

[10]See remarks on κλύδων below (19:7) regarding the connection between the Flood and the Exodus.

[11]For Winston, for example, this is the seventh such contrast (224, 323), as it is for J. Marböck ("'Denn in allem, Herr, hast du dein Volk großgemacht!' Weish 18,5-19,22 und die Botschaft der Sapientia Salomonis," *Lehrerin der Gerechtigkeit: Studien zum Buch der Weisheit* [eds. G. Hentschel and E. Zenger; ETS 19; Leipzig: Benno, 1991] 158) and Schwenk-Bressler (*Sapientia Salomonis*, 47). For Reider (215), it is the fifth contrast, as it is for A. G. Wright ("The Structure of the Book of Wisdom," *Bib* 48 [1967] 169, and

25, where the Israelites are preserved in the desert despite their egregious rebellion (cf. Num 16:41-50). But whereas God remains faithful to his people even in the midst of their disobedience (18:20-25), nothing can save the Egyptians from God's wrath (19:1-5). With respect to 19:1a specifically, we see another example of the broad stokes and bold colors with which Ps-Solomon paints the Egyptians: *But the ungodly were assailed to the end by merciless anger* (Τοῖς δὲ ἀσεβέσιν μέχρι τέλους ἀνελεήμων θυμὸς ἐπέστη).[12] As the remainder of vv. 1-9 shows, the "end" to which the ungodly were assailed certainly refers to the death of the Egyptians in the sea. By referring to the Egyptians as "the ungodly" (ἀσεβής), Ps-Solomon begins this pericope in the same way he began his discussion of 10:15-21, with a clear example of his uncompromising moral categories.

Ps-Solomon's use of certain words and phrases to contrast Israel to her enemies is a noticeable feature not only in 10:15-21 and 19:1-9, but throughout the entire book. He accomplishes this in two ways. First, in chaps. 10-19, he describes the Israelites of biblical times in ways that are similar, if not identical, to his description of the "godly" (his Jewish contemporaries) in chaps. 1-9, thereby establishing some sort of identification between the two groups. He then uses a different set of terms to describe the Egyptians of chaps. 10-19 (and the other enemies of the Exodus generation, i.e., the Canaanites of chap. 12 and idolaters of chaps. 13-15), which parallels his description of the "ungodly" (persecutors of the Jews) in chaps. 1-9. This identification in similar language of the Israelites and Egyptians in chaps. 10-19 with, respectively, the "godly" and "ungodly" in chaps. 1-9 leads to the conclusion that the description of the deliverance of God's people from her "enemies" in chaps. 1-9 is an attempt on Ps-Solomon's part to recontextualize the Exodus for his audience. In other words, the "departure" (ἔξοδος, 3:2; 7:6) of the godly from this life to the next in chaps. 1-9 is for Ps-Solomon an "Exodus;" it is another example of God's faithfulness in bringing his people out of oppression into the "promised land," in this case, immortality.[13] This thematic connection has been suggested by some, particularly G. Ziener[14] and J. M. Reese,[15] but

---

"Numerical Patterns in the Book of Wisdom," *CBQ* 29 [1967] 227).

[12]Deane perceptively shows how 19:1a explicitly contrasts God's punishment of the Egyptians to his care for the Israelites in 18:20, where God's anger against Israel in the desert is said to last "only for a while" (οὐκ ἐπὶ πολὺ ἔμεινεν ἡ ὀργή) (214). This contrast is suggested by δέ in 19:1. In 16:5, God's wrath is also said to be temporary (οὐ μέχρι τέλους ἔμεινεν ἡ ὀργή σου) against the Israelites in the desert.

[13]See, too, my comments in Part III, pp. 145-47.

[14]*Begriffssprache*, 95-96. See also, G. Ziener, *Das Buch der Weisheit* (Düsseldorf:

neither one develops thoroughly Ps-Solomon's consistent use of vocabulary throughout the book in an effort to establish this thematic connection more clearly.

A second means whereby Ps-Solomon contrasts the two groups of people is by using the same term to describe both groups, but, with the help of certain modifiers, in exactly the opposite way. For example, the Israelites are a "*holy* seed" (10:15), but the Canaanites are an "*accursed* seed" (12:11).

An exhaustive examination of Ps-Solomon's vocabulary throughout the entire book is justified, but would go far beyond the boundaries of this study. Therefore, in drawing out these two methods of contrasting the "good" and the "bad" in the Wisdom of Solomon, I will restrict myself to the two pericopes under consideration, 10:15-21 and 19:1-9, both of them rich in contrasting imagery.[16] Also, what follows summarizes and extends at several points the discussion in Part II.

Patmos, 1970) 125.

[15]*Hellenistic Influence,* 122-45. Similar comments, albeit in passing, are made by Y. Amir, "Measure for Measure," 37, and "The Figure of Death," 172; J. M. Reese, "Plan and Structure in the Book of Wisdom," *CBQ* 27 (1965) 398; M. Kolarcik, *The Ambiguity of Death,* 61; 84-85; 111-13, and "Creation and Salvation," 97-107; R. E. Murphy, *Seven Books of Wisdom* (Milwaukee: Bruce, 1960) 130-31, and "'To Know Your Might,'" 91-92; P. Beauchamp, "Le salut corporal," 491-526, esp. 497; Heinisch, 191; M. Dell 'Omo, "Creazione," 320-22; M. Gilbert, "Sagesse de Salomon," 90-91. To these modern treatments, one may also add *m. Pesaḥ.* 10.5: "In every generation a man must so regard himself as if he came forth himself out of Egypt" (H. Danby, *The Mishnah* [Oxford: Clarendon, 1933] 151). In contrast, note the negative opinion of S. S. Stuart: "The Exodus has virtually no function in Wisd 1:1-10:15" ("The Exodus Literature in Late Jewish and Early Christian Literature. A General Survey on the Literature and a Particular Analysis of the Wisdom of Solomon, II Esdras, and the Epistle to the Hebrews" [Ph.D. diss.; Vanderbilt University, 1973] 114). Stuart concedes, however, that there are "perhaps allusions to the Exodus theme" in part one of Wisdom, but nothing that "specifically calls to mind the Exodus" (52). I and others contend, however, that it is precisely these many allusions to the Exodus in part one that in fact serve to call to mind the Exodus.

[16]My work here has been greatly aided by the concordance/dictionary compiled by Eugen Gärtner, although an updated effort with fewer errors would be welcome (*Komposition und Wortwahl des Buches der Weisheit* [Berlin: Mayer & Müller, 1912] 107-229).

10:15-21

10:15

λαός/ἔθνος- These words are used throughout the book to contrast God's
  people (12:19; 15:14; 16:2, 20; 18:7, 13; 19:5, 22) to the enemies of
  God's people (3:8; 6:2; 8:14; 12:12; 14:11; 15:15).

ὅσιος- This is typically used throughout the book to describe the "godly"
  of chaps. 1-9 and the Israelites of chaps. 10-19 (3:9 [2]; 4:15 [2];
  6:10; 7:27; 18:1, 5, 9). See also ὁσιότης (2:22; 5:19; 9:3; 14:30)
  and ὁσίως (6:10). This word appears again in 10:17.

σπέρμα- The "holy seed" (cf. 14:6 and the children of Noah) here contrasts
  with the "accursed" (κατηραμένον) seed of the Canaanites in 12:11.
  See also 3:16 and the seed "of an unlawful union" (παρανόμου
  κοίτης σπέρμα).

θλίβω- This word occurs elsewhere only in 5:1 and refers to the
  oppressors of the righteous man. Both the Israelites of the Exodus
  and the righteous of Ps-Solomon's own day were "oppressed."

10:16

εἰσέρχομαι- Wisdom is said here to "enter Moses." This contrasts to 1:4
  where, "Wisdom will not enter a deceitful soul" (εἰς κακότεχνον
  ψυχὴν οὐκ εἰσελεύσεται σοφία).

θεραπών- Both Moses here and Aaron (18:21) are referred to as
  "servants." See also the verb θεραπεύω in 10:9 introducing Ps-
  Solomon's comments on Jacob.

ἀνθίστημι- That Wisdom is said to "withstand" kings during the plagues is
  consistent with what Ps-Solomon says in 11:3 and 18:21 about the
  Israelites resisting their enemies in the desert. This also contrasts
  nicely to 11:21 and 12:12. Having reviewed the plagues upon the
  Egyptians (11:15-20), Wis 11:21 asks the rhetorical question, "who
  can withstand (ἀντιστήσεται) the might of your arm?" In 12:12 we
  see another rhetorical question, this time following upon a
  condemnation of the Canaanites: "who will resist (ἀντιστήσεται)
  your judgment?" The contrast between the Israelites and her
  enemies is evident: Israel by God's strength resists her enemies, but
  her enemies cannot resist God.

φοβερός- Although this is the only occurrence of the adjective, the
  punishment of "dread kings" here in the plagues may be compared to

the fear that "dread monarchs" (τύραννοι φρίκτοι) have for the Solomonic king in 8:15.

τέρας- "Signs" also describes the plague of darkness in 17:15 and the miracles at the sea in 19:8.

10:17

ὅσιος- See appendix above on 10:15.

μίσθος- The wages Israel received upon leaving Egypt may be understood as an adumbration of the final reward, i.e., immortality, of the godly in 2:22 and 5:15. There are no other instances of this word in the book. This use of μίσθος supports the notion that the Exodus is depicted by Ps-Solomon as a type of immortality.[17]

κοπός- The only other use of this word is in 3:11 (πόνος is the preferred reading in 10:10): whereas the Israelites receive their due compensation for their years of servitude, the labors of the ungodly are unprofitable (οἱ κόποι ἀνόνητοι).

ὁδηγέω- As Wisdom guided Israel through the sea, she also guided Jacob in his flight from Esau (10:10), and "Solomon" in his effort to rule justly (9:11).

ὁδός- This word also occurs in an Exodus context in 19:7 (see below), calling the departure from Egypt "an unhindered way out of the Red Sea" (ἐξ ἐρυθρᾶς θαλάσσης ὁδὸς ἀνεμπόδιστος). Likewise, in 14:3, God safely guides a vessel by providing for it a "way in the sea" (ἐν θαλάσσῃ ὁδόν), which is to be read in conjunction with God's guidance of the ark (14:6-7). These "ways" of deliverance may be contrasted with idolatry as "paths of error" (τῶν πλάνης ὁδῶν) in 12:24. God's way brings his people to deliverance, yet the way of the ungodly leads to punishment.

θαυμαστός- The only other occurrence is the similar context of 19:8.

φλόγα ἄστρων- The contrast here is with 17:5, as discussed under #3.

10:18

θάλασσα/ὕδωρ- Both words appear together also in 5:22. In both passages, sea and water are at God's disposal, either for the punishment of the ungodly (5:22) or for the deliverance of the Israelites (10:18; see also 19:7). 5:15-23 as a whole, where creation is called upon to fight the enemies of God's people, is an

---

[17]See also Reese's comment: "The reward given to the chosen people at the Exodus serves as a type of the eternal reward of the just" (*Hellenistic Influence*, 126).

explicit example of the recontextualization of creation imagery (16:24-29; 19:6).

10:19

ἐχθρός- Ps-Solomon's evaluation of Egypt as Israel's ἐχθρός is consistent with what he says throughout the second part of the book. Contrasting Israel to her "enemies" is a frequent occurrence in Wis 10:15-19:22. Along with 10:19, seven other passages in part two (11:5; 15:14; 16:4, 8, 22; 18:7, 10) refer to Egypt as ἐχθρός. Also, 11:3 refers to the enemies in the desert, while 12:20, 22 and 24 refer to idolaters. The word is used once in part one (5:17) to describe the enemies of the Lord who are repulsed by the power of creation.[18]

κατακλύζω- The word is used elsewhere only in 10:4 to describe the Flood in Noah's day. See comments on κλύδων below under 19:7.

10:20

δίκαιος/ἀσεβής- Mention of the righteous and the ungodly in vv. 19b-20a helps put these verses in their broader context of 10:15-19:22. The Israelites as δίκαιοι are mentioned in the context of the desert (11:14 and 18:20), the conquest (12:9), and the plagues (16:17, 23; 18:7). As we have here in 10:20 δίκαιος and ἀσεβής are explicitly contrasted in 11:9-14, 12:9, and 16:16-18. The "ungodly" also refer to the Egyptians in 19:1 and idolaters in 14:16. With the close juxtaposition of the "righteous" and the "ungodly," we see a clear example of our author's contrasting portrayal of Israel and her enemies.

χείρ- The use of "hand" in v. 20c is another example of our author's attempt to contrast God's people with her enemies. In 19:8 "hand" is also used with reference to the Exodus. Its use in 14:6 with reference to Noah helps establish the connection between the Exodus and the Flood (see comments on κλύδων below under 19:7). Finally, in 11:1, we read, "She [=wisdom] prospered their works [those wandering in the desert] by the hand of a holy prophet [=Moses] (ἐν χειρὶ προφήτου ἁγίου)." This use of χείρ highlights God's salvific activity and contrasts in two ways with its use

---

[18]H. Eising connects ἐχθρός to related terms found throughout the Book of Wisdom: ἁμαρτωλός, ἀσεβής, ἄνομος, and ἄδικος ("Die theologische Geschichtsbetrachtung im Weisheitsbuch," *Vom Wort des Lebens: Festschrift für Max Meinertz* [ed. N. Adler; Münster: Aschendorffsche Verlagsbuchhandlung, 1951] 33).

elsewhere in 10:15-19:22. First, whereas God's hand delivers Israel, God's hand punishes the ungodly (11:17 and 16:15). Second, whereas God has "hands," idols do not (13:19 and 15:15).

ὁμοθυμαδόν- Whereas the Israelites here praise God "with one accord" at the sea for their deliverance, the Egyptians at the sea meet their doom "with one accord" (18:5).

10:21

στόμα/γλῶσσα- Both words also appear in 1:11. The mouth and tongues of the Israelites are made to praise God at the sea, but those of the ungodly engage in "slander" (καταλαλιᾶς) and "lying" (καταψευδόμενον). Also in 1:11, the ungodly are said to "murmur" (γογγυσμός), which recalls the murmuring of the Exodus generation. (Γογγυσμός is used in Exod 16:7-12; Num 17:5, 10; see also Sir 46:7. The cognates γόγγυσις and γογγύζω are also used of the Exodus generation in Exod 16:7; 17:3; Num 11:1; 14:27-29; 16:41; 17:5; LXX Ps 105:25.)

νήπιος- For God's people, even the infants are accorded special abilities: they sing as do the adults. These "babes" who praised YHWH at the sea are to be contrasted to the Egyptian infants who die in the tenth plague (18:5-19). Furthermore, whereas the babes of God's people are given special care, it is their adult enemies who are said to act like babes by oppressing God's people (15:14) or worshipping idols (12:24).

19:1-9

19:1

ἀσεβής- See appendix above on 10:20.

ἀνελεήμων- God's "merciless" punishment of the Egyptians may be compared to the Canaanites' merciless slaughter of their children in 12:5, the only other use of this term in the book.

μέχρι τέλους- Whereas God's anger against the Egyptians brought about their ultimate demise (16:5), God's anger (ὀργή) against Israel in 19:1 did not remain "to the end" (οὐ μέχρι τέλους ἔμεινεν). This phrase occurs nowhere else in the book. As mentioned above, God's punishment of the Egyptians here is to be contrasted directly to

18:20 where God's anger against Israel in the desert "did not continue for long" (οὐκ ἐπὶ πολὺ ἔμεινεν).

θυμός- This describes God's attitude toward the ungodly in 11:18 as well. God's wrath against the Israelites, however, although real, is not lasting (16:5 and 18:21; see previous comment on μέχρι τέλους).

ἐφίστημι- This word occurs only in 6:5 and 8 where God's judgment is said to come upon haughty rulers. In 19:1, God's judgment comes upon the Egyptians. This reinforces the notion of the recontextualization of the Exodus theme in chaps. 1-9: in both 6:5/8 and 19:1, the oppressors of God's people are punished. In this sense, the rulers of the first part of the book may be thought of as Pharaoh figures.

19:2-3

διώκω- Egypt is said to be pursued by "God's justice" (δίκη) in 11:20 and by rain and hail in 16:16. Whereas God's pursuit achieves its goal, the Egyptians in 19:2-3 make an aborted attempt at pursuing those who are under God's care.

19:3

πένθος- This word appears elsewhere only in 14:15 where a father, grieving for his dead child, makes an idolatrous image of the child. In 19:3, the Egyptians are also lamenting the death of their children. Furthermore, as the Egyptian oppressors were punished with death, not only in the tenth plague but at the sea as well, the oppressors of the ungodly in the first part of the book are also punished by death (chaps. 3-4, esp. 4:18-19).

ἐπισπάω- This verb is used twice, here and in 1:12. Reese has commented that this rare compound serves to "tie the entire exhortation [i.e., the book] together."[19] Both the ungodly of 1:12 and the Egyptians of 19:3 "bring on" their own destruction, the former by the conduct of their lives and the latter by pursuing the Egyptians.

λογισμὸς ἀνοίας- The "foolish reasoning" of the Egyptians to pursue the Israelites compares nicely to the "perverse thoughts" (σκολιοὶ...λογισμοὶ) of the ungodly in 1:3 and their "foolish

---

[19]Reese, 196. There is a typographical error, however, in attributing the first instance of this compound to 1:2 rather than 1:12. Reese (*Hellenistic Influence*, 139) and Gregg (181) also connect the "foolish decision" of 19:3 to the "counsel of folly" (σκολιοὶ λογισμοὶ) of 1:3.

thoughts" (λογισμῶν ἀσυνέτων) in 1:5. See also the "foolish and wicked thoughts" (λογισμῶν ἀσυνέτων ἀδικίας) of idolaters in 11:15, and the irascible wickedness of the Canaanites in 12:10. Throughout the book, Ps-Solomon portrays the enemies of God's people as displaying faulty reasoning. Also, ἀνοία is used elsewhere only in 15:18 regarding idolatry.

φυγάς- Jacob, too, is described as a fugitive from his brother Esau (10:10). The only other use of φυγάς (17:2) turns the tables on the Egyptians: in the plague of darkness, Ps-Solomon describes the Egyptians as "exiles from eternal providence" (φυγάδες τῆς αἰωνίου προνοίας). The verb φεύγω describes Lot's flight from Sodom (10:6). But whereas Lot's flight brings safety, we read in 16:15 that it is impossible for the ungodly to escape (φυγεῖν) from God's hand.

19:4

ἄχιος- As Egypt is worthy of its watery fate in 19:4, Israel's enemies meet a similarly "worthy" punishment in 1:16 (covenant with death) and in 12:26 and 15:6 (idolaters). The same word is also used to describe Egypt's punishment in the plagues in 16:9 and 18:4. God's people, on the other hand, are said to be "worthy of God" (3:5 and 6:16).

ἀνάγκη- This word occurs elsewhere only in 17:17 where it describes the Egyptian fate in the ninth plague.

βάσανος- Egypt is likewise the object of God's torment in 17:13. Torment, however, will never touch the righteous (3:1), regardless of the attempts of the ungodly (2:19). See also the verb βασανίζω and the torment of the ungodly Egyptians in 11:9, 16:1 and 4, and of the idolaters in 12:23.

κόλασις- Egypt is also said to receive punishment in 11:13, 16:2 and 24. See also the verb κολάζω where Egypt (11:5, 8, 15-16; 16:1, 9; 18:11, 22) and idolaters (14:10) are punished (also 12:14, 15, 27). God's people by contrast, although punished before men, have the hope of immortality (3:4).

19:5

λαός- See appendix above on 10:15.

παράδοξος- Describing Israel's journey through the sea as "incredible"
compares to the behavior of the elements in the plagues in 16:17, the
only other use of this word.

ὁδοιπορία- The same word is used for the Exodus (or perhaps the desert
wanderings) in 18:3.

πειράζω- The Israelites experience deliverance through the sea, but the
ungodly in 2:24 experience death.[20] Idolaters in 12:26 will be sure
to experience God's punishment.   By contrast, the Israelites
experience of death in the desert (18:20-21) was only temporary.

19:6

κτίσις- God's use of creation to repulse Israel's enemies is also found in
5:17 and 16:24. The ungodly by contrast attempt to use creation,
ironically the very means of their impending punishment, for their
own godless purpose (2:6).

ὑπηρετέω- Creation also obeys God's commands in the plagues (16:21,
24, 25).

ἐπιταγή- The plague of death also occurs at God's command (18:16).

παῖς- God's people are his children/servants in 2:13; 9:4; 12:7 and 20.

φυλάσσω- As God guards Israel here, he also kept Abraham safe in his
ordeal with Isaac (10:5) and "Solomon" in his effort to be a just
ruler (9:11). See also Adam (10:1) and Jacob (10:12), both of whom
are protected (διαφυλάσσω) by Wisdom.

19:7

ἐρυθρᾶς θαλάσσης- The phrase is used elsewhere only in 10:17.

ὁδός- See appendix above on 10:17.

ἀνεμπόδιστος- Israel's unhindered way through the sea may be an implicit
contrast to the Egyptians' hindered crossing (Exod 14:25). This
word also describes the ability of the "whole world" (ὅλος κόσμος)
to maintain normal activities while Egypt was shrouded in darkness
(17:20).

κλύδων- Ps-Solomon seems to make a typological connection between the
Red Sea and the Flood. The noun κλύδων is used only twice, in 19:7

---

[20]See also A. M. Dubarle, "La tention diabolique (πειράζω) dans le livre de la Sagesse
(2,24)," *Mélanges Eugène Tisserant* (Citte del Vaticano: Biblioteca Apostolica Vaticina,
1964) 187-95, and S. Lyonnet, "Le sens de πειράζειν en Sap. 2.24 et la doctrine du péché
original," *Bib* 39 (1938) 27-33. Dubarle offers a defense for reading 2:24 not as "they [the
people] experienced it [death]," but as "they [evil angels] tempted it [the world (κόσμος)]."

to describe the Red Sea, and in 14:5 concerning the raft (σχεδία) by which even the unskilled may safely put to sea and pass through the κλύδωνα. The point of 14:1-5 is not merely to discuss sea travel, but to show Wisdom to be the "craftswoman" (τεχνῖτις[21] according to whose purpose (14:5) ships safely make their way through the waves (14:3). In this respect, both the "raft" of 14:2 (σχεδία) and the ark of 14:6 (also called σχεδία,[22] its only other use in the book) are "guided" on their journeys (διακυβερνάω in 14:3; κυβερνάω,[23] in 14:6 and elsewhere only in 10:4 regarding the ark), albeit for very different purposes. This at least suggests that Ps-Solomon sees a typological connection between the waters of the Flood and the Red Sea. This Flood/Exodus connection finds further support in 10:19a where Wisdom is said have *drowned her enemies* (τοὺς δὲ ἐχθροὺς αὐτῶν κατέκλυσαν). Ps-Solomon is the lone extant witness to use κατακλύζω ("to Flood") to describe the Egyptians' death at the sea.[24] His only other use of this verb is in 10:4, where he refers to the Flood in Noah's day: "Because of him [=Cain] the earth was Flooded" (δι' ὃν κατακλυζομένην γῆν). The fact that κατακλύζω/κλύδων are used in the book to describe both the Flood and the Red Sea, coupled with the fact that nowhere else in the LXX is either event described by these words,[25] indicates that Ps-Solomon sees a typological connection between Noah's deliverance from the Flood and Israel's from Egypt: the enemies of both were "flooded" by water.[26]

---

[21]Both Reese (*Hellenistic Influence*, 7, 46, 131) and Winston (264-65) attribute Ps-Solomon's description of Wisdom as a "craftswoman" to Hellenistic influence.

[22]Note also Reese's comment: "σχεδία is literally 'raft,' but its use to describe Noah's ark becomes intelligible to the reader who knows that Homer uses this word for the bark used by Odysseus to escape from the Calypso" (*Hellenistic Influence*, 5).

[23]J. S. Kloppenburg argues that the use of κυβερνάω is another example of the influence of the Isis myth on Ps-Solomon's description of Wisdom ("Isis and Sophia," 69-70).

[24]Exod 15:4 has the verb טבע/καταποντίζω, "to sink" or "throw into the sea."

[25]The cognate κατακλυσμός, to be sure, describes the flood in Gen 6:17; 7:6, 7, 10, 17; 9:11 (2), 15, 28; 10:1, 32; 11:10. Nowhere, however, in the LXX does this cognate describe the death of the Egyptians at the sea. This fact highlights Ps-Solomon's intentional juxtaposition of these two events.

[26]On this connection, see also J. D. Levenson, *Creation and the Persistence of Evil: The Jewish Drama of Divine Omnipotence* (San Francisco: Harper and Row, 1985) 66-77, esp. 75-77. M. Gilbert sees 14:3b as an allusion to the crossing of the sea (*La critique des dieux dans le Livre de la Sagesse [Sg 13-15]* [AnBib 53; Rome: Biblical Institute Press, 1973] 104-9). J. Fichtner attributes Ps-Solomon's word choice to the influence of prophetic literature, which eschatologized the Exodus and Wilderness periods, citing Jer

19:8

διέρχομαι- Like κλύδων, this word occurs in 14:5 and further establishes
the Exodus/Flood connection. Its only other occurrence in the book
is in 5:10 and describes the transient prosperity of the ungodly as "a
ship that sails through the billowy water" (ὡς ναῦς διερχομένη
κυμαινόμενον ὕδωρ).

σκεπάζω- God's protection of Israel here compares nicely to Wisdom's
protection of the godly against their oppressors in, once again, 5:16,
a passage rich in Exodus imagery. The word occurs nowhere else.

χείρ- See appendix above on 10:20.

θαυμαστός- This word occurs only in the similar context of 10:17.

τέρας- See appendix above on 10:16.

19:9

αἰνέω- This word occurs elsewhere only in 10:20.

ῥύομαι- This word also describes the Exodus in 10:15 as well as Israel's
protection in the plagues in 16:8. It is also used to describe the
deliverance of Lot (10:6), Jacob (10:9), Joseph (10:13), and the
Israelites from the plagues (16:8). Its only appearance in chapters 1-
9 is in 2:18, where it describes the deliverance of the righteous man
from his adversaries.

29:2 (MT 47:2); Isa 13:11-13; 38:22; Dan (Theod) 11:10, 22, 26, where κατακλύζω is
used ("Der AT-Text," 176). Although this probably does not account for Ps-Solomon's
word choice entirely, it is interesting to consider Fichtner's comment in light of Ps-
Solomon's eschatological recontextualization of the Exodus for his readers.

Bibliography

Ackerman, J. "The Literary Context of Moses' Birth Story [Exodus 1-2]." *Literary Interpretations of Biblical Narratives*, eds. K. G. Louis, J. Ackerman, and T. S. Warshaw, 74-119. Nashville: Abingdon, 1974.

Aland, K. et al., eds. *The Greek New Testament*. 3rd edition. United Bible Societies, 1975.

Albeck, Ch. and Theodor, J. *Midrash Bereshit Rabbah*. 3 vols. Jerusalem: Wahrmann, 1965.

Alexander, T. D. "Lot's Hospitality: A Clue to his Righteousness." *JBL* 104 (1985) 289-91.

Alt, A. et al., eds. *Biblia Hebraica Stuttgartensia*. Stuttgart: Deutsche Bibelgesellschaft, 1984.

Amir, Y. "Authority and Interpretation of Scripture in the Writings of Philo." *Mikra: Reading, Translation and Interpretation of the Hebrew Bible in Ancient Judaism and Early Christianity*, ed. J. M. Mulder, 421-53. CRINT 2/1. Philadelphia: Fortress, 1990.

____. "Measure for Measure in Talmudic Literature and in the Wisdom of Solomon." *Justice and Righteousness: Biblical Themes and Their Influence*, eds. H. G. Reventlow and Y. Hoffman, 29-46. JSOTSup 137. Sheffield: JSOT, 1992.

____. "The Figure of Death in the 'Book of Wisdom.'" *JJS* 30 (1979) 154-78. Reprinted in *Studien zum antiken Judentum*, ed. Y. Amir. Frankfurt am Main/New York: Peter Lang, 1985.

Anderson, B. W., ed. *Creation in the Old Testament*. IRT 6; Philadelphia: Fortress/London: SPCK, 1984.

Anderson, G. "The Interpretation of the Purification Offering (חטאת) in the *Temple Scroll* (11QTemple) and Rabbinic Literature." *JBL* 111 (1992) 17-35.

____. "Sacrifice and Sacrifical Offerings." *ABD* 5.870-86.

Antoine, P. "Sagesse palestinienne et sagesse alexandrine." *Revue apologétique* 50 (1930) 531-48.

Bamberger, B. J. "The Dating of Aggadic Materials." *JBL* 68 (1949) 115-23.

Barclay, J. M. G. *Jews in the Mediterranean Diaspora: From Alexander to Trajan (323 BCE - 117 CE)*. Edinburgh: T & T Clark, 1996.

Barthélemy, D. and Rickenbacher, O. *Konkordanz zum Hebräischen Sirach, mit Syrisch-Hebräischem Index*. Göttingen: Vandenhoeck & Ruprecht, 1973.

Barton, J. *Oracles of God: Perceptions of Ancient Prophecy in Israel after the Exile*. London: Darton, Longman and Todd, 1986.

____. *Reading the Old Testament: Method in Biblical Study*. Philadelphia: Westminster, 1984.

Baskin, J. R. *Pharaoh's Counsellors: Job, Jethro, and Balaam in Rabbinic and Patristic Tradition*. BJS 47. Chico: Scholars Press, 1983.

Basser, H. W. *Midrashic Interpretations of the Song of Moses*. New York: Peter Lang, 1984.

Bauer, W. *A Greek-English Lexicon of the New Testament and Other Early Christian Literature*. Translated by Arndt, W. F. and Gingrich, F. W. 2nd revised edition. Chicago: University of Chicago Press, 1979.

Beaucamp, E. *Man's Destiny in the Books of Wisdom.* Staten Island, N.Y.: Alba House, 1970.

———. *The Bible and the Universe: Israel and the Theology of History.* Translated by D. Balhatchet. London: Burns & Oates, 1963.

Beauchamp, P. "Èpouser la Sagesse—ou n'épouser qu'elle? Une énigme du Livre de la Sagesse." *La Sagesse de l'Ancien Testament: Nouvelle édition mise à jour,* ed. M. Gilbert, 347-69. BETL 51. 2nd edition. Gembloux, Belgium: Leuven University Press, 1990.

———. "La cosmologie religieuse de Philon et la lecture de l'Exode par le Livre de la Sagesse: le thème de la manne." *Philon d'Alexandrie. Colloques Nationaux du Centre National de la Recherche Scientifique,* 207-18. Paris: Centre National de la Recherche Scientifique, 1967.

———. "Le salut corporel des justes et la conclusion du livre de la Sagesse." *Bib* 45 (1964) 491-526.

———. "Typologie et 'figures du lecteur.'" *RSR* 78 (1990) 221-32.

Beentjes, P. C. *The Book of Ben Sira in Hebrew: A Text Edition of all Extant Hebrew Manuscripts and a Synopsis of All Parallel Hebrew Ben Sira Texts.* VTSup 68. Leiden: E. J. Brill, 1997.

———. "'You Have Given a Road in the Sea.' What is Wisdom 14,3 Talking About?" *ETL* 68 (1992) 137-41.

Beer, G. *Exodus.* HAT 1, Reihe 3. Tübingen: JCB Mohr (Paul Siebeck), 1939.

Belkin, S. *Philo and the Oral Law: The Philonic Interpretation of Biblical Law in Relation to the Palestinian Halakah.* HSS 11. New York: Johnson Reprint, 1968.

Ben-Ḥayyim, Z. *Tibat Marqe: A Collection of Samaritan Midrashim.* Jerusalem, 1988.

Berwick, W. P. "The Way of Salvation in the Book of Wisdom." Ph.D. diss., Boston University, 1957.

Bissell, E. C. *The Apocrypha of the Old Testament.* New York: Charles Scribner's Sons, 1880.

Blass, F. and Debrunner, A. *A Greek Grammar of the New Testament and Other Early Christian Literature.* Translated by A. Funk. Chicago: University of Chicago Press, 1961.

Blenkinsopp, J. *Wisdom and Law in the Old Testament: The Ordering of Life in Israel and Early Judaism.* Oxford: Oxford University Press, 1983.

Blidstein, G. J. "The Importance of Early Rabbinic Writings for an Understanding of Judaism in the Hellenistic-Roman Period." *Jewish Civilization in the Hellenistic-Roman Period,* ed. S. Talmon, 64-72. Philadelphia: Trinity Press International, 1991.

Bloch, R. "Ecriture et tradition dans le judaïsme: aperçus sur l'origine du Midrash." *CaSi* 1 (1954) 9-34.

———. "Midrash." *DBSup* 5. Paris: Letouzey & Ané, 1950. Reprinted in *Theory and Practice. Approaches to Ancient Judaism,* ed. W. S. Green, 29-50, vol. 1. Translated by M. H. Callaway. Missoula: Scholars Press, 1978.

———. "Note méthodologique pour l'étude de la littérature rabbinique." *RSR* 43 (1955) 194-227. Reprinted in *Theory and Practice. Approaches to Ancient Judaism,* ed. W. S. Green, 51-75, vol. 1. Translated by W. S. Green. Missoula: Scholars Press, 1978.

———. "Quelques aspects de la figure de Moïse dans la tradition rabbinique." *Moïse: L'Homme de l'Alliance,* ed. H. Cazelles, 93-167. Paris: Desclée, 1955.

Boccaccini, G. *Middle Judaism: Jewish Thought, 300 B. C. E. to 200 C. E.* Minneapolis: Fortress, 1991.

Bokser, B. M. "Recent Developments in the Study of Judaism 70-200 C.E." *Second Century* 3/1 (1983) 1-68.

Boman, T. *Hebrew Thought Compared with Greek.* Translated by J. L. Moreau. New York: Norton, 1970.

Bousset, W. *Jüdisch-Christlicher Schulbetreib in Alexandria und Rom: Literarische Untersuchungen zu Philo und Clemens von Alexandria, Justin und Irenäus.* Göttingen: Vandenhoeck & Ruprecht, 1915.

Bowker, J. *The Targums and Rabbinic Literature: An Introduction to Jewish Interpretations of Scripture.* Cambridge: Cambridge University Press, 1969.

Bowman, J. "The Exegesis of the Pentateuch among the Samaritans and among the Rabbis." *OTS* 8, ed. P. A. H. DeBoer, 220-62. Leiden: E. J. Brill, 1950.

Boyarin, D. "Re-citing the Torah: Toward a Theory of Midrash." *Orim* 3 (1988) 22-30.

____. *Intertextuality and the Reading of Midrash.* Bloomington: Indiana University Press, 1990.

Braude, W. G. *Pesikta Rabbati.* 2 vols. New Haven: Yale University Press, 1968.

____. *The Midrash on Psalms.* 2 vols. New Haven: Yale University Press, 1959.

Brenton, L. C. L. *The Septuagint Version, Greek and English.* Reprint of 1844 edition. Grand Rapids: Zondervan, 1970.

Broekhoven, H. van. "Wisdom and World: The Functions of Wisdom Imagery in Sirach, Pseudo-Solomon and Colossians." Ph.D. diss., Boston University, 1988.

Brown, F., Driver, S. R., and Briggs, C. A. *The New Brown-Driver-Briggs-Gesenius Hebrew and English Lexicon with an Appendix Containing the Biblical Aramaic.* Peabody, MA.: Hendrickson, 1979.

Brown, R. E. *The Birth of the Messiah: A Commentary on the Infancy Narratives in Matthew and Luke.* Garden City, N.Y.: G. Chapman, 1977.

Brown, R. "Midrashim as Oral Traditions." *HUCA* 47 (1976) 181-89.

Bruce, F. F. and Rupp, E. G., eds. *Holy Book and Holy Tradition.* Grand Rapids: Eerdmans, 1968.

Bruns, G. L. "Midrash and Allegory: The Beginnings of Scriptural Interpretation." *The Literary Guide to the Bible*, eds. R. Alter and F. Kermode, 625-46. Cambridge: Harvard University Press, 1987.

____. "The Hermeneutics of Midrash." *The Book and the Text: The Bible and Literary Theory*, ed. R. Schwartz, 189-213. Oxford: Basil Blackwell, 1990.

Bückers, H. *Die Unsterblichkeitslehre des Weisheitsbuches: ihr Ursprung und ihre Bedeutung.* Alttestamentliche Abhandlungen 13/4. Münster: Aschendorffschen Verlagsbuchhandlung, 1938.

Burrows, E. "Wisdom X 10." *Bib* 20 (1939) 405-7.

Camps, G. M. "Midrash sobre la historia de les plagues." *Miscellanae Biblica B. Ubach*, 97-113. Montserrati, 1953.

Charlesworth, J. H. *The Pseudepigrapha and Modern Research with A Supplement.* SBLSCS 7. Missoula: Scholars Press, 1981.

____, ed. *The Old Testament Pseudepigrapha.* 2 vols. Garden City, N.Y.: Doubleday, 1983.

Charlesworth, J. H. and Evans, C. A., eds. *The Pseudepigrapha and Early Biblical Interpretation.* JSPSup 14. Sheffield: JSOT, 1993.

Childs, B. "Midrash and the Old Testament." *Understanding the Sacred Text: Essays in Honor of Morton S. Enslin on the Hebrew Bible and Christian Beginnings*, ed. J. Reumann, 45-59. Valley Forge, PA: Judson Press, 1972.

____. "The Birth of Moses." *JBL* 84 (1965) 118-22.

____. *The Book of Exodus*. Philadelphia: Westminster, 1974.

Churton, W. R. *The Uncanonical and Apocryphal Scriptures*. London: J. Whitaker, 1884.

Clark, D. K. "Signs in Wisdom and John." *CBQ* 45 (1983) 201-9.

Clarke, E. G. *Targum Pseudo-Jonathan of the Pentateuch: Text and Concordance*. Hoboken: Ktav, 1984.

____. *The Wisdom of Solomon*. Cambridge: Cambridge University Press, 1973.

Clements, R. *Exodus*. CBC. Cambridge: Cambridge University Press, 1972.

Cogan, M. "A Technical Term for Exposure." *JNES* 27 (1968) 133-35.

Cohen, J. *The Origins and Evolution of the Moses Nativity Story*. Studies in the History of Religions 58. Leiden: E. J. Brill, 1993.

Cohen, N. J. "Analysis of an Exegetic Tradition in the *Mekilta de-Rabbi Ishmael*: The Meaning of *Amanah* in the Second and Third Centuries." *AJSR* 9 (1984) 1-25.

____. "Miriam's Song: A Modern Midrashic Reading." *Judaism* 33 (1984) 179-90.

Collins, J. J. "Apocalyptic Eschatology as the Transcendence of Death." *CBQ* 36 (1974) 21-43.

____. "Cosmos and Salvation: Jewish Wisdom and Apocalyptic in the Hellenistic Age." *HR* 17 (1977) 121-42

____. "The Root of Immortality: Death in the Context of Jewish Wisdom." *HTR* 71/3-4 (1980) 177-82.

Collins, J. J. and Nickelsburg, G. W. E. *Ideal Figures in Ancient Israel: Profiles and Paradigms*. SBLSCS 12. Chico, CA: Scholars Press, 1980.

Colson, F. H. *Philo, With an English Translation*. 11 vols. LCL. Cambridge: Harvard University Press, 1929-64.

Cross, F. M. *Canaanite Myth and Hebrew Epic: Essays in the History of the Religion of Israel*. Cambridge: Harvard University Press, 1973.

Dähne, A. F. *Geschichtliche Darstellung der jüdische-alexandrinischen Religions-Philosophie*. Halle: Buchhandlung der Waisenhauses, 1834.

Dalbert, P. *Die Theologie der hellenistisch-jüdischen Missionsliteratur unter Anschluss von Philo und Josephus*. Hamburg-Volksdorf: H. Reich, 1954.

Danby, H. *The Mishnah: Translated from the Hebrew with Introduction and Brief Explanatory Notes*. Oxford: Clarendon, 1933.

Daube, D. "Alexandrian Methods of Interpretation and the Rabbis." *Festschrift Hans Lewald*, 27-44. Basel: Helbing and Lichtenhahn, 1953. Reprinted in *Essays in Greco-Roman and Related Talmudic Literature*, ed. H. A. Fischel, 165-82. New York: Ktav, 1977.

____. "Rabbinic Methods of Interpretation and Hellenistic Rhetoric." *HUCA* 22 (1949) 239-64.

____. *The Exodus Pattern in the Bible*. Westport, CT: Greenwood, 1979.

____. *The New Testament and Rabbinic Judaism*. Jordan Lectures in Comparative Religion 2. London: University of London, Athlone, 1956.

Davies, G. F. *Israel in Egypt: Reading Exodus 1-2*. JSOT 135. Sheffield: Sheffield University Press, 1992.

Davies, W. D. and Allison, D. C. *The Gospel According to Matthew*. ICC. Edinburgh: T & T Clark, 1988.

Deane, W. J. *The Book of Wisdom*. Oxford: Clarendon, 1881.

Delcor, M. "L'immortalité de l'âme dans le Livre de la Sagesse et dans les documents de Qumrân." *NRT* 77 (1955) 614-30.

Dell 'Omo, M. "Creazione, Storia Della Salvezza e Destino Dell' Uomo." *RevistB* 37 (1989) 317-27.

Delling, G. *Bibliographie zur jüdisch-hellenistischen und intertestamentarischen Literatur 1900-1970*. TU 106. Berlin, 1975.

Des Places, E. "Le Livre de la Sagesse et les influences grecques." *Bib* 4 (1969) 536-42.

____. "Un emprunt de la 'Sagesse' aux 'Lois' de Platon." *Bib* 40 (1959) 1016-17.

Di Lella, A. A. "Conservative and Progressive Theology: Sirach and Wisdom." *CBQ* 28 (1966) 139-54. Reprinted in *Studies in Ancient Israelite Wisdom*, ed. J. L. Crenshaw, 401-16. New York: Ktav, 1976.

Dimant, D. "Literary Typologies and Biblical Interpretations in the Hellenistic-Roman Period." *Jewish Civilization in the Hellenistic-Roman Period*, ed. S. Talmon, 73-80. Philadelphia: Trinity Press International, 1991.

____. "Use and Interpretation of Mikra in the Apocrypha and Pseudepigrapha." *Mikra: Reading, Translation and Interpretation of the Hebrew Bible in Ancient Judaism and Early Christianity*, ed. J. M. Mulder, 379-419. CRINT 2/1. Philadelphia: Fortress, 1990.

Drazin, I. *Targum Onkelos to Exodus: An English Translation of the Text with Analysis and Commentary (Based on the A. Sperber and A. Berliner Editions)*. Denver: Ktav, 1990.

Drubbel, A. "La tension diabolique (πειράζω) dans le livre de la Sagesse (2,24)." *Mélanges Eugène Tisserant*, 187-95. Citte del Vaticano: Biblioteca Apostolica Vaticana, 1964.

____. "Le Conflict entre la Sagesse profane et la Sagesse religieuse." *Bib* 17 (1936) 45-70, 407-28.

____. "Une Source du Livre de la Sagesse." *RSPT* 37 (1953) 425-43.

Dumbrell, W. J. *Covenant and Creation: An Old Testament Covenant Theology*. Grand Rapids: Baker, 1993.

Dunsky, S. *Midrash Rabbah: Shir ha-Shirim*. Jerusalem/Tel Aviv: Dvir, 1980.

Durham, J. I. *Exodus*. WBC 3. Waco: Word, 1987.

Eberlein, K. *Gott der Schöpfer—Israels Gott: Eine exegetische-hermeneutische Studie zur theologischen Funktion alttestamentlicher Schöpfungsaussagen*. Beiträge zur Erforschung des Alten Testaments und des antiken Judentums 5. Frankfurt am Main: Peter Lang, 1986.

Eising, H. "Der Weisheitslehrer und die Götterbilder." *Bib* 40 (1959) 393-408.

____. "Die theologische Geschichtsbetrachtung im Weisheitsbuch." *Vom Wort des Lebens: Festschrift für Max Meinertz*, ed. N. Adler, 28-40. Münster: Aschendorffsche Verlagsbuchhandlung, 1951.

Emerton, J. A. "Commentaries on the Wisdom of Solomon." *Theology* 68 (1965) 376-80.

Enns, P. "A Retelling of the Song at the Sea in Wisdom 10,20-21." *Bib* 76 (1995) 1-24.

____. "Creation and Re-creation: Psalm 95 and Its Interpretation in Hebrews." *WTJ* 55 (1993) 255-80.

____. "The 'Moveable Well' in 1 Cor 10:4: An Extrabiblical Tradition in an Apostolic Text." *Bulletin for Biblical Research* 6 (1996) 23-38.

Epstein, I., ed. *Hebrew-English Edition of the Babylonian Talmud*. Translated by M. Simon. London: Soncino, 1960—.

Evans, C. A. "Luke and the Rewritten Bible: Aspects of Lukan Hagiography." *The Pseudepigrapha and Early Biblical Interpretation.* eds. J. H. Charlesworth and C. A. Evans, 170-201. JSPSup 14/SSEJC 2. Sheffield: JSOT, 1993.

Evans, C. A. and Stinespring, W. F., eds. *Early Jewish and Christian Exegesis: Studies in Memory of William Hugh Brownlee.* Atlanta: Scholars Press, 1987.

Even-Shoshan, A. *New Concordance to the Torah, Nevi'im and Ketuvim.* Jerusalem: Kiryat Sepher, 1983.

Farrar, F. W. *The Wisdom of Solomon. Apocrypha,* ed. H. Wace, 403-584. London: J. Murray, 1888.

Feldmann, F. "Die literarische Art von Weisheit Kap. 10-19." *TGl* 1 (1909) 178-84

_____. *Textkritische Materialien zum Buch der Weisheit.* Freiburg: Herdershe Verlagshandlung, 1902.

Fichtner, J. "Der AT-Text der Sapientia Salomonis." *ZAW* 57 (1939) 155-92.

_____. "Die Stellung Sapientia Salomonis in der Literatur- und Geistesgeschichte ihrer Zeit." *ZNW* 35 (1936) 113-32.

_____. "Zum Problem Glaube und Geschichte in der israelitisch-jüdischen Weisheitsliteratur." *TLZ* 76 (1951) 145-50. Reprinted in *Gottes Weisheit: Gesammelte Studien zum Alten Testament* (J. Fichtner Festschrift), ed. K. D. Fricke, 9-17. Stuttgart: Calver, 1965.

_____. *Weisheit Salomos.* HAT 2, Reihe 6. Tübingen: J. C. B. Mohr, 1938.

Field, F. *Origenis Hexaplorum Quae Supersunt sive Veterum Interpretetum Graecorum in Totem Vetus Testamentum Fragmenta.* 2 vols. Oxford: Clarendon, 1925.

Fields, W. W. *Sodom and Gomorrah: History and Motif in Biblical Narrative.* JSOTSup 231. Sheffield: Sheffield Academic Press, 1997.

Finan, T. "Hellenistic Humanism in the Book of Wisdom." *ITQ* 27/1 (1960) 30-48.

Finkel, J. "The Alexandrian Tradition and the Midrash Ha-Ne`elam." *The Leo Jung Jubilee Volume: Essays in his Honor on the Occasion of his Seventieth Birthday,* eds. M. Kasher, N. Lamm, and L. Rosenfeld, 77-103. New York, 1962.

Finkelstein, L. "The Sources of the Tannaitic Midrashim." *JQR* 31 (1940-41) 211-43.

Fischel, H. A. "The Transformation of Wisdom in the World of Midrash." *Aspects of Wisdom in Judaism and Christianity,* ed. R. L. Wilken, 67-101. Notre Dame: University of Notre Dame Press, 1975.

_____. *Rabbinic Literature and Greco-Roman Philosophy.* Leiden: E. J. Brill, 1973.

_____, ed. *Essays in Greco-Roman and Related Talmudic Literature.* New York: Ktav, 1977.

Fishbane, M. *Biblical Interpretation in Ancient Israel.* Oxford: Clarendon, 1985.

_____. "From Scribalism to Rabbinism: Perspectives on the Emergence of Classical Judaism." *The Sage in Israel and the Ancient Near East,* eds. J. G. Gammie and L. G. Perdue, 439-56. Winona Lake, IN: Eisenbrauns, 1990.

_____. "Torah and Tradition." *Tradition and Theology in the Old Testament,* ed. Douglas A. Knight, 275-300. Philadelphia: Fortress, 1977.

Focke, F. *Die Entstehung der Weisheit Salomos.* FRLANT 5.5. Göttingen: Vandenhoeck & Ruprecht, 1913.

Fraade, S. D. "The Early Rabbinic Sage." *The Sage in Israel and the Ancient Near East,* eds. J. G. Gammie and L. G. Perdue, 417-36. Winona Lake, IN: Eisenbrauns, 1990.

Frankel, I. *Peshat in Talmudic and Midrashic Literature.* Toronto: La Salle, 1956.

Frankfurt, H. *Kingship and the Gods.* Chicago: University of Chicago Press, 1948.

Freedman, H. and Simon, M., eds. *The Midrash Rabbah.* 10 vols. London: Soncino, 1977.

Friedlander, G. *Pirke de-Rabbi Eliezer.* 4th edition. New York: Sepher-Hermon, 1981.

Friedmann, M. *Midrash Pesikta Rabbati.* Tel Aviv, 1962/63.

Gager, J. *Moses in Greco-Roman Paganism.* Nashville: Abingdon, 1972.

Gammie, J. G. "The Sage in Sirach." *The Sage in Israel and the Ancient Near East,* eds. J. G. Gammie and L. G. Perdue, 355-72. Winona Lake, IN: Eisenbrauns, 1990.

Gärtner, E. *Komposition und Wortwahl des Buches der Weisheit.* Berlin: Mayer & Müller, 1912.

Gaster, M. *The Asatir: The Samaritan Book of the "Secrets of Moses."* London: Royal Asiatic Society, 1927.

George, S. "Der Begriff Analogos im Buch der Weisheit." *Parousia: Studien zur Philosophie Platons und zur Problemgeschichte des Platonismus. Festgabe für Johannes Hirschberger,* ed. K. Flasch, 189-97. Frankfurt am Main: Minerva, 1965.

Georgi, D. "Der vorpaulinische Hymnus Phil 2,6-11." *Zeit und Geschichte: Dankesgabe an Rudolf Bultmann zum 80. Geburtstag,* ed. E. Dinkler, 263-93. Tübingen: J. C. B. Mohr (Paul Siebeck), 1964.

____. *Weisheit Salomos.* JSHRZ 3/4. Gütersiohe Verlagshaus Gerd Mohn, 1980.

Gerhardsson, B. *Memory and Manuscript: Oral Tradition and Written Transmission in Rabbinic Judaism and Early Christianity.* Translated by E. Sharpe. Lund: G. W. K. Gleerup, 1961.

Gesenius, W., Kautzsch, E., and Cowley, A. E. *Gesenius' Hebrew Grammar.* 2nd Eng. ed. Oxford: Clarendon, 1910.

Geyer, J. *The Wisdom of Solomon.* London: SCM, 1963.

Gilbert, M. *La critique des dieux dans le Livre de la Sagesse (13-15).* AnBib 53. Rome: Biblical Institute, 1973.

____. *La Sagesse de l'Ancien Testament: Nouvelle édition mise à jour.* BETL 51. 2nd edition. Gembloux, Belgium: Leuven University Press, 1990.

____. "Sagesse de Salomon." *DBSup* 60, 58-119. Paris: Letouzey & Ané, 1986.

____. "Wisdom Literature." *Jewish Writings of the Second Temple Period,* ed. M. E. Stone, 283-324. CRINT 2/2. Philadelphia: Fortress, 1984.

____. "La Relecture de Gn 1-3 dans le Livre de la Sagesse." *La Création dans l'Orient Ancien.* LD 127, eds. P. Beauchamp et al., 323-44. Paris: Éditions du Cerf, 1987.

Ginzberg, L. *The Legends of the Jews.* 15th edition. 7 vols. Translated by H. Szold. Philadelphia: Jewish Publication Society of America, 1988.

Glatt, M. J. "Midrash: The Defender of God." *Judaism* 35 (1986) 87-97.

Glatzer, N. N. *The Passover Haggadah, with English Translation and Commentary.* New York: Schocken Books, 1953.

Goldin, J. "This Song." *Salo Wittmayer Baron Volume,* vol. 1, eds. S. Lieberman and A. Hyman, 539-54. Jerusalem: American Academy for Jewish Research, 1975. Reprinted in *Judah Goldin: Studies in Midrash and Related Literature,* eds. B. L. Eichler and J. H. Tigay, 151-61. Philadelphia: JPS, 1988.

____. *The Fathers According to Rabbi Nathan.* New Haven: Yale University Press, 1955.

____. *The Song at the Sea.* New Haven: Yale University Press, 1971.

Goodenough, E. R. *By Light, Light: The Mystic Gospel of Hellenistic Judaism.* Amsterdam: Philo, 1969.

Goodrick, A. T. S. *The Book of Wisdom.* New York: Macmillan, 1913.

Grant, R. M. "The Book of Wisdom at Alexandria: Reflections on the History of the Canon and Theology." TU 92, *Studia Patristica* 7, 462-72. Berlin: Akademie-Verlag, 1966. Reprinted in R. M. Grant, *After the New Testament*, 70-82. Philadelphia: Fortress, 1967.

Gray, R. *Prophetic Figures in Late Second Temple Jewish Palestine: The Evidence from Josephus.* New York/Oxford: Oxford University Press, 1993.

Greenspahn, F. E., Hilgert, E., and Mack, B. L., eds. *Nourished with Peace: Studies in Hellenistic Judaism in Memory of Samuel Sandmel.* Chico, CA.: Scholars Press, 1984.

Gregg, J. A. F. *The Wisdom of Solomon.* Cambridge: Cambridge University Press, 1909.

Grelot, P. "L'eschatologie des Esséniens et le livre d'Hénoch." *RevQ* 1 (1958) 113-31.

———. "Sagesse 10,21 et le Targum de l'Exode." *Bib* 42 (1961) 49-60.

Gressmann, H. *Mose und seine Zeit: Ein Kommentar zu den Mose-sagen.* Göttingen: Vandenhoeck & Ruprecht, 1913.

Grimm, C. L. W. *Kurtzgefasstes exegetisches Handbuch zu den Apokryphen des Alten Testaments.* Sechste Lieferung. Leipzig: S. Hirzel, 1860.

Gunkel, H. *Einleitung in die Psalmen.* 4th edition. Göttingen: Vandenhoeck & Ruprecht, 1985.

Gutmann, M. *Die Apocryphen des Alten Testaments, übersetzt und erläutert.* Altona, 1841.

Haas, L. "Bibliography on Midrash." *The Study of Ancient Judaism I: Mishnah, Midrash, Siddur,* ed. J. Neusner, 93-103. New York: Ktav, 1981.

Halivni, D. "The Early Period of Halkhic Midrash." *Tradition: A Journal of Orthodox Thought* 22/1 (1986) 37-58.

Hammill, L. "Biblical Interpretation in the Apocrypha and Pseudepigrapha." Ph.D. diss., University of Chicago, 1950.

Harrington, D. J. "Birth Narratives in Pseudo-Philo's Biblical Antiquities and the Gospels." *To Touch the Text: Biblical and Related Studies in Honor of Joseph A. Fitzmyer, S. J.,* eds. M. P. Hogan and P. J. Kobelski, 316-24. New York: Crossroad, 1989.

——— et al., eds. *Pseudo-Philon: Les Antiquités Bibliques.* 2 vols. Paris: Les Éditions du Cerf, 1976.

Hartmann, G. H. and Budrick, S., eds. *Midrash and Literature.* New Haven: Yale University Press, 1986.

Heinemann, I. "Die Kontroverse über das Wunder im Judentum der hellenistischen Zeit." *Jubilee Volume in Honour of Prof. Bernhard Heller (at 70),* ed. S. Scheiber, 170-91. Budapest, 1941.

———. "Synkrisis oder aüssere Analogie in der Weisheit Salomos." *TZ* 4 (1948) 242-51.

Heinemann, J. and Werses, S., eds. *Studies in Hebrew Narrative Art through the Ages.* ScrHier 27. Jerusalem: Magnes, 1978.

Heinemann, J. "The Messiah of Ephraim and the Premature Exodus of the Tribe of Ephraim." *HTR* 68 (1975) 1-15.

Heinisch, P. *Das Buch der Weisheit.* EHAT 24. Münster: Aschendorffsche Verlagsbuchhandlung, 1912.

———. *Die griechische Philosophie im Buche der Weisheit.* Alttestamentliche Abhandlungen 1/4. Münster: Aschendorff, 1908.

Hengel, M. *Judaism and Hellenism: Studies in Their Encounter in Palestine During the Early Hellenistic Period.* 2nd edition. Translated by J. Bowden. Minneapolis: Fortress, 1981.

Hentschel, G. and Zenger, E. eds. *Lehrerin der Gerechtigkeit: Studien zum Buch der Weisheit.* ETS 19. Leipzig: St. Benno-Verlag, 1991.

Hoftijzer, J. and Jongeling, K. *Dictionary of North-West Semitic Inscriptions.* Handbuch der Orientalistik 2. Leiden: E. J. Brill, 1995.

Holladay, W. L. *A Concise Hebrew and Aramaic Lexicon of the Old Testament.* Grand Rapids: Eerdmans, 1986.

Holtz, B., ed. *Back to the Sources: Reading the Classic Jewish Texts.* New York: Summit Books, 1984.

Horbury, W. H. "The Christian Use and the Jewish Origins of the Wisdom of Solomon." *Wisdom in Ancient Israel: Essays in Honor of J. A. Emerton,* eds. J. Day, R. P. Gordon, and H. G. M. Williamson, 182-96. Cambridge: Cambridge University Press, 1996.

Horovitz, H. S. and Rabin, I. A. *Mechilta D'Rabbi Ismael.* Jerusalem: Bamberger & Wahrman, 1960.

Horowitz, C. M. *Pirke de-Rabbi Eliezer.* Jerusalem: Makor, 1972.

Hübner, H., ed. *Weisheit Salomos im Horizont biblischer Theologie.* Biblische-Theologische Studien 22. Neukirchen-Vluyn: Neukirchener Verlag, 1993.

_____. *Wörterbuch zur Sapientia Salomonis.* Göttingen: Vandenhoeck & Ruprecht, 1985.

Humbert, P. "'Qâna'' en Hébreu Biblique." *Festschrift Alfred Berthold,* eds. W. Baumgartner et al., 259-66. Tübingen: J. C. B. Mohr (Paul Siebeck), 1950.

Hyatt, J. *Commentary on Exodus.* NCB. London: Oliphants, 1971.

Hyman, A. *Torah Ha-kethubah ve-Hamessurah: A Reference Book of the Scriptural Passages Quoted in Talmudic, Midrashic and Early Rabbinic Literature.* Tel-Aviv: Dvir, 1979.

Jacobson, H. *A Commentary on Pseudo-Philo's* Liber Antiquitatum Biblicarum, *With Latin Text and English Translation.* AGJU 31. 2 vols. Leiden: E. J. Brill, 1996.

_____. *The* Exagoge *of Ezekiel.* Cambridge: Cambridge University Press, 1983.

Jaffee, M. S. "*Halakhah* in Early Rabbinic Judaism: Innovation beyond Exegesis, Tradition before the Oral Torah." *Innovations in Religious Traditions: Essays in the Interpretation of Religious Change,* 109-142. Berlin/NY: de Gruyter, 1992.

Jastrow, M. *A Dictionary of the Targumim, the Talmud Babli and Yerushalmi, and the Midrashic Literature.* New York: Judaica, 1992.

Kasher, R. "The Interpretation of Scripture in Rabbinic Literature." *Mikra: Reading, Translation and Interpretation of the Hebrew Bible in Ancient Judaism and Early Christianity,* ed. J. M. Mulder, 547-94. CRINT 2/1. Philadelphia: Fortress, 1990.

Keil, C. F. and Delitzsch, F. *Biblical Commentary on the Old Testament.* Translated by J. Martin. Grand Rapids: Eerdmans, 1949.

Keller, C. A. "Glaube in der Weisheit Salomos." *Wort, Gebot, Glaube: Beiträge zur Theologie des Alten Testaments. Walter Eichrodt zum 80. Geburtstag,* ed. H. J. Stoebe, 11-20. ATANT 59. Zürich: Zwingli Verlag, 1970.

Kenner, J. K. "Der zweite Teil des Buches der Weisheit." *ZKT* 35 (1911) 21-29; 449-65; 665-73.

Kloppenborg, J. S. "Isis and Sophia in the Book of Wisdom." *HTR* 75/1 (1982) 57-84.

Kohler, K. "Wisdom of Solomon, Book of the." *The Jewish Encyclopedia* 12 (1907) 538-40.

Kolarcik, M. "Creation and Salvation in the Book of Wisdom." *Creation in the Biblical Traditions*, eds. R. J. Clifford and J. J. Collins, 97-107. CBQMS 24. Washington, D.C.: Catholic Biblical Association of America, 1992.

_____. *The Ambiguity of Death in the Book of Wisdom 1-6: A Study of Literary Structure and Interpretation*. AnBib 127. Rome: Biblical Institute, 1991.

Kraft, R. A. "Philo (Josephus, Sirach and Wisdom of Solomon) on Enoch." SBLSP 13 (1978) 253-57.

Kraft, R. A. and Nickelsburg, G. W. E., eds. *Early Judaism and Its Modern Interpreters*. Philadelphia: Fortress/Atlanta: Scholars Press, 1986.

Kraus, H.-J. *Psalmen*. 2 vols. BKAT 15. Neukirchener Verlag, 1960.

Kugel, J. L. "On the Bible and Literary Criticism." *Prooftexts* 1 (1981) 217-36.

_____. "The Bible's Earliest Interpreters." *Prooftexts* 7 (1987) 269-83.

_____. "The Story of Dinah in the *Testament of Levi*." *HTR* 85/1 (1992) 1-34.

_____. "Two Introductions to Midrash." *Prooftexts* 3 (1983) 131-55. Reprinted in *Midrash and Literature*, eds. G. H. Hartman and S. Budick, 77-103. New Haven: Yale University Press, 1986.

_____. *In Potiphar's House: The Interpretive Life of Biblical Texts*. San Francisco: HarperCollins, 1990.

_____. *The Idea of Biblical Poetry: Parallelism and Its History*. New Haven: Yale University Press, 1981.

Kugel, J. L. and Greer, R. A. *Early Biblical Interpretation*. Philadelphia: Westminster, 1986.

Kuhn, G. "Beiträge zur Erklärung des Buches der Weisheit." *ZNW* 28 (1929) 334-41.

Kümmel, W. G. et al., eds. *Jüdische Schriften aus hellenistisch-römischer Zeit*. Gütersloh: Gerd Mohn, 1973-.

Kuntz, J. K. "The Retribution Motif in Psalmic Wisdom." *ZAW* 89 (1977) 223-33.

_____. "The Wisdom Psalms of Ancient Israel—Their Rhetorical, Thematic, and Formal Dimensions." *Rhetorical Criticism: Essays in Honor of James Muilenburg*, eds. J. J. Jackson and M. Kessler, 186-222. PTMS 1. Pittsburgh: Pickwick, 1974.

Kutsch, E. "'Du sollst dir kein Gottesbild machen.' Zu Weisheit Salomos 14,15." *Alttestamentlicher Glaube und Biblische Theologie: Festschrift für Horst Dietrich Preuß zum 65. Geburtstag*, eds. J. Hausmann and H-J. Kraus, 279-86. Stuttgart: W. Kohlhammer, 1992.

Lagrange, M.-J. "Le Livre de la Sagesse, sa doctrine des fins dernières." *RB* 4 (1907) 85-104.

Lange, S. "The Wisdom of Solomon and Plato." *JBL* 55 (1936) 293-302.

Larcher, C. *Études sur le Livre de la Sagesse*. Paris: Librairie LeCoffre, 1969.

_____. *Le Livre de la Sagesse ou la Sagesse de Salomon*. 3 vols. Paris: Librairie LeCoffre, 1983.

Lasine, S. "Guest and Host in Judges 19: Lot's Hospitality in an Inverted World." *JSOT* 29 (1984) 37-59.

Lauterbach, J. Z. *Mekilta de-Rabbi Ishmael*. 3 vols. Philadelphia: The Jewish Publication Society of America, 1933.

Le Déaut, R. "A propos d'une définition du midrash." *Bib* 50 (1969) 395-413. Reprinted as "Apropos a Definition of Midrash." Translated by M. Howard. *Int* 25 (1971) 259-82.

_____. *La Nuit Pascale: Essai sur la signification de la Pâque juive à partir du Targum d'Exode XII 42*. Rome: Biblical Institute, 1963.

_____. *Targum du Pentateuque*. Vol. 2, *Exode et Lévitique*. Paris: Éditions du Cerf, 1979.

Levenson, J. D. *Creation and the Persistence of Evil: The Jewish Drama of Divine Omnipotence*. San Francisco: Harper and Row, 1985.

Levi, J. *Die Inkongruenz im biblischen Hebräisch*. Wiesbaden: Harrassowitz, 1987.

Lewis, J. P. *A Study of the Interpretation of Noah and the Flood in Jewish and Christian Literature*. Leiden: E. J. Brill, 1968.

Liddell, H. G. and Scott, R. *Greek-English Lexicon*. Oxford: Clarendon, 1925.

Lieberman, S. "How Much Greek in Jewish Palestine." *Biblical and Other Studies*, ed. A. Altmann, 123-41. TextsS 1. Cambridge: Harvard University Press, 1963. Reprinted in *Essays in Greco-Roman and Related Talmudic Literature*, ed. H. A. Fischel, 325-43. New York: Ktav, 1977.

_____. *Hellenism in Jewish Palestine: Studies in the Literary Transmission, Beliefs and Manners of Palestine in the I Century B.C.E.-IV Century C.E.* New York: Jewish Theological Seminary, 1950.

Liebowitz, N. *Studies in Shemot*. Translated by A. Newman. Jerusalem: The World Zionist Organization, 1976.

Lightstone, J. N. "Form as Meaning in Halakic *Midrashim*: A Programmatic Study." *Semeia* 27 (1983) 23-35.

Lillie, B. J. "A History of the Scholarship on the Wisdom of Solomon from the Nineteenth Century to Our Time." Ph.D. diss., Hebrew Union College, 1982.

Loader, J. A. *A Tale of Two Cities: Sodom and Gomorrah in the Old Testament, Early Jewish and Early Christian Traditions*. Kampen: J. H. Kok, 1990.

Loewenstamm, S. E. *The Evolution of the Exodus Tradition*. Translated by B. Schwartz. Jerusalem: Magnes, 1992.

Lothar, R. "Gerechte und Frevler [Gottlose] in Sap 1,1-6,21. Zum Neuverständnis und zur Aktualisierung alttestamentlicher Traditionen in der Sapientia Salomonis." *Weisheit Salomos im Horizont biblischer Theologie*. Biblische-Theologische Studien 22; ed. H. Hübner, 1-54. Neukirchen-Vluyn: Neukirchener Verlag, 1993.

Lyonnet, S. "Le sens de πειράζειν en Sap. 2.24 et la doctrine du péché original." *Bib* 39 (1958) 27-33.

Maass, F. "Von den Ursprüngen der rabbinischen Schriftauslegung." *ZTK* 52 (1955) 129-61.

MacDonald, J. *Memar Marqah: The Teaching of Marqah*. BZAW 84. Berlin: Alfred Töpelmann, 1963.

Mack, B. L. "Imitatio Mosis: Patterns of Cosmology and Soteriology in the Hellenistic Synagogue." *Studia Philonica* 1 (1972) 27-55.

_____. "Under the Shadow of Moses: Authorship and Authority in Hellenistic Judaism." *SBLSP* 21 (1982) 299-318.

_____. *Logos und Sophia: Untersuchungen zur Weisheitstheologie in hellenistischen Judentum*. Göttingen: Vandenhoeck & Ruprecht, 1973.

Maher, M. *Targum Pseudo-Jonathan: Exodus: Translated with Notes*. The Aramaic Bible 2. Collegeville, Minnesota: The Liturgical Press, 1994.

Maier, J. and Schreiner, J., eds. *Literatur und Religion des Frühjudentums: Eine Einführung*. Würzburg: Echter Verlag, 1973.

Mandelbaum, B. *Pesikta de Rav Kahana*. 2 vols. New York: Jewish Theological Seminary of America, 1962.

Maneschg, H. "Gott, Erzieher, Retter und Heiland seines Volkes: Zur Interpretation vom Num 21,4-9 in Weish 16,5-14." *BZ* 28 (1984) 214-29.

____. *Die Erzählung von der ehernen Schlange (Num 21, 4-9) in der Auslegung der frühen jüdischen Literature: eine traditions-geschichtliche Studie.* Frankfurt am Main: Peter Lang, 1981.

Mann, T. W. "The Pillar of Cloud in the Reed Sea Narrative" *JBL* 90 (1971) 15-30.

Marböck, J. "'Denn in allem, Herr, hast du dein Volk großgemacht!' Weish 18,5-19,22 und die Botschaft der Sapientia Salomonis." *Lehrerin der Gerechtigkeit: Studien zum Buch der Weisheit*, eds. G. Hentschel and E. Zenger, 156-78. ETS 19. Leipzig: Benno, 1991.

Marcus, R. "On Biblical Hypostases of Wisdom." *HUCA* 23/1 (1950-1) 157-71.

Margoliouth, D. S. "Was the Book of Wisdom Written in Hebrew?" *JRAS* 6 (1890) 263-97.

Marmorstein, A. "The Background of the Haggadah." *HUCA* 6 (1929) 141-204. Reprinted in *Essays in Greco-Roman and Related Talmudic Literature*, ed. H. A. Fischel, 48-69. New York: Ktav, 1962.

Matthews, V. H. "Hospitality and Hostility in Gen 19 and Judg 19." *BTB* 22 (1992) 3-11.

Mayser, E. *Grammatik der griechischen Papyri aus der Ptolemäerzeit mit Einschluß der gleichzeitigen Ostaka und der Ägypten verfassten Inschriften.* 2 vols. Berlin: de Gruyter, 1926.

McKane, W. *Proverbs: A New Approach.* Philadelphia: Westminster, 1970.

Meeks, W. *The Prophet-King: Moses Traditions and the Johannine Christology.* Leiden: E. J. Brill, 1967.

Ménard, J.-E., ed. *Exégèse biblique et judaïsme.* Strasbourg: Université des sciences humaines de Strasbourg, 1973.

Metzger, B. M. *An Introduction to the Apocrypha.* New York: Oxford University Press, 1957.

Midrash Rabbah ha-Mevoar (Exodus). Jerusalem: Mekhon ha-Midrash ha-Mevoar, 1982/83.

Miller, M. P. "Midrash." *IDBSup.* Nashville: Abingdon, 1962 593-97.

____. "Targum, Midrash and the Use of the Old Testament in the New Testament." *JSJ* 1-2 (1970-71) 29-82.

Miller, P. D., Jr. "El, The Creator of Earth." *BASOR* 239 (1980) 43-46.

Mintz, A. "The Song at the Sea and the Question of Doubling in Midrash." *Prooftexts* 1 (1981) 185-92.

Morgenstern, J. "Despoiling the Egyptians." *JBL* 68 (1949) 1-28.

Moulton, J. H. *A Grammar of New Testament Greek.* Vol 3, *Syntax*, by N. Turner. Edinburgh: T & T Clark, 1963.

Mowinckel, S. "Psalms and Wisdom." *Wisdom in Israel and in the Ancient Near East*, eds. M. Noth and D. Winton Thomas, 205-24. VTSup 3. Leiden: E. J. Brill, 1955.

Mulder, J. M. *Mikra: Reading, Translation and Interpretation of the Hebrew Bible in Ancient Judaism and Early Christianity.* CRINT 2/1. Philadelphia: Fortress, 1990.

Murphy, F. J. *Pseudo-Philo: Rewriting the Bible.* New York/Oxford: Oxford University Press, 1993.

Murphy, R. E. "'To Know your Might is the Root of Immortality' (Wis 15,3)." *CBQ* 25 (1963) 88-93.

____. "A Consideration of the Classification, 'Wisdom Psalm.'" *Congress Volume: Bonn 1962.* VTSup 9, 156-67. Leiden: E. J. Brill, 1963. Reprinted in *Studies in Ancient Israelite Wisdom*, ed. J. L. Crenshaw, 456-67. New York: Ktav, 1976.

____. *Seven Books of Wisdom*. Milwaukee: Bruce Publishing Company, 1960.

Neusner, J. *Invitation to Midrash: The Workings of Rabbinic Bible Interpretation. A Teaching Book*. San Francisco: Harper & Row, 1989.

____. *Mekhilta Attributed to R. Ishmael. An Analytical Translation*. 2 vols. BJS. Atlanta: Scholars Press, 1988.

____. *Pesiqta deRab Kahana. An Analytical Translation and Explanation*. 2 vols. BJS. Atlanta: Scholars Press, 1987.

____. *Song of Songs Rabbah. An Analytical Translation*. 2 vols. BJS. Atlanta: Scholars Press, 1990.

____. *The Fathers According to Rabbi Nathan. An Analytical Translation and Explanation*. BJS. Atlanta: Scholars Press, 1986.

____. *The Rabbinic Traditions about Pharisees Before 70*. 3 vols. Leiden: E. J. Brill, 1971.

____. *What is Midrash?* Philadelphia: Fortress, 1987.

____. *A Midrash Reader*. Minneapolis: Augsburg-Fortress, 1990.

Newman, H. L. "The Influence of the Book of Wisdom on Early Christian Writings." *Crozer Quarterly* 8 (1931) 361-72.

Newman, J. *Halachic Sources: From the Beginning to the Ninth Century*. Leiden: E. J. Brill, 1969.

Nickelsburg, G. W. E., Jr. *Jewish Literature Between the Bible and the Mishnah: A Historical and Literary Introduction*. Philadelphia: Fortress, 1981.

____. *Resurrection, Immortality and Eternal Life in Intertestamental Judaism*. HTS 26. Cambridge: Harvard University Press, 1972.

Niditch, S. "The 'Sodomite' Theme in Judges 19-20: Family, Community, and Social Disintegration." *CBQ* 44 (1982) 365-78.

Noth, M. *Exodus, A Commentary*. Philadelphia: Westminster, 1962.

Offerhaus, U. *Komposition und Intention der Sapientia Salomonis*. Rheinischen Friedrich-Wilhelms-Universität Bonn, 1981.

Osty, E. *Le Livre de la Sagesse*. La Sainte Bible. Paris: Éditions du Cerf, 1955.

Padora, A. M. *Midrash Shoher Tov (Midrash Tehillim)*. Jerusalem: H. Vagshal, 1980, 1986 (?).

Patte, D. *Early Jewish Hermeneutic in Palestine*. SBLDS 22. Missoula: Scholars Press, 1975.

Perdue, L. *Wisdom and Cult: A Critical Analysis of the Views of Cult in the Wisdom Literatures of Israel and the Ancient Near East*. SBLDS 30. Missoula: Scholars Press, 1977.

Peters, N. *Der jüngst wiederaufgefundene hebräische Text des Buches Ecclesiasticus*. Freiburg: Herdersche Verlagshandlung, 1902.

Pfeiffer, R. H. "The Wisdom of Solomon." *History of New Testament Times with an Introduction to the Apocrypha*, 313-51. New York: Harper, 1949.

Ponizy, B. "High-priestly Ministrations according to the Book of Wisdom." *Goldene Äpfel in silbernen Schalen: Collected Communications to the XIIIth Congress of the International Organization for the Study of the Old Testament, Leuven, 1989*, eds. K. D. Schunck and M. Augustin, 135-46. Beiträge zur Erforschung des Alten Testaments und das antiken Judentums 20. Frankfurt am Main: Peter Lang, 1992.

Pope, M. H. *Song of Songs: A New Translation with Introduction and Commentary*. AB 7c. Garden City: Doubleday, 1977.

Porton, G. "Defining Midrash." *The Study of Ancient Judaism I: Mishnah, Midrash, Siddur*, ed. J. Neusner, 55-92. New York: Ktav, 1981.

_____. "Midrash: Palestinian Jews and the Hebrew Bible in the Greco-Roman Period." *ANRW* II.19.2 (1979) 103-38.

Priotto, M. "Il Significto del Confronto Egitto-Sodoma in *Sap*.19,13-17." *RevistB* 32 (1894) 370-94.

Purinton, C. E. "Translation Greek in the Wisdom of Solomon." *JBL* 47 (1928) 276-304.

Rad, G. von. *Genesis: A Commentary*. OTL. Philadelphia: Westminster, 1972.

_____. *Wisdom in Israel*. Translated by J. D. Martin. London: SCM, 1972.

Rahlfs, A. *Septuaginta*. Stuttgart: Deutsche Bibelgesellschaft, 1979.

Rappaport, S. *Agada und Exegese bei Flavius Josephus*. Frankfurt am Main, 1930.

Reese, J. M. "A Semiotic Critique: With Emphasis on the Place of the Wisdom of Solomon in the Literature of Persuasion." *Semeia* 50 (1990) 229-42.

_____. "Can Paul Ricoeur's Method Contribute to Interpreting the Book of Wisdom?" *La Sagesse de l'Ancien Testament: Nouvelle édition mise à jour*, ed. M. Gilbert, 384-96. BETL 51. 2nd edition. Gembloux, Belgium: Leuven University Press, 1990.

_____. "Plan and Structure in the Book of Wisdom." *CBQ* 27 (1965) 391-99.

_____. *Hellenistic Influence on the Book of Wisdom and Its Consequences*. AnBib 41. Rome: Biblical Institute, 1970.

_____. *The Book of Wisdom, Song of Songs*. OTM 20. Wilmington, Delaware: Michael Glazier, Inc., 1983.

Reider, J. *The Book of Wisdom*. New York: Harper & Row, 1957.

Ringgren, H. *Word and Wisdom: Studies in the Hypostatisation of Divine Qualities and Functions in the Ancient Near East*. Lund: H. Ohlssons, 1947.

Romaniuk, C. "Le Livre de la Sagesse dans le Nouveau Testament." *NTS* 14 (1967-68) 498-514.

Rooden, P. T. van. "Die antike Elementarlehre und der Aufbau von Sapientia Salomonis 11-19." *Tradition and Re-interpretation in Jewish and Early Christian Literature: Essays in Honor of Jürgen C. H. Lebram*, eds. J. W. van Henten et al., 81-97. SPB 36. Leiden: E. J. Brill, 1986.

Rost, L. *Judaism Outside the Hebrew Canon*. Translated by D. E. Green. Nashville: Abingdon, 1976.

Roth, W. M. W. "For Life He Appeals to Death: A Study of Old Testament Idol Parodies." *CBQ* 37 (1975) 21-47.

Russell, D. S. *The Old Testament Pseudepigrapha: Patriarchs and Prophets in Early Judaism*. Philadelphia: Fortress, 1987.

Rylaarsdam, J. C. *Revelation in Jewish Wisdom Literature*. Chicago: University of Chicago Press, 1946.

Safrai, S., ed. *The Literature of the Sages: First Part: Oral Torah, Halakah, Mishna, Tosefta, Talmud, External Tractates*. CRINT 2/3. Philadelphia: Fortress, 1987.

Saldarini, A. J. *The Fathers According to Rabbi Nathan (Abot De Rabbi Nathan) Version B*. SJLA 11. Leiden: E. J. Brill, 1975.

Sandmel, S. *The First Christian Century in Judaism and Christianity*. New York: Oxford University Press, 1969.

Sarna, N. *Exodus*. JPS. Philadelphia: JPS, 1991.

_____. *Genesis*. JPS. Philadelphia: JPS, 1989.

Schaberg, J. "Major Midrashic Traditions in Wisdom 1,1-6,25." *JSJ* 13 (1982) 75-101.

Schäfer, P. *Rivalität zwischen Engeln und Menschen: Untersuchungen zur rabbinischen Engelvorstellung.* SJ 8. Berlin/New York: de Gruyter, 1975.

Schechter, S. *Aboth de Rabbi Nathan.* New York: Philipp Feldheim, 1945.

Schmitt, A. "Struktur, Herkunft und Bedeutung der Beispielreihe in Weish 10," *BZ* 21 (1977) 1-22.

____. *Das Buch der Weisheit.* Würzburg: Echter, 1986.

Schnabel, E. J. *Law and Wisdom from Ben Sira to Paul.* WUNT 2, Reihe 16. Tübingen: J. C. B. Mohr (Paul Siebeck), 1985.

Schniedewind, W. M. *The Word of God In Transition From Prophet to Exegete in the Second Temple Period.* JSOTSup 197. Sheffield: Sheffield Academic Press, 1995.

Schütz, R. *Les idées eschatologiques du Livre de la Sagesse.* Paris-Strasbourg: P. Geuthner, 1935.

Schwenk-Bressler, U. *Sapientia Salomonis als ein Beispiel frühjüdischer Textauslegung: die Auslegung des Buches Genesis, Exodus 1-15 und Teilen der Wüstentradition in Sap 10-19.* Beiträge zur Erforschung des Alten Testaments und des antiken Judentums 32. Frankfurt am Main: Peter Lang, 1993.

Scott, R. B. Y. *Proverbs—Ecclesiastes.* AB 18. Garden City, N. Y.: Doubleday, 1965.

____. *The Way of Wisdom in the Old Testament.* New York: Macmillan, 1971.

Seeley, D. "Narrative, the Righteous Man and the Philosopher: An Analysis of the Story of the *Dikaios* in Wisdom 1-5." *JSP* 7 (1990) 55-78.

Seeligmann, I. L. "Voraussetzungen der Midrash." *Congress Volume: Copenhagen 1953.* 150-81. VTSup 1. Leiden: E. J. Brill, 1953.

Shafer, B. E., ed. *Religion in Ancient Egypt: Gods, Myths, and Personal Practice.* Ithaca: Cornell University Press, 1991.

Sheppard, G. T. *Wisdom as a Hermeneutical Construct: A Study in the Sapientializing of the Old Testament.* BZAW 151. Berlin/New York: de Gruyter, 1980.

Siebeneck, R. T. "The Midrash of Wisdom 10-19." *CBQ* 22 (1960) 176-82.

____. "Wisdom (Book of)." *NCE* 14 (1967) 974.

Silberman, L. H. "Toward a Rhetoric of Midrash: A Preliminary Account." *The Biblical Mosaic,* eds. R. M. Polzin and E. Rothman, 15-26. Philadelphia: Fortress, 1982.

Silbermann, A. M., ed. *Pentateuch with Targum Onkelos, Haphtaroth and Prayers for Sabbath and Rashi's Commentary.* Translated by M. Rosenbaum and A. M. Silbermann. London: Shapiro, Vallentine & Co., 1930.

Skehan, P. W. "Borrowings from the Psalms in the Book of Wisdom." *CBQ* 10 (1948) 384-97. Reprinted in Skehan's *Studies in Israelite Poetry and Wisdom,* 149-62. CBQMS 1. Washington, D.C.: The Catholic Biblical Association of America, 1971.

____. "Isaias and the Teaching of the Book of Wisdom." *CBQ* 2 (1940) 289-99. Reprinted in Skehan's *Studies in Israelite Poetry and Wisdom,* 163-71. CBQMS 1. Washington, D.C.: The Catholic Biblical Association of America, 1971.

____. "Notes on the Text of the Book of Wisdom," *Tradition* 3 (1945) 9-12. Reprinted in Skehan's *Studies in Israelite Poetry and Wisdom,* 132-36. CBQMS 1. Washington, D.C.: The Catholic Biblical Association of America, 1971.

____. "The Literary Relationship of the Book of Wisdom to Earlier Wisdom Writings." *Studies in Israelite Poetry and Wisdom,* 172-236. CBQMS 1. Washington, D.C.: The Catholic Biblical Association of America, 1971.

____. "Structures in Poems on Wisdom: Proverbs 8 and Sirach 24." *CBQ* 41 (1979) 365-79.

Smend, R. *Die Weisheit des Jesus Sirach.* Berlin: Georg Reimer, 1906.

_____. *Greichisch-Syrisch-Hebräischer Index zur Weisheit des Jesus Sirach.* Berlin: Georg Reimer, 1907.

Smith, M. "A Comparison of Early Christian and Early Rabbinic Tradition." *JBL* 82 (1963) 169-76.

Smyth, H. W. *Greek Grammar.* Cambridge: Harvard University Press, 1956.

Soggin, J. A. *Joshua: A Commentary.* OTL. Philadelphia: Westminster, 1972.

Sowers, S. "On the Reinterpretation of Biblical History in Hellenistic Judaism." *Oikonomia: Heilsgeschichte als Thema der Theologie* (O. Cullmann Festschrift), ed. F. Christ, 18-25. Hamberg-Bergstedt: Reich, 1967.

Sparks, I. A. "Fragment of Sapientia Salomonis from Oxyrhynchus." *JSJ* 3 (1972) 149-52.

Stein, E. "Ein jüdisch-hellenistischer Midrash über den Auszug aus Ägypten." *MGWJ* 78 (1934) 558-75.

_____. *Die allegorische Exegese des Philo aus Alexandria.* BZAW 51. Giessen: A. Töpelmann, 1929.

_____. *Philo und der Midrasch: Philos Schilderung der Gestalten des Pentateuch verglichen mit der Midrasch.* BZAW 57. Giessen: A. Töpelmann, 1931.

Stern, D. "Midrash and Indeterminacy." *Critical Inquiry* 15 (1988) 132-61.

Stern, M., ed. *Greek and Latin Authors on Jews and Judaism.* 3 vols. Jerusalem: Israel Academy of Sciences and Humanities, 1974.

Stone, M. E. "Ideal Figures and Social Context: Priest and Sage in the Early Second Temple Age." *Ancient Israelite Religion: Essays in Honor of Frank Moore Cross*, eds. P. D. Miller, P. D. Hanson, and S. D. McBride, 575-86. Philadelphia: Fortress, 1987.

_____, ed. *Jewish Writings of the Second Temple Period.* CRINT 2/2. Philadelphia: Fortress, 1984.

Strack, H. L. and Stemberger, G. *Introduction to the Talmud and Midrash.* Translated by M. Bockmuehl. Minneapolis: Fortress, 1992.

Stuart, S. S. "The Exodus Traditions in Late Jewish and Early Christian Literature. A General Survey on the Literature and a Particular Analysis of the Wisdom of Solomon, II Esdras, and the Epistle to the Hebrews." Ph.D. diss., Vanderbilt University, 1973.

Suggs, M. J. "Wisdom of Solomon 2 10-5: A Homily Based on the Fourth Servant Song." *JBL* 76 (1957) 26-33.

Sweet, J. M. P. "The Theory of Miracles in the Wisdom of Solomon." *Miracles*, ed. C. F. D. Moule, 113-26. London: A. R. Mowbray, 1965.

Tapp, A. M. "An Ideology of Expendability: Virgin Daughter Sacrifice in Gen 19:1-11, Judg 11:30-39 and 19:22-26. *Anti-Covenant: Counter-Reading Women's Lives in the Hebrew Bible* , ed. M. Bal, 157-74. JSOTSup 81. Sheffield: Almond, 1989.

Taradach, M. *Le Midrash: Introduction á la littérature midrashique.* Genève: Labor et Fides, 1991.

Taylor, R. J. "The Eschatological Meaning of Life and Death in the Book of Wisdom." *ETL* 42 (1966) 72-137.

Teeple, H. *The Mosaic Eschatological Prophet.* JBLMS 10. Philadelphia: SBL, 1957.

Tennant, F. R. "The Teaching of Ecclesiasticus and Wisdom on the Introduction of Sin and Death." *JTS* 2 (1901) 207-23.

Thackeray, H. St. J. et al., eds. *Josephus.* 9 vols. LCL. London: William Heinemann Ltd., 1926-65.

Thomson, C. *The Old Covenant Commonly Called the Old Testament.* 2 vols. London: Skeffington & Son, 1904.

Tigay, J. "An Early Technique of Aggadic Exegesis." *History, Historiography and Interpretation: Studies in Biblical and Cuneiform Literature,* eds. H. Tadmor and M. Weinfeld, 169-89. Jerusalem: Magnes, 1983.

Towner, W. S. "Hermeneutical Systems of Hillel and the Tannaim: A Fresh Look." *HUCA* 53 (1982) 101-35.

_____. "Retribution Theology in the Apocalyptic Setting." *USQR* 26/2 (1971) 203-14.

_____. *The Rabbinic "Enumeration of Example": A Study of a Rabbinic Pattern of Discourse with Special Reference to* Mekilta D'R. Ishmael. SPB 22. Leiden: E. J. Brill, 1973.

Urbach, E. E. *The Sages: Their Concepts and Beliefs.* Translated by I. Abrahams. Cambridge: Harvard University Press, 1979.

Vermes, G. "Bible and Midrash: Early Old Testament Exegesis." *The Cambridge History of the Bible.* Vol. 1, *From the Beginnings to Jerome,* eds. P. R. Ackroyd and C. F. Evans, 199-231. Cambridge: Cambridge University Press, 1970.

_____. "La Figure de Moïse au Tournant des deux Testaments." *Moïse: L'Homme de l'Alliance,* ed. H. Cazelles, 63-92. Paris: Desclée, 1955.

_____. *Post-biblical Jewish Studies.* SJLA 8. Leiden: E. J. Brill, 1975.

_____. *Scripture and Tradition in Judaism.* SPB 4. 2nd edition; Leiden: E. J. Brill, 1973.

Visotzky, B. L. "Two Types of Midrash Study." *Conservative Judaism* 41 (1989) 65-71.

Vogels, W. "The God Who Creates is the God Who Saves: The Book of Wisdom's Reversal of the Biblical Pattern." *Église et Theologie* 22 (1991) 315-35.

Wacholder, B-Z. "The Date of the Mekilta de-Rabbi Ishmael." *HUCA* 39 (1968) 117-44.

Wallach, L. "A Palestinian Polemic Against Idolatry [A Study in Rabbinic Literary Forms]." *HUCA* 19 (1946) 389-404. Reprinted in *Essays in Greco-Roman and Related Talmudic Literature,* ed. H. A. Fischel, 111-126. New York: Ktav, 1977.

Waltke, B. K. and O'Connor, M. *An Introduction to Biblical Hebrew Syntax.* Winona Lake, IN: Eisenbrauns, 1990.

Weber, W. "Der Auferstehungsglaube im Eschatologischen Buche der Weisheit Salomos." *ZWT* 54 (1912) 205-39

_____. "Die Composition der Weisheit Salomo's." *ZWT* 47 (1904) 145-69.

_____. "Die Seelenlehre der Weisheit Salomos." *ZWT* 51 (1909) 314-32.

_____. "Die Unsterblichkeit der Weisheit Salomo's." *ZWT* 48 (1905) 409-44.

_____. "Heimat und Zeitalter des Eschatologischen Buches der Weisheit Salomos." *ZWT* 53 (1911) 322-45.

Webster, E. C. "Structural Unity in the Book of Wisdom." *East Asia Journal of Theology* 4 (1986) 94-112.

Weimar, P. and Zenger, E. *Exodus: Geschichten und Geschichte der Befreiung Israels.* SBS 75. Stuttgart: KBW Verlag, 1975.

Weinfeld, M. "'They Fought from Heaven'—Divine Intervention in War in Ancient Israel." ErIsr 14 (1978) 23-30 (Hebrew, English summary).

Weingreen, J. "Exposition in the Old Testament and in Rabbinic Literature." *Promise and Fulfillment,* ed. F. F. Bruce, 187-201. Edinburgh: T & T Clark, 1963.

_____. *From Bible to Mishna: The Continuity of Tradition.* Manchester: Manchester University Press, 1976.

Weisengoff, J. P. "Death and Immortality in the Book of Wisdom." *CBQ* 3 (1941) 104-33.

_____. "The Impious of Wisdom 2." *CBQ* 11 (1949) 40-65.

Weiser, A. *The Psalms*. OTL. London: SCM, 1962.

Weitzman, S. P. "Sing to the Lord a New Song: The Role of Songs within Biblical Narrative and their Resonance in Early Biblical Interpretation." Ph.D. diss., Harvard University, 1993.

Wenham, G. J. *Genesis 1-15*. WBC 1. Waco: Word, 1987.

Westermann, C. *Genesis 1-11: A Commentary*. Translated by J. J. Scullion. Minneapolis: Augsburg Publishing House, 1984.

_____. *Genesis 12-36: A Commentary*. Translated by J. J. Scullion. Minneapolis: Augsburg Publishing House, 1985

Wevers, J. W. *Exodus*. Septuaginta: Vetus Testamentum Graecum. Vol.II/1. Göttingen: Vandenhoeck & Ruprecht, 1991.

_____. *Notes of the Greek Text of Exodus*. SBLSCS 30. Atlanta: Scholars Press, 1990.

Wilken, R., ed. *Aspects of Wisdom in Judaism and Early Christianity*. Notre Dame: University of Notre Dame Press, 1975.

Winston, D. "Solomon, Wisdom of." *ABD* 6, eds. D. N. Freedman et al., 120-27. New York: Doubleday, 1992.

_____. "The Book of Wisdom's Theory of Cosmogony." *HR* 11/2 (1971) 185-202.

_____. "The Sage as Mystic in the Wisdom of Solomon." *The Sage in Israel and the Ancient Near East*, eds. J. G. Gammie and L. G. Perdue, 383-98. Winona Lake, IN: Eisenbrauns, 1990.

_____. "Wisdom in the Wisdom of Solomon." *In Search of Wisdom: Essays in Memory of John G. Gammie*, ed. L. G. Purdue et al., 149-64. Louisville: Westminster/John Knox, 1993.

_____. *The Wisdom of Solomon*. AB 43. New York: Doubleday, 1979.

Wright, A. G. "Numerical Patterns in the Book of Wisdom." *CBQ* 29 (1967) 524-38.

_____. "The Literary Genre Midrash." *CBQ* 28 (1966) 105-38; 417-57. Reprinted, New York: Society of St. Paul, 1967.

_____. "The Structure of the Book of Wisdom." *Bib* 48 (1967) 165-84

_____. "The Structure of Wisdom 11-19." *CBQ* 27 (1965) 28-34.

Zeitlin, S. "Midrash: A Historical Study." *JQR* 44 (1953-54) 21-36.

Zerwick, M. *Biblical Greek*. Scripta Pontificii Instituti Biblici 114. Rome: Pontifical Biblical Institute, 1963.

Ziegler, J. *Sapientia Salomonis*. Septuaginta: Vetus Testamentum Graecum. Vol.XII/1. Göttingen: Vandenhoeck & Ruprecht, 1980.

Ziener, G. *Das Buch der Weisheit*. Düsseldorf: Patmos, 1970.

_____. *Die theologische Begriffssprache im Buche der Weisheit*. Bonn: Peter Hanstein, 1956.

_____. "Die Verwendung der Schrift im Buche der Weisheit." *TTZ* 66 (1957) 138-52.

_____. "Weisheitsbuch und Johannesevangelium." *Bib* 38 (1957) 396-418 and (1958) 37-60.

Zimmermann, F. "The Book of Wisdom: Its Language and Character." *JQR* 57 (1966) 1-27 and (1967) 101-35.

Index of Ancient Works